Sunset

Hawaii

A GUIDE TO ALL THE ISLANDS

By the Editors
of Sunset Books
and
Sunset Magazine

Sunset Publishing Corporation • Menlo Park, California

CONTENTS

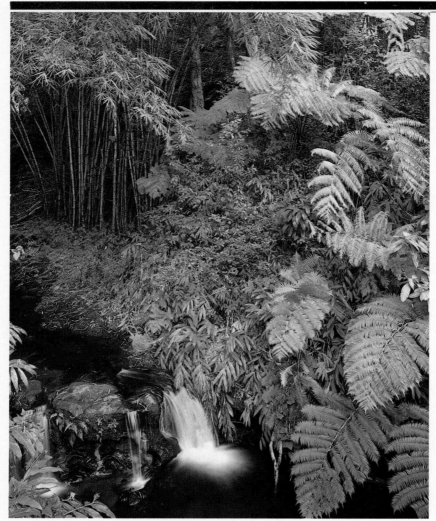

Bamboo forest, Akaka Falls State Park

Book Editor
Barbara J. Braasch

Coordinating Editor
Joan Beth Erickson

Design
JoAnn Masaoka Van Atta

Two-Color Maps
Eureka Cartography

Full-color Illustrations
H. Tom Kamifuji

Cover:
Among Molokai's pristine and scenic treasures lies Kapuaiwa Coconut Grove in Kiowea Beach Park. Design by Susan Bryant. Photography by Jeff Gnass.

Mahalo...

The editors of Sunset gratefully acknowledge the help provided by the many people and organizations of Hawaii's travel industry. We particularly appreciate the assistance of the Hawaii Visitors Bureau. Our special thanks also go to Fran Feldman for her careful editing of this edition.

Special Features

Editorial Director, Sunset Books:
Kenneth Winchester

Second printing December 1994

Hours, admission fees, prices, telephone numbers, and highway designations in this book are accurate as of the time this edition went to press.

Nene, the state bird

Kauai

Niihau

Oahu

Honolulu

The

Flying across the Pacific from the mainland, you strain your eyes to see the first of the eight major islands that compose the state of Hawaii. Seven of these islands are inhabited; the eighth, Kahoolawe, was used by the U.S. Navy for bombing practice until 1990.

Hawaii—the largest island—is usually referred to as the "Big Island." With an area of 4,050 square miles, Hawaii is almost twice as large as all the other islands combined. It boasts two mountain peaks that rise more than 13,000 feet from sea level, two active volcanoes, and a national park.

Maui is the second largest island. It contains some of the state's most magnificent beaches, a variety of resort areas, a refurbished whaling port, and the vast, colorful crater of dormant Haleakala.

West and northwest of Maui, the islands of Lanai and Molokai are quiet and still comparatively undeveloped. But new resorts and golf courses are beginning to attract more visitors.

Oahu, third in size, is first in number of people. Honolulu, the state capital, is located here, as are such famous landmarks as Diamond Head, Waikiki, and Pearl Harbor.

Westernmost of the main islands are Kauai and Niihau. A 1992 hurricane devastated lush Kauai, the Garden Isle, but, thanks to community effort and a beneficial climate, it will soon recover. Privately owned Niihau is viewed only by helicopter.

Stretching beyond Niihau lie a series of tiny islets and atolls officially named the Northwestern Hawaiian Islands. Military installations on Midway and Kure and small wildlife facilities are the only marks of habitation.

Aloha Spirit

Molokai

Maui

Lanai

Kahoolawe

Hawaii

You'll stand on volcanoes...

Devastation Trail, a volcanic reminder

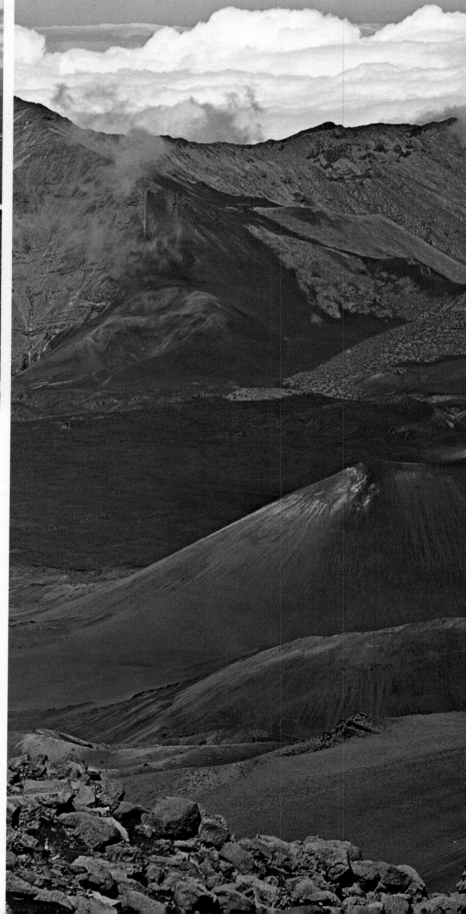

Everywhere you travel in Hawaii you're atop a volcano. The volcanic activity that formed the Hawaiian Islands began at the northwest end of a chain commonly called the Leeward Islands. These islands are estimated to be 5 to 10 million years old, the main Hawaiian Islands 1 to 5 million. On the Big Island, volcanic activity still continues; it's said that Pele, the goddess of fire, traveled from island to island looking for a home before settling down in Hawaii.

To view Madam Pele's latest handiwork, visit Hawaii Volcanoes National Park. Here Kilauea, the nation's "drive-in volcano" (so named for its accessibility) still smokes and intermittently belches fire and rock. Mauna Loa, though quieter, erupted in early 1984, sending streams of molten lava down her slopes. By comparison, Maui's mighty Haleakala last erupted some 200 years ago.

Haleakala, Maui's "House of the Sun"

6 THE ALOHA SPIRIT

Steaming Kilauea caldera

...splash in the sea

A windsurfing capital

Swimming, surfing, snorkeling, scuba diving, boating, windsurfing—these are all part of Hawaii's water world. Even if you're not a sports enthusiast, sometime during your stay you'll toast on a beach or test the ocean's temperature with your toes.

The Recreation Guide for each island provides specific information on the activity for which the area is noted. On page 53 we provide a guide to "The Perfect Wave"; on page 92 we caution against the ocean's vagaries.

From the early-morning splashing of the surf against the shore until the late-evening painting of the sun on the waves, you'll notice the sea. It blends with the land to create the vacation destination that is Hawaii.

Sailboats in Waikiki

Underwater look at Kealakekua Bay

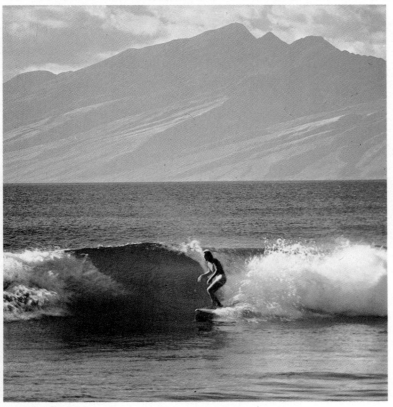

Surfing off Maui coast

...meet the people

The people of Hawaii are a fascinating mixture of races and cultures. Each succeeding wave of migration added a dash to the melting pot of the island society—Polynesian, Oriental, and Caucasian.

Today, the pure Hawaiian is only a small percentage of the total population, but there is an increasing number of part-Hawaiians. And a new cultural awareness preserves the language and customs of the past.

At the Polynesian Cultural Center on Oahu, you'll catch glimpses of the South Seas cultures represented in the islands; tours of Japanese shrines, Chinese markets, and Filipino restaurants add a second dimension; and a visit to Kauai's Grove Farm Homestead, Oahu's Plantation Village, or Maui's Alexander & Baldwin Sugar Museum offers a peek into the sugar plantation era. Whalers and missionaries are long gone, but you can walk in their footsteps in Lahaina, Maui.

Shinto priest

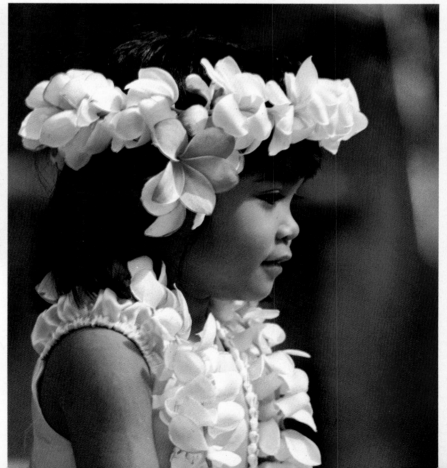

Aspiring hula enthusiast

...smell the flowers

Creamy plumeria

Showy blossoms, pervasive perfume, and riotous hues characterize Hawaii's exotic floral display. Hibiscus and *hau*, a cousin of the state flower, and bougainvillea sprays decorate roadsides. Orchids, anthuriums, plumeria, and ginger are only a few of the other tropical blooms that delight the eye.

Showy torch ginger

Bird of paradise

Vanda tricolor orchid

...enjoy the music and dance

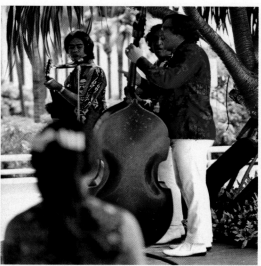

Melody of the islands

First used as a religious ritual or war dance and performed only by men, the hula still conveys a story by means of movements and gestures.

Accompanying chants and songs performed by drum, ukulele, and guitar linger in a visitor's memory even after the return to the mainland.

Exhorting the gods in dance

...savor the food

Coconut milk shake

Dining in Hawaii can become an adventure in food. Most menus include island specialties like teriyaki steak and mahimahi. You'll find coconut, pineapple, and macadamia nut waffles, pancakes, and ice creams; guava and *liliko'i* (passion fruit) sherbets; curries; and Kona coffee. Among the array of fresh fruits are papayas, mangoes, pineapples, and bananas.

Try the various kinds of Chinese noodles and *dim sum* (stuffed pastries). Sample *sashimi* (raw fish) and different kinds of Japanese *sushi* (stuffed rice). *Saimin*, a filling noodle soup, is unique to the islands.

Most visitors want to join in at least one luau, complete with roast pig, raw fish, *lomi lomi* salmon, poi, *lau laus* (taro tops or spinach, chicken, and fish steamed in ti leaves), *haupia* (coconut pudding), and fresh fruits. By all means sample "crack seed," the Chinese dried and preserved whole fruits, and the fruit-flavored "shave ice" (snow cones) that children love.

Food from the sea

...admire the pageantry

Hula—Tahitian style

Portrait of ali'i

Costuming, history, and ritual combine to create the colorful performances enjoyed by vacationers to the islands.

Hawaiians love to celebrate on every possible occasion, and there's usually an occasion someplace on the islands. Many events are local festivals, others are all-island activities.

Everything from the opening of the Hawaii State Legislature in January (music, hula, flowers, prayers), narcissus and cherry blossom fetes, pageants honoring King Kalakaua (Merrie Monarch in April) and King Kamehameha (June 11), to Aloha Week (September and October) includes flowers, parades, music, and dance.

For a partial listing of year-round events, see pages 20–21. For information on exact dates and times, check the local Hawaii Visitors Bureau office or newspapers.

A fire performance

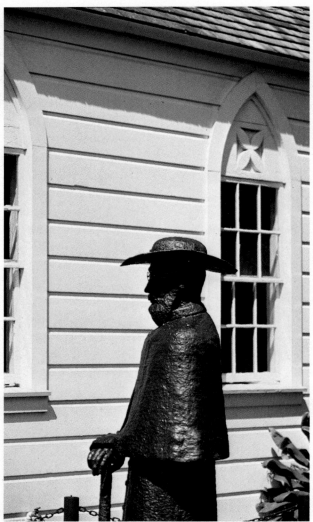

Statue of Father Damien *stands beside his church on Molokai's Kalaupapa peninsula where he served leprosy victims, before succumbing himself.*

W hen you first approach the Hawaiian Islands you may wonder how explorers centuries ago ever found these bits of land. Actually, they discovered them not by chance, but through impressive feats of navigation.

The Early Polynesians

Polynesians from the Marquesas as early as A.D. 500 and from Tahiti about 500 years later crossed the uncharted ocean in large sailing canoes and landed in Hawaii with their families, plants, animals, and personal belongings. For hundreds of years, they knew only a Stone Age life, making *tapa* cloth, grass houses, outrigger canoes, and carvings. They subsisted on fish, poi, and other fruit of the land.

A United Hawaii

When British navigator Captain James Cook discovered the islands in 1778 (he named them the Sandwich Islands for the Earl of Sandwich) during the third and last of his famous South Pacific voyages, he found each a separate kingdom organized in a feudal manner with chiefs, priests, and commoners. By 1810 the king of Hawaii island, Kamehameha, had brought all of the islands under his domain. He and his descendants reigned until 1872. They were followed by rulers from another ancient family of chiefs that included Queen Liliuokalani, who was ruler in 1893 when the monarchy was overturned. A provisional government was set up at that time.

An Immigrant Society

The waves of immigrants who came to Hawaii during the 19th century rearranged Hawaiian society. Traders landed from Captain Cook's time on. In the middle years, whalers beached, seeking provisions and entertainment. Companies of missionaries arrived starting in 1820. These stern, dedicated New Englanders braved the hazardous journey to the mid-Pacific to convert natives to Christianity and to introduce plantation agriculture, commerce, and democratic government. Many of their descendants are still prominent in the islands.

In the last half of the century came Chinese, then Portuguese and Japanese, and later on Filipinos to work the sugarcane and pineapple plantations started by early New Englanders.

The 50th State

On July 4, 1894, the Republic of Hawaii came into existence with Sanford B. Dole (another missionary descendant) as president. The islands were annexed by the United States in 1898 and made a territory in 1900. Dole was appointed governor of the territory and Prince Kuhio (a nephew of Queen Liliuokalani) became one of the first delegates to Congress. A tireless fighter for the rights of the native Hawaiians, Prince Kuhio also introduced the first Hawaiian statehood bill in 1919.

During the time between Hawaii's annexation and World War II, the sugar and pineapple industries continued to prosper and the number of immigrants brought in to work the vast holdings increased. And the military became interested in the islands. In 1908, a gigantic naval base at Pearl Harbor was approved by Congress—the scene of the bombing on December 7, 1941, that drew the U.S. into war.

Though Hawaii was still seen by some as too far away, statehood was assured when Alaska joined the Union in January of 1959. On March 12, 1959, Congress passed the bill that made Hawaii the 50th state, ending a statehood campaign waged for nearly half a century.

Hawaii has more than 1 million residents and plays host to some 7 million visitors annually.

PLANNING YOUR TRIP

Information on getting to and around each of Hawaii's major islands can be found in "The Essentials" section for that island. You'll also discover information on accommodations, sightseeing trips, restaurants, and shops. Details on camping and picnicking, swimming, surfing, diving, snorkeling, beachcombing, boating, bicycling, golf, tennis, hiking, horseback riding, and fishing are contained in the "Recreation Guide" for each island. See pages 20–21 for a roundup of festivals and special events.

Getting to the Islands

Hawaii lies about 2,400 miles/3,840 km southwest of California. By air, the trip takes approximately 5 hours from West Coast cities, 9 hours from Chicago, and 11 hours from New York. Honolulu is a port of call on some round-the-world and Pacific cruises, and there is some cargo-liner service. By sea, the trip takes about 4½ days from West Coast cities.

Mainland-to-Hawaii air service. You'll have your choice of airlines to Hawaii. Most have been flying to the islands for many years. Among the largest and best known are American, Continental, Delta, Hawaiian, Northwest, TWA, United, and USAir. Most flights land at Honolulu International Airport on Oahu, though direct service from the mainland to neighboring islands is growing. American, Hawaiian, and United all offer nonstop or connecting service to Maui, Hawaii, and Kauai from some mainland cities.

Honolulu is also a stopover point for many foreign carriers, but they are prohibited by law from carrying passengers solely between two U.S. cities (San Francisco and Honolulu, for example). Passengers can stop in Hawaii en route to or from a foreign destination.

Interisland air travel. Five scheduled carriers offer frequent commuter flights to all islands. Aloha and Hawaiian airlines provide service from Oahu to Maui, Hawaii, and Kauai. Aloha's sister carrier, IslandAir, flies to Princeville (Kauai); Hana, Kahului, and Kapalua (Maui); Molokai; Lanai; and Kamuela (Hawaii). Air Molokai flies from Kahului (Maui) to Molokai, Lanai, and Honolulu. Mahalo Air operates from Honolulu to Lihue (Kauai), Kahului (Maui), and Kona (Hawaii). Charter service is also available on all islands.

Boat service. American Hawaii Cruises offers 7-day interisland sailings aboard the S.S. *Constitution* and the S.S. *Independence*. These round-trip cruises from Honolulu stop at Kauai, Maui, and both Hilo and Kona on the Big Island. They also spend a leisurely day passing along the shores of Molokai, Lanai, and Kahoolawe, off the coast of Maui.

Ships travel from port to port at night. En route, a variety of activities keep passengers entertained. Daytime shoreside options include excursions to major attractions, trips for golf and tennis, snorkeling sallies, volcano tours, and shopping expeditions.

All meals, shipboard activities, entertainment, and services are included in the ticket price. Land tours, beverages, and tips are added expenses. For information on cruises, add-on land packages, and special air fares, contact your travel agent or American Hawaii Cruises, 500 Kearny Street, San Francisco, CA 94108; (800) 765-7000.

Honolulu is a port of call for several cruise lines, including Cunard, Holland America, and Princess. Though you cannot travel solely between U.S. ports on foreign ships, some lines include Hawaii on sailings between Baja California and the West Coast, or stop at Hawaii going to or from Polynesian ports.

Special tours. Packaged tours have come a long way from the no-time-alone travel regimens of the past. By purchasing a travel package, vacationers can often save money. Choices range from fully escorted, special-interest tours to independent fly-and-drive packages. Most tours are sold through travel agents. Stop by their offices to check your options or to book a tour.

Handicapped Travel

Hawaii is one of the most accessible vacation options for disabled travelers. The Commission on Persons with Disabilities (5 Waterfront Plaza, 500 Ala Moana Boulevard, Suite 210, Honolulu, HI 96813) publishes a register of statewide handicapped services and a useful guide to wheelchair access at hotels, restaurants, and attractions.

Where to Stay

Hawaii's accommodations range from mountain cabins to plush seaside hotel suites. Among the hotel chains represented are Aston, Colony, Embassy Suites, Four Seasons, Hilton, Hyatt, Marriott, Outrigger, Prince, Ritz-Carlton, Sheraton, Stouffer, and Westin. Check with a travel agent for details on these and other hotels and on condominiums.

Getting Around the Islands

Before you rent a vehicle in Hawaii, check the various rates and special packages that are offered. There are many from which to choose—flat rates with no mileage charge, weekly specials covering cars on several islands, fly-drive combinations, and others. By checking the possibilities in advance, you can select the plan best suited to the type of driving you intend to do. There is sometimes a shortage of cars during big conventions, school vacation periods, holiday weekends, or when a major event (such as a golf tournament) is scheduled. For this reason, it is a good idea to make car reservations in advance.

It's impossible to list in our limited space every car rental agency in the islands; you'll find most national agencies (Alamo, Avis, Budget, Dollar, Hertz, and National) as well as several local companies, such as Roberts and

...Planning Your Trip

United, on the larger islands. If you shop around after you arrive, you may find lower rates at other island-only agencies; you'll also run across companies specializing in convertibles, "wrecks," and such. For complete listings, check the Yellow Pages.

Rent minivans for camping or 4-wheel-drive vehicles at the time you book your trip, since supplies are limited. Four-wheelers are almost necessary to explore Lanai; they're useful on Maui, Hawaii, and Kauai.

How's the Weather?

The islands are in the tropics, but fresh trade winds from the east and northeast prevail most of the year, keeping the air pleasantly balmy. In lowland areas, such as Waikiki, temperatures range from an average low of 65° to an average high of 80° in winter, and from 73° to 88° in summer. Atop the highest mountains, the temperature occasionally drops into the 20s, and in many upland sections the range is from the low 50s to low 70s.

Sometimes the trades break down and a spell of *kona* (a leeward wind) weather sets in, with southwesterly breezes and high humidity. In summer and early fall, a kona wind is synonymous with sticky weather; in winter it brings a few storms (gales and torrential rain) but also some of the islands' clearest days.

Winter trades can get blustery and drop frequent showers even on dry areas such as Waikiki, which receives only 20 to 25 inches of rain a year. In spring and summer, showers are few and come mostly at night, drifting down from the mountain peaks. The surprise of island weather is that a year's rain may amount to more than 100 inches of rain in one place and less than 20 in another just a few miles away.

What to Wear

Lightweight clothing is the rule throughout the year. Around resorts and for touring, women wear casual attire (short *mu'umu'us*, shorts, or pants); men wear sport shirts with shorts or slacks. Women may want a scarf or other covering to protect hairdos from island breezes. Informal clothes are also suitable in the evening; a few restaurants do require men to wear a coat and tie. In business offices, the dress is the same as in any mainland city in the summertime.

A sweater or lightweight jacket is sometimes welcome on a cool evening or in an air-conditioned restau-

BRING THE KEIKIS (KIDS)

With its variety of vacation options, its pleasant weather, and its numerous child-friendly accommodations, Hawaii is a perfect place to bring the kids—and enjoy *your* stay at the same time. The islands brim with family-pleasing destinations, many, like the miles of beaches, free. Hawaii has long been playing host to families and even planned some of its man-made attractions with children in mind. In Oahu, Foster Botanic Garden added bewildering mazes, and Hawaii Maritime Center set up a separate Children's Touch and Feel Museum.

Hawaiians love children and your little ones will be welcomed almost everywhere. Most major hotels and resort condominiums cater to families, offering discounted rates or allowing kids to stay free if no extra bed is needed. Restaurants have children's menus.

Best of all, thoughtfully designed children's programs at most large resorts allow parents carefree time on their own while their offspring are busy learning to surf, taking nature tours, or enjoying beach barbecues. Most camps charge a small daily fee; some programs are basically free, charging only for transportation and sightseeing admissions. All camps are active in summer; many remain open throughout the year.

These kiddie camps are much more than supervised day-care centers. Children learn Hawaiian arts and crafts, take nature walks, enjoy beach activities with pint-size equipment, and go sightseeing.

Teenagers are not forgotten. Maui's Grand Wailea Resort and Four Seasons Resort offer scavenger hunts, theme parties, and evening movies. Mauna Lani Bay Hotel on the Big Island has an Eco-Teen Adventures program with petroglyph tours of lava fields, a sea turtle program, sports, and two or three-day coastal excursions. The Ritz-Carlton schedules Hawaiiana classes plus sports-oriented activities. At nearby Kona Village, tennis, sailing, and snorkeling occupy teens.

Hawaii is also a premier vacation spot for those times when you want to sightsee together. With attractions ranging from A(quariums) to Z(oos), there's something for every member of the family. The following places are particularly appealing to children:

Oahu: Honolulu Zoo, Pacific Submarine Museum, Polynesian Cultural Center, Sea Life Park.

Kauai: Fern Grotto boat ride, Kilauea Point National Wildlife Refuge, Smith's Tropical Paradise.

Maui: Maui Tropical Plantation, Sugar Cane Train, Whalers Village Museum.

Hawaii: Nautilus Submarine, Panaewa Rainforest Zoo, Hawaii Volcanoes National Park.

Molokai: Molokai Ranch Wildlife Park.

rant. A fold-up umbrella is useful during occasional rainy periods (a raincoat is usually too warm); take lightweight rain gear, though, if you plan to do much hiking or camping.

Shopping—A Potpourri from Many Lands

Shopping centers and resort shop complexes on all the islands carry a tremendous selection of clothes, handicrafts, jewelry, food, flowers, homewares, and decorative items. You'll find much repetition; the more you browse, the more selective you will probably become. Prices are similar to mainland prices, but Hawaii offers a wider selection of merchandise from the Pacific islands and Asia. You'll find unusual items in Japanese department stores (Hawaii has several), Honolulu's Chinatown, and country stores on all the islands. Here are some buying suggestions:

Clothes and fabrics. Stores are full of shirts, gowns, and sportswear turned out by more than 100 Hawaii garment manufacturers. Many island-design prints are also sold on yard goods counters and racks, along with interesting fabrics from Asia. Most plentiful are easy-care cotton and synthetic prints, ranging from bright modern florals to traditional Pacific motifs. Well worth searching out are the small fabric shops that feature such imported fabrics as batiks, Japanese printed *yukata* cotton, and silks. Even though these places offer smaller selections, fabric pieces are frequently one-of-a-kind.

Handicrafts. Locally made handicrafts are featured in gift and specialty shops in the big, new shopping complexes that are springing up everywhere in the islands, in gift sections of department stores, and in isolated small shops and factories. At many places you can watch craftspeople at work on their products. Look for bowls and trays of monkeypod, koa, and some rare native woods; *lauhala* handbags, hats, and mats; jewelry of pink and black coral, seeds and shells, obsidian, olivines, wood, and hand-wrought silver; lava curios; ceramics; ukuleles; hula accessories and Hawaiian dolls in all sizes, shapes, and materials.

Oriental and South Pacific imports. Almost every store has imports; many shops are exclusively devoted to the products of one country. Consulates and ethnic chambers of commerce can tell you where to buy the wares of the countries they represent. Look for jade and pearl jewelry; basketry and other woven articles; oriental tableware and cookware; china, pottery, lacquer, bronze, and brass ware; rattan and wicker furniture; masks; bamboo fishing poles, nets, floats, and reef-walking *tabi*; and costly *objets d'art*.

Foods, flowers, plants. Many Hawaiian foods come giftboxed, separately or in combinations. Favorites to bring or mail home are pineapples, jams, jellies, syrups, maca-

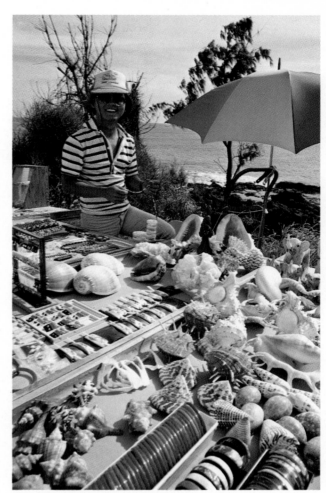

He sells shells *at a stall near Kauai's blowhole, Spouting Horn.*

damia and coconut confections, and Kona coffee. Avocados and papayas must be treated before shipment; bananas and litchis can't be shipped. (For more information contact the Agricultural Quarantine office of the U.S. Department of Agriculture in Honolulu.)

At street stands, in flower shops, and at the airport, you can buy leis of plumeria, *pikake,* orchids, carnations, tuberoses, crown flowers, and ginger. Cut flowers include anthuriums and bird of paradise. Dried arrangements of coconut sheaths, woodroses, papyrus, and koa pods are popular.

All baggage of air travelers going from Hawaii to the U.S. mainland is subject to inspection at the airport by the U.S. Department of Agriculture. Not permitted to enter the mainland are fruits other than pineapples and treated papayas and avocados; mauna loa, gardenia, and jade vine; coffee berries; other berries and pulpy seeds; cactus plants; sugarcane; and plants in soil. You can take plants potted in a fiber medium and bare-root plants, properly packed and inspected by the State Department of Agriculture. Many flower shops and nurseries carry preinspected potted plants.

Aloha Week float

Cherry Blossom Festival. Honolulu, Oahu. A series of events presented by the Japanese community continues through March.

Captain Cook Festival. Waimea, Kauai. A two-day party in the port where Cook first landed in Hawaii.

Great Waikoloa Horse Races and Rodeo. Waikoloa, Hawaii. A combination of rodeo events and horse races.

March

Prince Kuhio Day. All islands. A state holiday honoring Prince Kuhio, a delegate to Congress from 1902 to 1922. Kauai's week-long celebration of its native son includes songs, dances, canoe races, and a royal ball.

Prince Kuhio Ironman/Ironwoman Canoe Race. Kauai's venerable race from Kealia Beach to Wailua Beach.

LPGA Women's Kemper Open Golf Tournament. Wailea, Maui. Stars of the women's golf tour compete.

Mauna Kea Ski Meet. Mauna Kea, Hawaii. Two international cup races and one cross-country race on the volcano snow. Other meets in April and June.

April

Easter Sunrise Service. Honolulu, Hawaii. Service is held at Punchbowl National Memorial Cemetery.

Buddha Day. All islands. The birth of Guatama Buddha is commemorated.

Merrie Monarch Festival. Hilo, Hawaii. A competition among the best hula schools from all islands highlights this tribute to Kalakaua, Hawaii's fun-loving last king.

May

Lei Day. All islands. Islanders don leis to greet spring during this annual celebration; statewide lei competitions and exhibits are the highlights.

Memorial Day. Honolulu, Oahu. The many thousands of markers at Punchbowl Crater are heaped with flower leis strung by school children on all the islands. A memorial service is held in the morning.

50th State Fair. Honolulu, Oahu. The fair continues into June. A special highlight is Hawaiian crafts.

June

King Kamehameha Day. All islands. A state holiday with parades and pageantry honoring King Kamehameha I, who founded the all-islands kingdom.

Kapalua Music Festival. Kapalua Bay Hotel, Maui. Chamber music by internationally acclaimed musicians.

Hawaii State Farm Fair. Honolulu, Oahu. Hawaii's largest agricultural show, with produce, flowers, livestock, and poultry competitions and exhibits—and a carnival. Continues into July.

July

Bon Odori Festival. All islands. The Buddhist festival of souls, with colorful *bon* dances Friday and Saturday nights at each temple ground, in turn. A few temples have nighttime floating lantern ceremonies.

Cowboys and canoes, festivals and feasts, pageants and parades all combine in the kaleidoscope of special events that Hawaii offers its visitors. Flower and craft shows, rodeos, athletic competitions, and religious ceremonies abound. Holiday periods, such as Christmas and the Fourth of July, are packed with a variety of activities. Hawaii Visitors Bureau offices on the major islands and hotel activities desks can provide information on events of interest during your stay.

January

Hawaiian Open International Golf Tournament. Honolulu, Oahu. Top professional golfers compete.

Opening of the State Legislature. Honolulu, Oahu. The legislature begins its session with a colorful ceremony, Hawaiian music and dancing, and the presentation of leis.

Narcissus Festival. Honolulu, Oahu. Five weeks of festivities, including fireworks and lion dances, coinciding with Chinese New Year.

Volcano Marathon and Rim Runs. Hawaii Volcanoes National Park, Hawaii. A race that crosses the Ka'u Desert, circles Kilauea Caldera, and dips into Kilauea Iki Crater.

February

NFL Pro Bowl. Honolulu, Oahu. All-star professional football game held in Aloha Stadium.

Maui Marine Art Expo. Locale varies. International marine artists display works.

Sandcastle Building Contest. Kailua, Oahu. Competition pits architectural students from the University of Hawaii against professionals.

Little Transpac. Oahu-Kauai. A biennial race that follows the Transpacific Yacht Race (see below).

Makawao Statewide Rodeo. Makawao, Maui. One of the top old-time rodeos, this is the biggest and oldest.

Prince Lot Hula Festival. Honolulu, Oahu. An ancient hula festival.

Puuhonua O Honaunau Cultural Festival. Kona Coast, Hawaii. A three-day festival where visitors can try *lauhala* weaving, lei making, and poi pounding under the watchful eyes of the feather-bedecked royal court.

Run to the Sea. Kahului, Maui. A 37.5-mile run from sea level to the 10,000-foot summit of Haleakala.

Transpacific Yacht Races. Oahu; Maui. In odd-numbered years the boats leave San Pedro, CA, for Diamond Head. In even-numbered years they sail from Victoria, B.C., to Lahaina, Maui, while multihulls race the San Pedro-Diamond Head course.

Ukulele Festival. Honolulu, Oahu. Hundreds of ukulele artists perform in this toe-tapping event.

Parker Ranch Rodeo and Horseraces. Waimea, Hawaii. Paniolos from the largest singly-owned ranch in the U.S.

Honomu Village Fair. Honomu, Hawaii. A 46-mile relay race from Volcano to Honomu, with 25 competing teams, is a highlight of the fair.

August

Establishment Day. Puukohala Heiau, Hawaii. Festival emphasizing Hawaiian traditions, with ancient hulas, an artifact show, and workshops in lei making, Hawaiian language, and ancient schools.

Hawaiian Canoe Racing State Championship Regatta. Site varies. Koa canoe championships, with top crews from each island. Individual island championships are held in July.

Hawaiian International Billfish Tournament. Kailua-Kona, Hawaii. The leading international marlin-fishing tournament.

Macadamia Nut Harvest Festival. Honokaa, Hawaii. Harvest celebration with a run, golf tournament, recipe contest, and other activities.

Gabby Pahinui/Atta Isaacs Slack-key Guitar Fest. Ala Moana Park, Honolulu, Oahu. A gathering of Hawaii's best slack-key guitar performers.

September

Aloha Week Festivals. All islands. Hawaiian pageantry, street entertainment, luaus, balls, parades, and canoe races are just some of the highlights of this week-long celebration of the aloha spirit. Each island has its own week of festivities; some are held in October.

Molokai to Oahu Women's Canoe Race. Molokai-Oahu. Endurance classic in the rough water between the two islands.

Waikiki Roughwater Swim. Honolulu, Oahu. Two-mile swim from Sans Souci Beach to Duke Kahanamoku Beach.

Kona Nightingale Race. Kailua-Kona, Hawaii. A donkey race and other zany activities commemorate the time when donkeys were used in the coffee farming industry.

October

Aloha Classic Pro Windsurfing World Cup Finals. Hookipa Beach Park, Maui. The best windsurfers from around the world compete for the cup.

Ironman Triathlon World Championships. Kailua-Kona, Hawaii. The original triathlon, with a 2.4-mile rough-water swim, 112-mile bicycle race, and a 26.2-mile marathon.

Makahiki Festival. Waimea Falls Park, Oahu. Ancient Hawaiian games, crafts, chants, dances, and a luau.

Maui County Fair. Kahului, Maui. The oldest county fair in Hawaii.

Molokai to Oahu Men's Canoe Race. Molokai-Oahu. This endurance race with Hawaiian canoes crosses the rough channel between Molokai and Oahu.

November

Kaluanui Country Christmas House. Makawao, Maui. Holiday craft fair at Hui Noeau Visual Arts Center.

Na Mele O Maui. Lahaina and Kaanapali Beach, Maui. Two-day festival of Hawaiian arts, crafts, and music.

Kapalua International Championship of Golf. Kapalua, Maui. Some of the world's finest professionals compete.

Kona Coffee Festival. Kailua, Hawaii. A celebration of the harvest of America's only commercially grown coffee.

December

A Christmas Tradition. Hilo, Hawaii. The Lyman House Museum's annual New England Christmas observance.

Hawaiian Pro-Surfing Championships. Oahu. Usually three big meets with dates and places determined by wave action; Men's Masters always at Banzai Pipeline.

Christmas in the Country. Volcano Art Center, Hawaii. Arts, crafts, Christmas music, and hot apple cider every day until Christmas up at 4,000 feet where the hearth fire is welcome.

Start of Parker Ranch rodeo

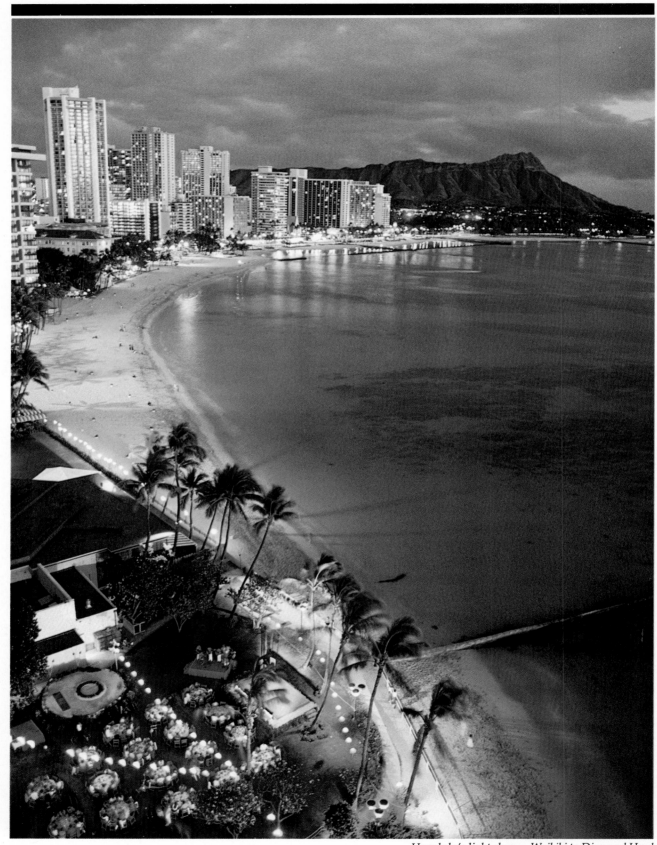

Honolulu's light show—Waikiki to Diamond Head

OAHU

• A MIX OF CITY AND COUNTRY •

Diamond Head, the Pali, Pearl Harbor, the long stretch of Waikiki Beach—you may see some of Oahu's famous sights as your plane circles the island's edge before landing at Honolulu International Airport.

Though Oahu ranks only third in size among the islands, it contains more than three-fourths of Hawaii's people, almost half of whom live in Honolulu. Appropriately named "The Gathering Place," this capital island of approximately 600 square miles/1,560 square km (40 miles/64 km long and 26 miles/42 km wide) lies between Kauai and Molokai.

The Koolau Range that runs from northwest to southeast and the Waianae Mountains along the west coast are the remains of two volcanic domes which formed the island. Lava flows and erosion joined the two ranges, creating the fertile Schofield (or Leilehua) plateau where much of Oahu's sugar and its pineapple are grown today.

Monarchy to Statehood

Evidence of human culture—bits of volcanic glass dated to A.D. 500—has been unearthed at Bellows Field Beach at Waimanalo, the earliest site of habitation yet discovered in these islands. Waikiki, with its coconut groves, fishponds, and walled taro patches, became a favorite seaside resort of early monarchs. Oahu was added to the all-island kingdom in 1795 when King Kamehameha and his warriors from Hawaii island landed at Maunalua Bay and Waikiki and took the Oahu king's forces in a famous battle; they supposedly pushed some of the Oahu men all the way up to the Nuuanu Pali, forcing them to leap from the precipice to their deaths.

With its fine harbors, the island gradually developed into the state's political, economic, military, educational, and cultural center. Honolulu Harbor, first investigated by an English sea captain in 1792, became a key Pacific port of call for whalers and sandalwood and fur traders. The sailing vessels used a mere reef-protected slip at the mouth of Nuuanu Stream; since then, men have dredged and widened it, carved two inlets, and added fill to make shelter and berths for the world's largest liners and freighters. Pearl Harbor came into importance decades later when ships exchanged sails for engines and nations set about building strategic bases.

In the mid-19th century the court moved permanently to Honolulu, which has been the seat of the islands' governments—monarchy, republic, territory, state—ever since. Until the governor and legislature moved into the monumental State Capitol in 1969, Hawaii's capitol was Iolani Palace; the first one stood from 1845 to 1879 and served five kings. The present palace, used for decades as the executive building after the monarchy was overthrown in 1893, has been restored to the grandeur it first enjoyed as the home of King Kalakaua and later his sister, Queen Liliuokalani. It's now a museum.

An Economic Center

Though other economic activities have long surpassed Oahu's agriculture, this island has more land planted with pineapple than any other; its sugar plantations produce more than 16 percent of the state's crop; its truck farms and orchards yield 15 to 20 percent of Hawaii's fruits and vegetables.

Most of the state's military personnel live on Oahu, where all the large bases are located. Including service people, the island's population numbers some 850,000.

Oahu hosts the majority of visitors, now about 7 million, who come to the islands each year, making tourism its largest source of revenue. Manufacturing—everything from petroleum to surfboards and Hawaiian apparel—is also important business; aquaculture and high technology are still infant industries. Construction has tapered off in the 1990s, but the bulldozer, pile driver, crane, and jackhammer are always at work somewhere around the island—in Waikiki, along the waterfront, downtown, or in former cane fields.

THE ESSENTIALS

Most flights across the central Pacific stop at Honolulu International Airport; except for a few trips directly to other islands, Honolulu is the terminus of all mainland-to-Hawaii flights. See page 17 for more on how to reach the islands.

While at the airport, stop by the Pacific Aerospace Museum, located in the lobby of the main concourse. Here, aviation buffs can enjoy a history of flight film, try a cockpit simulator to "fly" in or out of Honolulu, tour a space shuttle flight deck, and use state-of-the-art computers to design planes, trace flights around the Pacific, and predict the weather. The museum (open daily 8 A.M. to 5 P.M.) charges a small admission fee.

Getting Around

Buses, taxis, and limousines shuttle passengers the 9 miles/14 km between Honolulu International Airport and Waikiki. If you prefer to drive on your own, car rental agencies are located in both places. Many firms also have desks in hotel lobbies, a convenience if you want a car only for a day of sightseeing. Agencies will supply maps and help you plot routes around the island. See page 17 for a list of major car rental agencies; for local firms, many of which offer lower rates, consult the Yellow Pages. To rent 4-wheel-drive vehicles, minivans, motorcycles, mopeds, or bicycles, check with your hotel activities desk or look in the Yellow Pages.

Municipal buses reach all parts of the island; call 531-1611 for details. Hotels offer free shuttles to Ala Moana Shopping Center and downtown Honolulu. Commercial attractions, such as Hilo Hattie and Dole Cannery Square, also have Waikiki pickups. Transportation is included in Pearl Harbor and Polynesian Cultural Center tours.

You can best explore Oahu by dividing your sightseeing into three separate trips: a circuit of the greatest part of the island, crossing the Koolaus on the Pali or Likelike Highway, going around the north end, and returning to Honolulu by way of Wahiawa and Pearl Harbor (about 90 miles/144 km); a loop around the east end of the island past Koko Head, through Waimanalo and then the Pali tunnels (about 40 miles/64 km); and a drive through Leeward Oahu and along the Waianae Coast to Makua and back (about 85 miles/136 km). You can also include some city sights on each trip.

Where to Stay

Waikiki, Honolulu's resort district, has some 35,000 rooms in its thicket of hotels and condominiums. Of the more than 20 hotels, condominiums, and apartment complexes strung along the waterfront, a handful are in the luxury class. Most accommodations are in high-rises, but a few low-profile clusters still remain.

You'll find names and locations of major Waikiki hotels on the map on page 32. Look for descriptions of leading hotels in the Waikiki section of this chapter and in the sections where the following resorts are located: Kahala Hilton on the beach at the end of Kahala Avenue, Turtle Bay Hilton at Kahuku on Oahu's north tip, Sheraton Makaha in Makaha Valley on the Waianae Coast, and Ihilani Hotel at the new Ko Olina Resort near Ewa.

Makaha and Kahuku also have condominiums; the Windward Coast offers apartments in Pat's at Punaluu and hotel rooms in Laniloa Lodge at Laie; the North Shore's Mokuleia Beach Colony has condominium apartments. Near Ala Moana Center are the Ala Moana Americana and Pagoda hotels and, close to the airport, Holiday Inn-Airport, Pacific Marina Inn and the Plaza Hotel-Airport. Many apartment rentals are handled by condominium agencies, well known to travel agents.

Bed and breakfast accommodations are available at the John Guild Inn in Manoa Valley, a restored Victorian mansion, and in homes all about the island.

Sightseeing Tours

Honolulu tour agencies will usher you in buses, minibuses, vans, limousines, or sedans on sightseeing trips of the city and the Koko Head-Waimanalo-Pali loop (each a half day) and the greater Oahu circuit (all day). Their packages include various combinations of trips for a comprehensive look at such attractions as Sea Life Park, the Polynesian Cultural Center, Waimea Valley, Home of Waimea Falls; and the Arizona Memorial. Tour agencies or travel agents can also arrange customized tours.

Air tours. For an overview of the island, check the tours of Papillon Hawaiian Helicopters, 836-1566. Glider rides are offered daily from 10 A.M. until late afternoon from Dillingham Field at Mokuleia; reservations are not required. Panorama, 836-2122, and Scenic, 836-0044, give full-day air tours of all the islands in twin-engined craft. The Yellow Pages may list other options.

Boat tours. You'll notice a fleet of cruise boats and catamarans plying the waters off the city every evening. They are out on sunset and moonlight cruises that include dinner and Hawaiian entertainment, departing from Kewalo Basin, Honolulu Harbor, or Waikiki. In the daytime, some of the small craft you see are catamarans giving a fast sail to Waikiki beach-goers or large cats and motor vessels on three-hour cruises morning and afternoon to Pearl Harbor.

Commercial Pearl Harbor cruises from Kewalo Basin don't stop at the Arizona Memorial or Bowfin Submarine Museum and Park, but they do offer an inside look at the workings of the harbor and naval base. For information, call Paradise Cruise, 536-3641. The same company operates the largest dinner ship, *Star of Honolulu*. Tour prices include pickup from Waikiki hotels.

For underwater viewing, dive under the sea with Atlantis Submarines, 973-9811. One-hour tours leave from the Hilton Hawaiian Village pier.

FOR CITY SIGHTSEEING

Bold black and white letters identify "TheBus," part of Honolulu's transportation system throughout Oahu. The white and yellow buses are so popular with visitors that bus guides are sold everywhere; check with your hotel activities desk for further information. Buses run from 6 A.M. to 10:30 P.M. The current fare is $.60 (exact change) whether you're shuttling through Waikiki or making a 4-hour trip around the island. You're allowed a free transfer if you ask when boarding. The main bus terminus is at Ala Moana Center (King Street side of the ground-floor parking lot). The No. 8 bus runs between Kapiolani Park and Ala Moana Center; the No. 52 bus circles the island. To reach Pearl Harbor from Waikiki, take the No. 20 bus marked Airport.

Waikiki Trolley Tours has a fleet of open-air, motorized trolleys cruising between Waikiki and downtown Honolulu. The 2½-hour narrated city tour leaves from Royal Hawaiian Shopping Center every 30 minutes from 8 A.M. to 4:30 P.M. for Ala Moana Center, Iolani Palace, Chinatown, Bishop Museum, and other attractions. You can disembark and reboard at any of 18 locations along the route. An all-day pass is $15 for adults, $5 for children 12 and under.

...The Essentials

Special Interest Tours and Activities

Nothing can more effectively enhance your knowledge and appreciation of Oahu's unique attractions than the guided tour—on foot or by vehicle. In addition to tours offered by some museums, theme parks, and public gardens (details are included with their individual descriptions in this chapter), guides will take you walking through the Capital District (page 37) and Chinatown (page 45). You can take a self-guided tour of the University of Hawaii's Manoa Campus (page 51). Pick up a free map and map-guide to the fine trees and plants on the campus from the Office of University Relations in Hawaii Hall.

Local industries. You can visit factories producing Hawaiian apparel, tee shirts, and coral jewelry, or tour an operating pineapple cannery. Free buses take visitors to Hilo Hattie, Maui Divers' Jewelry Design Center, and for a tour and free, 25-minute movie at Dole Cannery Square. Also at Cannery Square are restaurants, shops, and a children's science museum.

Honolulu has any number of small factories that turn out unusual products—Chinese and Japanese noodles and *saimin*, Japanese fish cake, Portuguese sausage, ukuleles, monkeypod bowls and other wood articles, to name a few. Many places will let visitors watch their operation—but do call ahead. Look in the Yellow Pages under product and ethnic names and note factories mentioned in this chapter's area sections.

Fish auction. United Fishing Agency's lively fish auction is held Monday through Saturday from 6 to about 9 A.M. at 117 Ahui Street fronting Kewalo Basin. Much of the competitive bidding of wholesalers and retailers is in

pidgin English—language as colorful as the sights. Longline sampans and other vessels unload their catches of *ahi* (yellowfin and big-eye tuna), mahimahi, marlin, red snapper, and mackerel at Kewalo and at Piers 15, 17, and 18 starting about 4 A.M. Picturesque, high-prowed *aku* (skipjack tuna) boats unload at Kewalo in late afternoon or early evening as well as the wee hours, with some of their catch going to the basin's Hawaiian Tuna Packers cannery, producers of Bumble Bee and Coral brands.

Handicrafts. Free demonstrations of Hawaiian crafts at hotels and shopping centers are Waikiki institutions along with free hula lessons; in the Waikiki section we point out the spots with the most active programs. The Bishop Museum and Polynesian Cultural Center also sponsor regular shows and demonstrations. At Lanakila Crafts, a rehabilitation center at 1809 Bachelot Street, workers turn out many of the handicrafts you see in tourist gift shops. The center's gift shop is open weekdays from 8 A.M. to 3:30 P.M., and tours of the workshop are given Tuesday and Thursday at 1 P.M.

The Entertainment Scene

Complimentary programs of Hawaiian music and dance are presented by many hotels and shopping centers (see the Waikiki section and look for listings in the many visitor giveaway publications). Most famous is the Kodak Hula Show (Tuesday, Wednesday, and Thursday, 10 A.M.), staged especially for photographers next to the Waikiki Shell lawn. A tradition for more than 50 years, the hula show is great fun, its costumed performers mostly old-timers.

Dinner shows offer such popular entertainers as Don Ho (Hula Hut), Society of Seven (Outrigger Waikiki Hotel), Brothers Cazimero (Royal Hawaiian Hotel), Charo (Hilton Hawaiian Village), and Danny Kaleikini (Kahala Hilton).

Polynesian revues include Hilton Hawaiian Village's free salute to King Kalakaua (torch-lighting ceremony, hula dancing, and fireworks) every Friday night and the nightly (except Sunday) musical comedy in Aloha Showroom atop Waikiki's Royal Hawaiian Shopping Center. Two commercial luaus are held at the edge of Waikiki Beach, at Royal Hawaiian Hotel Monday night and at Outrigger Waikiki Hotel Sunday, Tuesday, and Friday nights. Luaus run by Germaine's or Paradise Cove are held almost every night on beaches near Ewa.

Music. The Honolulu Symphony, one of the country's major orchestras, performs both a classics and pops series of concerts from early fall to spring in Blaisdell Concert Hall and a Starlight pops series at Waikiki Shell in late summer (it also gives free community concerts around the island). Hawaii Opera Theatre presents three different operas in midwinter at Blaisdell Concert Hall. A half dozen or more chamber music ensembles perform

---

WHICH WAY
SHALL I GO?

Islanders have a simple way of giving directions. On every island, you either go toward the sea (*makai*) or toward the mountains (*mauka*). Since the mountains always form the center of each island and the sea always surrounds it, the directions are easy to follow.

Each island and each part of an island has its own terms for directions around the island's perimeter, based on local landmarks. In Honolulu, you might go *Waikiki* or *Diamond Head*. You'll hear someone say, "Go two blocks *Diamond Head* on Kalakaua, then *mauka* on Kaiulani." Beyond Diamond Head, the term will change to *Koko Head*. If you are going in the opposite direction from Waikiki in Honolulu, you are going *Ewa* (toward Ewa, beyond Pearl Harbor).

throughout the year, mostly at Orvis Auditorium, the Academy Theatre, Mamiya Theatre, and churches. The Royal Hawaiian Band (see page 34) plays some Hawaiian numbers along with good band music at its regular concerts. The Honolulu Boy Choir gives periodic shows that are always a delight. About 200 boys, aged 7 to 13 and of all ethnic strains, are trained to sing heartily and with expressive faces; the repertoire includes Hawaiian songs and hulas.

Dance. Ballet Hawaii and Hawaii Ballet Theatre For Youth present occasional concerts. Dances We Dance, Inc. stages modern dance programs periodically at its Jones-Ludin Dance Center, 930 McCully Street upstairs, and also presents monthly programs by local ethnic dance groups or visiting artists; among these may be performances by the best hula *halau* (hula schools), the Pamana or Pearl of the Orient Philippine dance companies, or perhaps Onoe Kikunobu Kai in Japanese classical dances. Be on the lookout for music and dance programs by every one of Hawaii's ethnic groups—Honolulu is a city hard to equal for its variety of cultural offerings.

Theater. Any month you can expect to find a production staged by at least one of these companies: Honolulu Community Theatre (at Ruger Theatre) and Windward Theatre Guild (at a school auditorium) perform popular plays and musicals; Hawaii Performing Arts Company (Manoa Valley Theatre) and University Theatre (Kennedy Theatre) present classical and contemporary works, some experimental; the University-sponsored Kumu Kahua (Kennedy) produces original plays with an island theme; and the Honolulu Theatre for Youth (school auditoriums) has won national acclaim for its plays for youngsters— that also delight their parents.

Art. Honolulu's prolific community of artists exhibits in office buildings, shopping centers, and at fairs in parks as well as in conventional galleries. Their associations range from the Hawaii Artists League, the most selective for artists in all media, to Hale Naua III, for artists of Hawaiian ancestry, to groups of artists who specialize in watercolors, prints, stained glass, weaving, pottery, various handicrafts, or stitchery and fiber arts; all present at least one exhibition each year. You'll find mention of good places to see and buy local art throughout this chapter.

Honolulu Academy of Arts (900 S. Beretania Street) houses one of the finest collections of Asian art outside the Orient, along with its American and European collections. Once a private estate, Contemporary Museum (2411 Makiki Heights Drive), on the slopes of Tantalus, is noted for its views, gardens, and cafe as well as its fine modern art. Don't miss the weekend Art Mart held along Honolulu Zoo's Monsarrat Avenue fence.

The Sporting Guide

On Oahu you'll find the sporting events you'd expect of a major urban and college center. This island is the home of

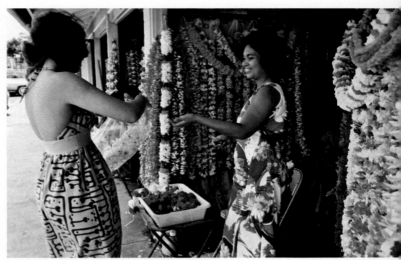

Airport lei stands *supply traditional island greeting, farewell to mainland-bound vacationers.*

the Hawaii Islanders of the Pacific Coast League (a Class AAA baseball league). The University of Hawaii at Manoa, a member of the Western Athletic Conference, has teams in most sports and, recently, outstanding baseball and women's volleyball teams. This island's four small private colleges and the University of Hawaii at Hilo are all members of the National Association of Intercollegiate Athletics (NAIA) and enter teams in several sports. Basketball is most popular; Chaminade's teams have earned that university a national reputation.

Look also for good swimming meets, road races, triathlons (swimming, bicycling, running), rodeos and horse shows, golf and tennis tournaments, periodic boxing and wrestling matches (professional sumo once in a while), and regular auto racing at Hawaii Raceway Park.

Because of its cultural diversity, Oahu provides a rare opportunity to observe sports that are unusual to many visitors. Amateur competition in the Oriental martial arts such as karate, judo, and kung fu continues all year. Check the Yellow Pages for lists of schools; the City-County Department of Parks and Recreation also sponsors classes. There's amateur sumo wrestling every Sunday from 2 to 5 P.M. at Aala Park and occasionally a tournament featuring amateurs from Japan. Cricket— especially popular with Samoans—is played in Kapiolani and Keehi Lagoon parks, rugby in several places including Kapiolani Park; check with the Department of Parks and Recreation. Outrigger canoe races—regattas or distance races—go on most of the year.

The islands' international, professional, big wave surfing meets are held on Oahu's west and north shore beaches in late fall and winter. Good amateur contests are scheduled in spring and summer in or near Waikiki, where waves are of average size. See "Annual Events" (pages 20-21) for details on the biggest crowd-pullers in all sports.

HONOLULU: A CAPITAL CITY

Sunlovers line sands *in front of Royal Hawaiian Hotel, city's venerable "Pink Palace."*

Honolulu sprawls over 25 miles/40 km of Oahu's south shore, from Hickam Air Force Base to Makapuu Point. Its residential sections burrow into the jungled valleys of the Koolaus and climb the steep ridges toward the city limits—the tops of the green-clad peaks. At night, lights of houses on the ridges, or heights, create a patchwork backdrop to the vast central plain, occupied largely by business, industry, apartments, and the resort community of Waikiki. Residential districts also extend from Diamond Head all the way to Koko Head.

A melange of Polynesia, the Orient, and the contemporary mainland, Honolulu is a city shaped by people of a dozen different ethnic strains, whose heritage and customs assert themselves in many ways upon the urban scene. You'll find both English and foreign-language newspapers, films, and programs on radio and TV; lunch wagons and "mom and pop" stores (often with a "shave ice" machine); and open-front markets full of strange foods popular in the Orient.

Because of its beautiful setting in the lee of the mountains and its large, protected harbor, Honolulu has burgeoned in recent years. Though the city is crowded (population 370,000), possesses thickets of concrete towers, and matches freeway congestion with any other major city, growth has also brought sophisticated modern squares studded with handsome sculpture, high-fashion stores, galleries with quality antiques and fine art, museums, concerts, theaters, and restaurants for almost every cuisine.

The land-scarce community retains old buildings in styles that bespeak its history, quaint box houses with "chop suey" gardens huddled together along narrow lanes, and elegant homes with expansive grounds. Forest trails with waterfalls and swimming holes, tree-lined boulevards, fine beaches, boat harbors, and generous city parks are used intensively for sports, family outings, group picnics, concerts, fairs, and festivals.

Still, Honolulu retains a friendly, small town atmosphere. People wear sports or "aloha" attire everywhere, with *zori* (go-aheads) on their feet, and navigate their autos over streets with seldom a honking of the horn.

Greater Waikiki

Officially, Waikiki is a peninsula about ½ mile/1 km wide by 2 miles/3 km long, bounded by the ocean, Ala Wai Canal, and Kapahulu Avenue. But Waikiki Beach extends almost to Diamond Head and thus so does Greater Waikiki, taking in the world of Kapiolani Park.

Most visitors spend at least part of their stay in this resort area. Formerly maligned for its tacky tourist shops and clogged streets, Waikiki spent millions of dollars sprucing up parks, hotels, streets, and shops. Sidewalks along Kalakaua Avenue, the main street, have been widened, repaved, and lined with trees and planter boxes. Much of the commercial traffic has been rerouted or restricted to off hours. And with grand city parks (Ala Moana and Kapiolani) at either end of the district, it's a great place to stroll.

More than just a tourist enclave for mainlanders, Waikiki is also a place to mingle with visitors from many foreign lands, especially Japanese newlyweds. An average day in the district finds about 100,000 visitors rubbing shoulders with the 25,000 people who live here and the 30,000 local people who work in the area. You'll meet islanders strolling, shopping, dining, swimming, surfing, and enjoying the parks.

Along with new hotels, apartments, and shopping centers has come an explosion of pools, fountains, gardens, and art works. Most shops are open well into the evening, when the balmy air invites you out for a stroll. You might catch a street-side Polynesian show or listen to music emanating from an open-air dining spot. Your choices for dinner or cocktails range from outdoor terraces to vantage points in the sky and, for food, everything from hamburgers to a nine-course Chinese feast. During the day, you can also sun, swim, surf, take a hula lesson, and visit the reef fish at the aquarium or rare tropical birds at the zoo.

Though Waikiki has less crime than many mainland tourist resorts, you'll want to take the usual precautions. Watch your wallet or purse and don't walk alone on back streets or dark stretches of beach at night. Keep to the well-lighted, busy main thoroughfares.

Waikiki Beach is not one continuous crescent of sand but a series of beaches, some natural, some manmade, each with its own flavor and habitués. The whole strip is public and accessible by right-of-ways; you can walk on sand and connecting sea walls from Duke Kahanamoku Beach to Kuhio Beach Park or on to Sans Souci Beach. And even when the ocean is rough, you can swim anywhere without fear of dangerous currents.

Several beaches are territories for outrigger canoes, catamarans, surfboards, and beachboys who give surfing lessons or take you on boat rides. Most of the action takes place a half-mile offshore where the waves break, beyond most swimmers but within view of beach-sitters.

Some of Waikiki's beach bustle is wacky and fun, but if your stretch of sand becomes overcrowded, change your location—or your tanning time. You'll find more

pristine sand and fewer people early in the morning or late in the day.

Ala Wai Canal was dredged in the 1920s to drain surrounding swamps and duck ponds and carry runoff from the streams that occasionally flooded Waikiki. Apartments strung along Ala Wai Boulevard look across the waterway to Ala Wai Golf Course and Field (the open lands that let the trade winds into Waikiki) and to the developed heights and wild green peaks beyond.

Early morning or late in the day, residents jog or just walk along the canal's promenade; in the afternoon, outrigger canoes skim the water as muscular paddlers train for forthcoming races. At any time of day, anglers sit comfortably on banks overhung with Chinese banyans between the Kalakaua and Ala Moana bridges, plucking *akule, papio,* mullet, and even crabs from the silty water.

Ala Wai Yacht Harbor shelters more than 1,000 private boats (no commercial craft). Broad piers make it easy to visit them. The State of Hawaii has 780 berths filled with 20 to 100-foot sailboats, including more than 100 "live-aboards." Waikiki Yacht Club on Ala Moana Park Drive has 185 slips and Hawaii Yacht Club at the end of Mole A, about 25 spaces for boats of up to 60 feet. Both clubs and the harbor have long waiting lists.

Exploring Waikiki's attractions takes you through several neighborhoods, each trying to make its major

Muumuu-clad musicians *entertain visitors at the Kodak Hula Show in Waikiki's Kapiolani Park.*

...Honolulu/Waikiki

hotels and shopping centers stand out from the others. The area's center includes the blocks along and off Kalakaua and Kuhio avenues from Waikiki Gateway Park to Kaiulani Avenue. Its beach and swimming area—from Royal Hawaiian Hotel to Kuhio Beach Park—is the most spacious but also accommodates Waikiki's largest concentration of surfers, outrigger canoes, and catamarans.

Start your tour at Ala Wai Yacht Harbor and proceed *Diamond Head*. If you travel on foot, you won't have to master the one-way street system. To cover longer distances, hop aboard TheBus or Waikiki Trolley. Buses travel on Kalakaua and Kuhio avenues, Saratoga and Kalia roads, and Ala Moana Boulevard; the trolley stops at Royal Hawaiian Shopping Center, at Hilton Hawaiian Village, and at Kalakaua Avenue and Kapiolani Boulevard.

Hawaii Prince Hotel, 100 Holomoana Street, is Waikiki's latest luxury entry. All rooms in the two 32-floor towers face the yacht harbor. The elegant Prince Court, an award-winning restaurant, features the best of the island's regional cuisine. Free shuttles ferry guests to nearby Ala Moana Shopping Center or downtown.

Discovery Bay Shopping Center, 1778 Ala Moana Boulevard, features shops and restaurants beneath twin apartment towers. Among the dining options is Bon Appetit, a superb French restaurant.

Eaton Square, 444 Hobron Lane, captures a touch of Europe with brick paving, lights made of London gas lamps, and imported iron gates and roof tiles, but its rubbish containers respond in "pidgin" when you feed them. Its several levels contain shops and restaurants, among them Chez Michel, renowned for its Continental and French fare.

Ilikai Waikiki, 1777 Ala Moana Boulevard, has 800 large units in 3 towers, with 6 garagetop tennis courts and a broad terrace with colored fountains, the scene of a torch-lighting ceremony. A glass elevator lifts you 30 stories for grand views at Champeaux's restaurant or Annabelle's lounge.

Duke Kahanamoku Beach, named for Hawaii's famous Olympic swimming champion, encloses the lagoon fronting Hilton Hawaiian Village (see below). The lagoon, with its clear water and soft, sandy bottom, is popular with small children and their parents.

Hilton Hawaiian Village, 2005 Kalia Road, is Waikiki's largest resort complex, with 4 towers, 2,523 rooms, 22 restaurants, 3 swimming pools, and beautifully landscaped gardens. The complex, which resembles a self-contained village, encompasses 100-plus shops, 22 restaurants and cocktail lounges, 3 pools, and a boat dock.

Both ends of Rainbow Tower are decorated with Millard Sheets's eye-catching murals, created from ceramic tile in 17 different colors and lighted after dark. The enormous aluminum geodesic dome by Buckminster Fuller is one of Waikiki's largest show rooms.

Casual attire *and indoor-outdoor settings make island dining an informal delight.*

Primary / Secondary

Honolulu

0 1 2 KM
0 .5 1.0 1.5 MI

At the Rainbow Bazaar, you view Hawaiian and Pacific wares in three areas: Imperial Japan, with a 400-year-old farmhouse imported and rebuilt without nails for Benihana of Tokyo (where a chef teppan-broils your entrée with great flourish); Hong Kong Alley, arranged around a court with moon gate; and the South Pacific, with buildings missionaries might have erected.

Fort DeRussy, built on filled fish and duck ponds as part of Oahu's coastal defense system, is now primarily a recreation base for military personnel—and an inviting greensward in Waikiki. The public is welcome on DeRussy's long wide beach of hard sand, but its hotel, Hale Koa, and other facilities are reserved for members of the armed forces and their families.

In the U.S. Army Museum (Tuesday through Sunday 10 A.M. to 4:30 P.M.; free), you can tour a labyrinth of corridors and concussion chambers in Battery Randolph and walk along its 22-foot-thick top. Displays cover the history of the Army in the Pacific and aspects of Hawaii military history. In the superstructure, the Corps of Engineers presents a film on its Pacific Basin projects.

Urasenke Foundation of Hawaii Tea Room, 245 Saratoga Road (Wednesday and Friday 10 A.M. to noon; free) makes a good spot to stop for a cup of tea. In a tranquil garden setting, kimono-clad Japanese hostesses perform the tea ceremony, serving sweets and green tea. They carefully explain the artistry and tradition behind *Chado,* the Way of Tea. The tea room, with its authentic *tatami* mats, is adjacent to Breakers Hotel, 1½ blocks *mauka* Kalia Road.

Gray's Beach borrowed its name from Grays-by-the-Sea, an early boarding house. Good swimmers head for "the rock," a remnant of an old mooring in the sandy channel part-way out to the reef.

Halekulani Hotel, 2199 Kalia Road, lives up to its name as "the house befitting heaven." The modern version of this luxurious hostelry contains 456 rooms clustered around a historic garden lanai and the handsome "Main Building," built by architect C. W. Dickey in 1931. The hotel began life in 1907 as a collection of cottages nestled in a coconut grove.

Among its ties with the past are a lounge named for Robert Lewers, the hotel's founder, and Sunset Terrace, a popular lunch and cocktail area with a century-old *kiawe* tree. A second House Without a Key replaces the original open-walled bar made famous in a Charlie Chan mystery. Both hotel dining rooms, casual Orchids and elegant La Mer, win rave reviews for setting, decor, and cuisine.

Waikiki Parc, 2233 Helumoa Road, lies adjacent to Halekulani, its sister hotel. The 298-room, 22-story hotel, with its 2 restaurants and 8th-floor pool, is a popular and less extravagant lodging alternative to its neighbor.

Lewers Street, a noisy, congested thoroughfare between Kalia Road and Kalakaua Avenue, is lined with reasonably priced hotels, including several Outriggers, and informal restaurants, such as Moose McGillicuddy's and Perry's Smorgy.

Waikiki Joy Hotel, 320 Lewers Street, is popular with people who don't care about views. A charming hotel with fewer than 100 rooms, it boasts a pool and a restaurant.

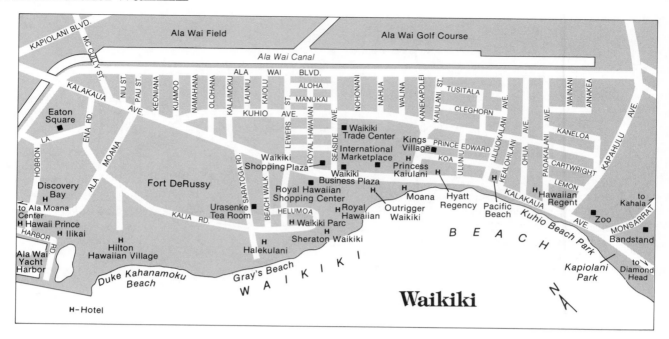

Waikiki

Woolworth's, 2224 Kalakaua Avenue, is the best-known occupant of an unusual tower with concrete arches. It offers an exotic selection of goods, including Hawaiian wear, curios, and take-out ethnic foods. Prices, though lower than specialty shops, may be higher than at the store's other location in Ala Moana Shopping Center.

Waikiki Shopping Plaza, 2250 Kalakaua Avenue, has escalators, open-front shops, and restaurants rising around a 75-foot-high lighted fountain made of acrylic bowls. Fast-food eateries on the lower level are topped by three floors of shops and two of specialty restaurants. Waldenbooks, Waikiki's only book store, is located here.

Waikiki Business Plaza, 2270 Kalakaua Avenue, is distinguished from other buildings by its mosaic mural and fountain. On the eighth floor are the offices of Hawaii Visitors Bureau, the best place to get information on hotels, restaurants, attractions, and upcoming events. Some of the wholesale fashion outlets on the 10th floor admit the public. A revolving restaurant on the 21st floor offers panoramic views.

Hawaii Imax Theatre, 325 Seaside Avenue, has a 35-minute film showing breathtaking island scenery, from the cliffs on Molokai to the formation 4,000 feet under the sea of the island of Loihi, south of the Big Island. The film ($7.50 adults, $5 children), which alternates with a space documentary, is shown on a screen 5 stories high and 70 feet wide. Also in the theater is a fast-food concession and a museum-quality gift shop. The theater is open daily from 11 A.M. to 9 P.M.

Waikiki Trade Center, 2255 Kuhio Avenue (corner of Kuhio and Seaside), attracts visitors to its out-of-the-way location with a shopping arcade located on the first floor of a 22-story sculptured tower (lots of black glass and portholes). It houses several haute couture shops and specialty restaurants (Baci is noted for its Italian food).

Royal Hawaiian Shopping Center, 2201 Kalakaua Avenue, extends across 6½ acres in front of Royal Hawaiian and Sheraton Waikiki hotels. More than 200 shops and restaurants fill 3 multistory buildings connected by bridges.

This upscale center has everything from international fashion outlets to native arts and crafts. Little Hawaiian Craft Shop boasts museum-quality handicrafts as well as appealing souvenirs. Suntory is considered one of the city's finest Japanese restaurants.

Vines and other plantings drape the lava rock and coral-textured walls and decorate atriums and interior promenades. Several restaurants, including a McDonald's that displays contemporary Hawaiian art inspired by ancient legends, open to Royal Hawaiian's garden.

Free entertainment takes place several times a week in the waterfall-laced courtyard facing Kalakaua. Demonstrations by Hawaiian artisans are offered in Building A's third-floor Bridge Room. The center's 1,000-seat Aloha Showroom is the nighttime setting for a lively Hawaiian musical comedy.

Sheraton Waikiki, 2255 Kalakaua Avenue, towers over nearby hotels, including its sister property, low-rise Royal Hawaiian. The hotel, Sheraton's largest in Hawaii, has 1,900 rooms and a vast, curved facade. The glass elevator shoots up 30 stories to Hanohano Room, where the view is spectacular at cocktail, dinner, or Sunday brunch time. Photographs of old Waikiki are displayed in Historical Room on the convention floor.

Royal Hawaiian Hotel, 2259 Kalakaua Avenue, is familiarly known as the "Pink Palace." Now under the Sheraton banner, the Spanish Mission style hotel was opened in 1927; the tower wing was added in the 1960s. Though the gardens have been reduced, they still include palms growing in 1870 when King Kamehameha V had a beach cottage on the site. Lovely shops off the lobbies and arcades offer oriental antiques and local artists' works. A stunning, mirror-backed floral arrangement, spotlighted for photographers, is at the end of the gallery to the Monarch Room, scene of good cocktail and dinner shows Tuesday through Saturday and a tea dance late Monday afternoon (except in summer). The Royal's Surf Room and Mai Tai Bar back up to the beach and are popular for food, drinks, and music.

Outrigger Waikiki, 2335 Kalakaua Avenue, is this chain's premier property. The high-rise hotel (529 rooms) stands on a good beach in the middle of the action. Other amenities include pools, restaurants, and cocktail lounges. The main show room has long been home to the Society of Seven, a popular performing group.

Sheraton Moana Surfrider, 2365 Kalakaua Avenue, was Waikiki's first large tourist hostelry. Opened in 1901, Victorian style Moana Hotel boasted 75 rooms in an old-fashioned central frame structure; the concrete wings were added in 1918. The Ocean Lanai wing was the original Surfrider Hotel, built in 1952. Meticulously restored in 1989, the 803-room hotel (the old section contains the most charming accommodations) has returned to its former glory.

Moana's Banyan Court is named for one of Honolulu's magnificent old banyans. More than a century ago, it provided shade and inspiration for writer Robert Louis Stevenson.

Princess Kaiulani Hotel, 120 Kaiulani Avenue, is named for the lovely heir to the throne who was only 23 when she died in 1899. Her estate, Ainahau, would today be a park had the government accepted the gift of her father, Archibald Cleghorn, a governor of Oahu who landscaped Honolulu's first parks. Hotel banquet rooms are named for the estate, Cleghorn, his wife (Princess Likelike), and author Stevenson, a family friend. The handsome Japanese-roofed shops that line Kalakaua are among the original parts of this Sheraton hotel built by Matson Navigation Company in 1955.

International Market Place, 2330 Kalakaua Avenue, is a two-level bazaar in wood and thatch beneath spreading banyan trees. It's unbelievably crammed with open-front restaurants, shops, kiosks, and carts; you'll find apparel, jewelry, baskets, and handicrafts from Hawaii, other Pacific islands, and Asia—everything from schlock to good folk art.

Duke's Lane, along the *Ewa* side of the bazaar, is lined with still more souvenir stands; adjoining Kuhio Mall has more shops and restaurants.

Hyatt Regency Waikiki, 2424 Kalakaua Avenue, is across the street from the beach and close to Kapiolani Park. With more than 1,200 rooms, the sleek twin-tower property features a block-long promenade that opens to three levels of shops, restaurants, and lounges.

Great Hall, an atrium between the two 40-story towers, contains a waterfall, a gigantic hanging metal sculpture, and Harry's Bar, a "sidewalk" cafe (drinks, coffee, light breakfasts and lunches).

In the late afternoon and evenings, the Great Hall fills with music. A Friday afternoon show at 5 P.M. features Hawaiian music and dance. On the second floor, an Hawaiiana expert displays artifacts and museum-quality Hawaiian art work, and shows you how they are made.

King's Village, 131 Kaiulani Avenue, features a cobblestoned Monarch's Walk that winds up three levels past shops and restaurants in buildings resembling those of Honolulu a century ago. At night the buildings are outlined with lights. Plaques commemorate Hawaii's *alii* (royalty). You can watch a Changing of the Guard ceremony, performed by guardsmen dressed like King Kalakaua's Royal Guard, at the entrance evenings at 6:15 P.M., and a children's hula show in Bishop Court Sunday at 1 P.M.

Pacific Beach Hotel, 2490 Kalakaua Avenue, has a 280,000-gallon oceanarium of tropical marine life that rises three stories from the lobby. A diver feeds the fish five or six times a day; you can watch from the lobby or from the first or second-floor restaurants. Diners in the Japanese restaurant, Shogun, on the third floor view the waterfall that fills the tank with sea water.

WAIKIKI WALKS

Waikiki, Honolulu's tourist mecca, boasts a colorful history. Thanks to the talents of storyteller-guides on five walking tours, its past comes alive.

A Journey to Old Waikiki: This 2½-hour morning stroll begins at the Duke Kahanamoku statue on Kuhio Beach and ends at International Market Place, where you see a film of early 20th-century days. Tours (fee) take place Tuesday, Thursday, and Saturday at 9 A.M. For reservations, call Passport Hawaii, 924-1911.

The Magic of Waikiki: Kapiolani Community College sponsors a 2-hour evening week on the second and fourth Tuesday of each month. The guided tour (fee) follows the shoreline from Kapiolani Park to Fort DeRussy. Call 734-9245 for reservations.

Aunty Malia's Historical Walking Tour: This 2-hour loop tour focuses on the area once home to Princess Kaulani (including the hotel named for her). The free tour, limited to those aged 18 and over, departs Tuesday and Wednesday at 10:30 A.M. May through September from the Hawaii Museum at Hyatt Regency Waikiki. For information, call 923-1234, ext. 6410.

Historic Waikiki Beach Stroll: The 3-hour walk starts at 9 A.M. weekdays at the Honolulu Zoo entrance and extends to Hilton Lagoon and Ilikai Hotel. The stroll is free. Reserve by calling 948-3299.

Moana Hotel Tour: The hour-long walk leads you through Waikiki's first luxury hotel, restored in 1989. The free tour starts at 11 A.M. daily at the concierge desk of Sheraton Moana Surfrider Hotel.

St. Augustine's Church, 130 Ohua Avenue, holds weekend masses featuring native songs by a choir of Hawaiians or Tongans. The Damien Museum, located behind the church, houses historical photographs and the personal possessions of Father Damien (see page 124).

Hawaiian Regent Hotel, 2552 Kalakaua Avenue, has a handsome open-to-the-sky court in its Kalakaua Tower with a dramatic stairway to The Library (a piano bar), and on to The Secret, a popular restaurant. Hawaiian music emanates nightly from the Kuhio Tower lobby.

Kuhio Beach Park stretches from the Moana Hotel to Kapiolani Park and is bordered by a broad promenade with trees, benches, and steps down to the sand. In the pavilions, chess, checkers, and card players gather day and night. Four legendary "wizard stones" stand on the sand beside the Moana, supposedly endowed with healing powers by four Tahitian *kahuna* (priests). The walkway jutting into the sea at the end of Kapahulu Avenue, takes you into the midst of local board and body surfers.

Kapiolani Park sprawls over some 170 acres between Kapahulu Avenue and Diamond Head. A gift to the people from King Kalakaua in 1877, the park was named for his queen. It has a zoo, aquarium, beaches, tennis courts, archery and golf-driving ranges, and an encircling jogging path. On the grass lawns people play softball, soccer, volleyball, cricket, and rugby; fly kites; feed the birds; exercise their dogs; and picnic under enormous shade trees.

Most park concerts and programs take place at the Waikiki Shell, an outdoor amphitheater, and the Kapiolani Bandstand, site of a 2 P.M. Sunday concert and a 7:30 A.M. Sunday marathon clinic. The old-fashioned green and gold pavilion nearby was a 1900s trolley station.

Monkeypods, weeping banyans, and ironwoods line the drives. Near the Louise Dillingham Memorial Fountain on Kalakaua Avenue are yellow and pink rainbow shower trees that bloom in spring and summer. In Queen Kapiolani Garden, stunning pink butterfly hibiscus trees border the *lokelani* roses.

Honolulu Zoo, 151 Kapahulu Avenue (daily 8:30 A.M. to 4:30 P.M.; admission fee), is a 42-acre tropical garden home for some 900 species of mammals, amphibians, fish, reptiles, and birds. Here children meet Mari, an Indian elephant, climb a spiral stair to get eye to eye with the giraffes, and venture into the African savanna exhibit. Picnicking is popular around the snack bar. In borders outside the zoo's Kapahulu and Paki fences, local people tend crops in a community recreational garden; outside the Monsarrat Avenue fence you'll find the colorful Art Mart.

Waikiki Aquarium, 2777 Kalakaua Avenue (daily 9 A.M. to 5 P.M., free, but adult donation requested), contains Hawaii's greatest variety of tropical Pacific marine life. In addition to giant clams, cuttlefish, and Hawaiian monk seals (an endangered species), there's an oceanfront "Edge of the Reef" tidepool exhibit with living coral and fish common to Hawaii's shallow reefs and tidepools.

The park waterfront starts with Queen's Surf Beach, popular with residents. Broad Sans Souci Beach (shallow, placid water ideal for children or novice swimmers) takes its name from the resort lodge built on this site in the 1880s. The sandy channel running out to the reef contains remnants of the first Honolulu–to–San Francisco oceanic

THE ROYAL HAWAIIAN BAND...MUSIC SINCE MONARCHY

Stroll by the bandstand at Iolani Palace on a Friday at noon and you'll find yourself part of a 100-year-old tradition as the Royal Hawaiian Band serenades listeners with selections ranging from Hawaiian tunes to European classics to Broadway showstoppers.

King Kamehameha III formed the band in 1836, and it has continued to play throughout Hawaii's transition from monarchy to statehood. Band membership has grown from 10 to 39; in 1909, after a number of changes, the group was officially named the Royal Hawaiian Band.

What saved the band from fading into obscurity was the arrival in 1872 of Henry Berger, sent from Prussia on a four-year loan. Four years stretched into 57, and Berger remained in the islands as a naturalized citizen until his death in 1929. During his 43 years as bandmaster, Berger welded the group into a harmonic unit that played over 32,000 concerts (as many as five a day).

Berger was more than just the bandmaster. A composer whose credits include Hawaii's state song, "Hawaii Ponoi," Berger taught at the local school for orphans and wayward youth, inviting promising musicians to join the band. It was Berger who began the tradition of playing during the festivities at Aloha Tower celebrating ship arrivals and departures. It was also Berger who pushed the band to the forefront of Hawaiian society. Berger is still honored in a yearly concert.

Today the Royal Hawaiian Band is the only full-time municipal band in the United States. Membership is a highly coveted prize and auditions for the occasional openings are rigorous.

Currently under the direction of Aaron Mahi, the band has toured the mainland and Europe. Back home, it continues to perform the Friday noon concerts as well as Sunday afternoon in Kapiolani Park and monthly at Bishop Square. The band can also be found marching in parades, giving benefit concerts, and participating in cultural events—performing the music that is a part of Hawaii's history.

ON THE PALACE GROUNDS

A palm-lined drive off King Street leads through iron-fenced lawns to picturesque Iolani Palace (guided tours Wednesday through Saturday 9 A.M. to 2:15 P.M.; admission; call 522-0832 for reservations), restored to look as it did a century ago when Hawaii's last king and queen lived in it.

Built by King Kalakaua and inspired by his European travels, the palace was completed in 1882. After his death it became the official residence of his sister, Queen Liliuokalani, until the monarchy ended in 1893. It later served as Hawaii's capitol for 75 years.

The turreted structure of cement-faced brick has double lanais on all sides, unusual upper-floor corner tower rooms, and delicate cast-iron columns and balustrades. The throne room, dining room, and the king's library upstairs are furnished. Royal portraits and niches with vases and statuary line the walls of the splendid main hallway with its curved staircase of koa.

Replacing the furniture sold at auction when the kingdom was toppled may take years, but there is still plenty to see on the hour-long tour: sculptured plaster, etched glass doors, carved woodwork, mirror-polished floor, and crystal and bronze light fixtures.

The palace shop and ticket office are in Iolani Barracks, the rebuilt 1871 headquarters of the kingdom's household guards. The fortresslike building has coral block walls, slate roof, crenelated parapets, and towers with decorative loopholes. It will become a military museum when the visitor center is moved to the Kanaina Building in the late 1980s.

This 1906 Classical Style structure on the other side of the palace was the first building in the country designed as a public archives; it now houses state offices. In front are legendary sacred boulders and Oahu's only memorial to Captain Cook. Across the lawn, a fenced, planted mound marks the site of the tomb where the bodies of Kamehameha II and Queen Kamamalu were buried from 1825 until 1865, when they were transferred to the Royal Mausoleum.

The present State Archives, built in 1954, has a wealth of research material, historical photographs, and drawings from which prints can be ordered. The building is separated from the palace by an enormous banyan (originally two trees) that Kalakaua's queen, Kapiolani, planted in the 1880s.

Iolani Palace Bandstand, an octagonal pavilion, was built by Kalakaua in front of the palace for his belated coronation in 1883. It soon became a bandstand and was moved to its present site on the *Ewa-makai* lawn.

On special occasions, the restored or reproduced gates to the palace grounds are manned by ceremonial guardsmen dressed in uniforms like those of Kalakaua's guard.

Conch shells signal start of festivities

Kamehameha the Great *presides from atop pedestal in front of the Judiciary Building.*

Diamond Head

The craggy profile of this crater, formed some 150,000 years ago in a series of underwater volcanic explosions, is as familiar as the Rock of Gibraltar. Diamond Head was once a coast defense fort, bristling with guns poked through its high walls. Now gardens of fine homes built upon the lower slopes create a greenbelt. Diamond Head won its name when some 19th century British sailors discovered calcite crystals on its slopes and mistook them for diamonds. The federal government bought Diamond Head in 1904, fortified and used it through World War II, and then gave it to the state in 1950. It's now a state park and monument and national natural landmark.

To circle the crater you take Diamond Head Road from Kapiolani Park, drive under the spreading trees of fine oceanfront estates, then climb the *kiawe*-covered Kuilei Cliffs to the lighthouse and turnouts. The panorama of residential Honolulu spreads below you, from Black Point to Koko Head and Koko Crater. Notice tobacco heiress Doris Duke's white-columned, Persian style "Shangri-La" at Black Point. One lookout has a monument to famous aviatrix Amelia Earhart.

Diamond Head Lighthouse, rising 55 feet from its cliffside perch, has an automatic light visible 17 miles out to sea. Beneath the cliffs, two unimproved beach parks make up an unbroken strip of sand fringing a sea floor grown with coral. Diamond Head Beach Park, on the *Ewa* side and reached by Beach Road, attracts reef-explorers and sunbathers. Surfers populate Kuilei Cliffs Beach Park *Koko Head* of the light, hauling their boards down paths from the lookouts above. You can walk the shore on sand or lava to Black Point and swim at Kaalawai Beach, where sandy pockets and channels stretch out to surfing grounds, or at breakwater-protected Duke's harbor.

From its highest point above the sea, Diamond Head Road descends between cliffside houses to a junction with Kahala Avenue, then climbs the crater's east side through Fort Ruger, the Army's first garrisoned coastal artillery fort in Hawaii.

Monsarrat Avenue takes you down the crater's western slope, past Fort Ruger's Cannon Club.

Drive into Diamond Head through a tunnel off Diamond Head Road near 18th Avenue (open 6 A.M. to 6 P.M.). The vast, desolate interior is open space except for the Hawaii National Guard Armory and the Federal Aviation Administration's Air Route Traffic Control Center, which directs aircraft over 10 million square miles.

A trail to the 761-foot seaward rim of the crater leads up a gently graded path, traversing the *kiawe* and *koa haole*-covered slopes to a fine lookout facing Koko Head and Koko Crater. From here, a series of steps, stairways, and a tunnel lead to the summit; your reward is a spectacular view over much of the island.

Action Hawaii Adventures offers morning crater hikes. The price of the package includes transportation; check with your hotel activities desk for information.

cable, completed in 1903. Sans Souci is also site of the New Otani Kaimana Beach Hotel, 2863 Kalakaua Avenue; an aged *hau* tree shelters the main dining spot.

The Outrigger Canoe Club Beach and swimming channel, also serving the Colony Surf and Colony East hotels (2895 Kalakaua) and the Elks Club (2933 Kalakaua), were manmade in the early 1960s. The clubs offer informal indoor-outdoor oceanfront dining. The hotel and condo complex houses Michel's, an elegant French restaurant with open windows and beach views, and Bobby McGee's Conglomeration, where salads are arrayed in a Victorian bathtub and waiters and waitresses appear as Attila the Hun, Wee Willie Winkie, and other characters.

The Outrigger Canoe Club (2909 Kalakaua) was on the site of the Outrigger Waikiki Hotel for 55 years. Its Hau Terrace, a dining institution, was reestablished in this handsome home.

Greater Downtown

The downtown area extends inland about 6 blocks from Honolulu Harbor. Each of its three districts (Capital, Downtown Center, and Chinatown) are just the right size to explore on foot; good walkers can cover the whole area, from South Street to Nuuanu Stream, in one visit. (Office buildings are open weekdays, generally from 7:30 or 8 A.M. to 4:30 or 5 P.M.; most stores are open until 5 P.M. and on Saturday.)

Hawaii Capital District

The Capital District, from South to Richards streets, contains architectural treasures arrayed in a gardenlike setting—structures of missionaries and monarchs and later bureaucrats span more than a century and a half. This is the center of Hawaii's state government. Guides take you through the museums—Iolani Palace (see page 35) and Mission Houses Museum (see page 38); the latter museum offers a guided walk through the district (weekday mornings by reservation) with tours inside Kawaiahao and St. Andrew's churches and the Capitol; or, for just the admission price to its historic structures, you'll receive a self-guiding tour booklet describing the area. When the legislature is in session the first months of the year, you can tag along with school classes touring the Capitol.

Hawaii State Capitol, between Beretania Street and Hotel Street Mall. Designed by architects John Carl Warnecke and Associates and Belt, Lemmon, and Lo, the Capitol rises out of its reflecting pool like the islands from the sea. The open-ended central court, flanked by conical legislative chambers, is topped by a volcano-shaped crown open to the sky. Concrete columns supporting the balconied office stories suggest royal palms. From spectator galleries in the House and Senate chambers, you can view Otto Piene's light spheres symbolizing the sun and moon and Ruthadell Anderson's Hawaiian-motif tapestries.

The court is always open and elevators are unlocked. On the court floor, note Tadashi Sato's circular mosaic, *Aquarius*. From the fifth floor you can look down upon the court, up to the sky, and out over the city; the reception rooms of the governor and lieutenant governor display works by local artists and make extensive use of Big Island koa in paneling and furniture.

A huge copper state seal, derived from the monarchy's coat of arms, hangs over both Capitol entrances. On the Beretania side is Marisol's striking bronze of Father Damien; on the grass mall between the Capitol and the palace grounds (see page 35) stands Marianna Pineda's melancholy figure of Queen Liliuokalani, her outstretched hand often bearing a flower lei.

Hawaii State Library, 478 South King Street (Monday through Saturday 9 A.M. to 5 P.M.; Tuesday and Thursday until 8 P.M.). On a monkeypod-shaded lawn stands the columned and tile-roofed library, built in 1913 with side wings added in 1929. Its open-air central court and surrounding loggias provide inviting spots for reading.

Honolulu Hale (City Hall), King and Punchbowl streets. This Spanish Colonial style building houses the offices of the mayor and city council around a tiled court open to the sky. Built in 1929 and expanded in 1952, the Hale has a grand staircase off the courtyard, a speaker's balcony, fine cast stone carving, coffered ceiling with frescoes, and bronze chandeliers and entrance doors. The court is the scene of frequent art shows and a free concert each month (tickets are available in advance from the building's information office).

On the expanse of green around City Hall you'll notice *Sky Gate*, a 24-foot-high black steel abstract sculpture by Isamu Noguchi.

Mission Memorial Buildings, 530–558 South King Street. The three Georgian style buildings of red brick and white trim beside City Hall were built for the association of Congregational churches in memory of their founders, the missionaries who reached the islands between 1820 and 1848. The large two-story building and attached auditorium were finished in 1916; the small Christian Education Building alongside was added in 1930. All three were converted to city and county offices after World War II.

Honolulu Municipal Building, 650 South King Street. Designed to accent the Capital District's *Waikiki* boundary without stealing any thunder from its decorative old-

A downtown landmark, *historic Aloha Tower welcomes marine traffic and affords visitors fine city and harbor views from 10th-floor decks.*

timers, this plain but well-articulated tower has housed most city departments since 1975. Broad entrance walks slope up through banks of tropical gardens to the open-walled lobby.

Kalanimoku Building, 1151 Punchbowl Street. The contemporary state office building features four stained glass murals by Erica Karawina, conceptions of the islands at different times of day using the four chief gods of old Hawaii. Though lighted for night viewing, the murals show off best against the sun from fourth-floor offices.

Board of Water Supply Headquarters, 630 South Beretania Street. Three distinct structures comprise the eclectic complex: the 1957 Public Service Building, its facade of vertical aluminum sun-control grilles inspired by Peking's Imperial Palace; the 1938 Engineering Building with bas-reliefs around its entrance; and the 1926 Beretania Pumping Station with tiled hip roof, arches, and a steam stack used until 1971, still the hub of Oahu's water-pumping network.

Mission Houses Museum, 553 South King Street (daily 9 A.M. to 4 P.M.; admission fee includes guided tours).

Falls of Clyde, *world's last full-rigged four-master, receives visitors in new role as floating maritime museum.*

Three houses, restored and furnished, depict the history of the early Protestant missionaries from New England: Hawaii's oldest frame house, prefabricated in Boston and shipped around the Horn in 1821; the 1841 coral stone printing house, outfitted with a working replica of the original Ramage press brought to Hawaii by the first missionaries aboard the brig *Thaddeus*; and a two-story, coral block home and storehouse built in 1831 by Levi Chamberlain, the mission's business agent. The Chamberlain house has changing exhibits and a fine shop.

Mission Historical Library, 560 Kawaiahao Street (Monday through Friday 10 A.M. to 4 P.M.). Built in 1950, the library houses the collections of books, pamphlets, and original manuscripts of the Hawaiian Mission Children's Society (missionary descendants and operators of Mission Houses Museum) and the Hawaiian Historical Society.

Kawaiahao Church, 957 Punchbowl Street (open daily 8 A.M. to 4 P.M.). Oahu's oldest remaining church was built in 1842 of coral and timber by Hawaiian converts led by King Kamehameha III. Named for "the waters of Ha'o," a nearby sacred spring, the church stands on the site of Hawaii's first mission (1820) and was preceded by four thatched structures. In the last century Kawaiahao was the setting for royal inaugurations, weddings, christenings, and funerals; it still knows pageantry when Hawaiian societies march in regalia to honor royal forebears, commemorated inside by pews, plaques, and paintings. The Sunday service (10:30 A.M.) in Hawaiian and English is highlighted by Hawaiian hymns and a talk afterwards on the church's history. The grounds contain congregation and mission cemeteries as well as King Lunalilo's tomb, completed in 1875.

Aliiolani Hale (Judiciary Building), 417 South King Street. It looks like a palace because that's what Kamehameha V had in mind. But when the government decided it needed an office building, plans were modified and the building was finished in 1874 to house the Supreme Court, the legislature, and some ministries. King Kalakaua used it at night for balls and receptions. When other departments moved to Iolani Palace in 1893, after the monarchy's overthrow, Aliiolani became the Judiciary Building.

This restored Renaissance style treasure has walls of precast concrete blocks, arched doors and windows, lanais with Ionic columns, balustrades, and a marvelous entrance tower rising four levels from arched portals to a clock with four faces.

Statue of Kamehameha the Great. In front of Aliiolani Hale stands a bronze figure with gilded clothing, a duplicate of the original statue in Kapaau on the Big Island (see page 164). Commissioned to commemorate the centennial of Captain Cook's discovery of Hawaii, the original statue was lost off the Falkland Islands en route from American sculptor Thomas Gould's workshop in Italy. It was recovered, but only after insurance money had paid for another casting of the statue, which was unveiled for Kalakaua's belated coronation ceremony in 1883. The original went to the island of Hawaii, where Kamehameha was born.

Richards Street YWCA, 1040 Richards Street. A beautiful 1927 Spanish Colonial style building, the work of pioneer woman architect Julia Morgan of San Francisco, faces the palace grounds; two-story wings arranged around dining and swimming pool courts are separated by loggias. The columns and whimsical pool-court wall decorations are among the late Mario Valdastri's earliest ornamental cast stone work in the islands. The patio dining room is open to the public. The Y offers inexpensive courses (a few short term) in such subjects as hula, ukulele, oriental cooking and flower arranging, and lei making.

St. Andrew's Cathedral, Queen Emma Square (open 6 A.M. to 6 P.M.). The cathedral of Hawaii's Episcopal Diocese took almost a century to complete. A year after King Kamehameha IV introduced the English Anglican Church, he died unexpectedly (in 1863) on the feast day of St. Andrew—inspiring the name of the Gothic Revival cathedral begun in 1867 by his queen and his brother, Kamehameha V. Queen Emma went to England for drawings and funds and shipped much of its stone around Cape Horn as ballast (local cut sandstone was used for later parts). Construction was intermittent throughout the next century: though the first services were held in 1886 and the church was consecrated in 1902 with only two bays complete, the present structure with square carillon tower and grand front stained glass window wall was not finished until 1958.

The columns of the nave arcades are ornamented with classical and Hawaiian floral designs. Most aisle windows have fine 19th century English stained glass. Gracing the plaza is a fountain with bronze sculptures of St. Andrew, the fisherman apostle, and his fish.

Queen Emma Square, 1275 Queen Emma Street. The lawn separating St. Andrew's Cathedral and Priory School was Honolulu's second park (after Thomas Square), set aside by Kámehameha IV in 1858 to honor his queen. Only a spreading Moreton Bay fig tree remains from the early landscaping. Midway in this century, the square gained a garden pool, seats, and a terra cotta bust of Queen Emma.

St. Andrew's Priory School, 224 Queen Emma Square (open weekdays 7 A.M. to 4 P.M.). Queen Emma founded the Episcopal college-preparatory day school in 1867 to prepare Hawaiian girls for careers as nurses, teachers, and Christian homemakers. The original wooden buildings have all been replaced by concrete, most with Gothic features; the main Kennedy Hall is a recently enlarged and remodeled 1909 structure.

St. Peter's Episcopal Church, 1317 Queen Emma Street (office open weekdays 8 A.M. to 3:30 P.M.). This charming Gothic church with crenelated parapets was built in 1914 by a Chinese rector for a Chinese congregation. One Sunday service is still conducted in Cantonese. Fine koa trusses and pews and a Chinese baptismal font decorate the interior.

Washington Place, 320 South Beretania Street. The governor's home and the oldest continuously occupied

house in Hawaii, the Greek Revival style mansion was built in 1846 of cement-faced coral stone and wood. The original owner, Captain John Dominis, disappeared at sea just after moving in; his widow rented rooms to the American commissioner, who named the mansion—his legation—in honor of George Washington. In 1862 the captain's son, John Owen Dominis, married Lydia Kapaakea, the future Queen Liliuokalani. The queen inherited the home and lived here after she was deposed in 1893 until her death in 1917.

The government acquired the estate and opened it as the executive mansion in 1922. Several downstairs rooms, on view only for receptions and special tours, display the queen's possessions, including the koa piano on which she played her compositions such as the famous "Aloha Oe."

Capitol Mall, across Beretania from the Capitol. In a promenade flanked by royal palms stands the *Eternal Flame,* Bumpei Akaji's abstract copper and bronze sculpture dedicated to all islanders who have died serving in the U.S. Armed Forces.

Queen's Medical Center, 1301 Punchbowl Street. King Kamehameha IV and Queen Emma opened the hospital in 1860 to treat the large numbers of Hawaiians dying of smallpox and measles. The current buildings were constructed piecemeal from the 1890s to the present. The grounds still have exceptional trees planted by the first medical director, Dr. William Hillebrand, whose own estate became Foster Botanic Garden. The Center's Historical Room (weekdays 10 A.M. to 4 P.M.) displays early photographs, letters, and medical records; Queen Emma Gallery (daily 9 A.M. to 4 P.M.) presents monthly exhibitions by local artists.

THE KINGDOM OF HAWAII

Standing in regal solitude in front of the Aliiolani Hale, the building housing the state's Supreme Court, the black and gold statue of Kamehameha I, Hawaii's first ruler, wears the feathered cape and helmet designed for ancient kings (see photo on page 36). It is a popular photo stop for tourists, especially on June 11, when the statue is draped with garlands of flowers.

Officially, that date commemorates Kamehameha Day, but for a growing number of Hawaiians, those flowers honor the 19th century Kingdom of Hawaii. This era included all of Hawaii's rulers, from Kamehameha I to Queen Liliuokalani.

A Royal Heritage

Kamehameha I, ruler of Hawaii, the Big Island, began his conquest of other Hawaiian islands in 1791. By 1810, he had created the first unified Hawaiian kingdom. He reigned until 1819, when he was succeeded by his son. During his brief tenure (1819–1824), Kamehameha II witnessed the arrival of the first whaling ships and the first New England missionaries.

Kamehameha III, who reigned from 1825–1854, signed Hawaii's first written constitution, which ensured the rights of residents and limited the king's power, and passed an act dividing kingdom lands among chiefs, government, and commoners.

Kamehameha IV (1854–1863), a nephew, succeeded the king and later married Emma Rooke, the granddaughter of the first king's English adviser. Their son, Prince Albert, who died at the age of 4, was the last child born to a ruling Hawaiian monarch. The king's brother, Kamehameha V (1863–1872), was a bachelor and the last of the line.

Lack of a clear heir to the throne resulted in a government crisis over succession. Finally, the legislature chose the popular chief "Prince Bill" Lunalilo, who ruled for only 13 months before dying in 1874 without an heir. His sucessor was David Kalakaua, who ruled until 1891.

Liliuokalani, Kalakaua's appointed successor, was crowned queen in 1891 but ruled only two years before being deposed in January, 1893, a preliminary step that led to the annexation of Hawaii by the United States in 1898. And the rest, they say, is history.

A New Hawaiian Nation?

Today, however, a growing number of native Hawaiians insist that history is about to change. Questions raised—and ignored—for more than a century are assuming critical importance: Was the overthrow legal? Were the civil and human rights of the natives violated? Who actually has legal rights to government lands in Hawaii?

Answers to these and other questions could profoundly affect the future of the 50th state. At stake are some 400,000 acres of federal lands (including military bases and national parks) and billions of dollars in potential reparations. Perhaps the most immediate issue facing the state is sovereignty. Should native Hawaiians, like other Native Americans, have rights to self-government and to establish their own separate nation within the United States?

The state Office of Hawaiian Affairs plans to introduce legislation that would call a constitutional convention to establish a Hawaiian nation, return all federal lands to the Hawaiian people, and give native Hawaiians the right to sue the federal government for damages from the overthrow of the kingdom. One impatient group, Ka Lahui Hawaii, has already formed the Hawaiian Nation and chosen a monarch—Owana Kaohelelani Salazar, a descendant of Keoua, father of Kamehameha I. Salazar would act as regent for her young son, who would become the *alii nui* (paramount chief).

A Tour of the Past

Although it has been a century since the last Hawaiian monarch, royal history and landmarks are still intact, including Iolani Palace, America's only royal residence. A visit to some of these historic sites will offer a greater understanding of Hawaii's royal past (to find those located in downtown Honolulu, see the map on page 39).

Make your first stop the restored Iolani Palace (see page 35), the crown jewel of Hawaii's historic buildings. It was one of the first palaces in the world with indoor plumbing and electric lights. The main floor, which includes a formal crimson and gold throne room, was used for functions of state; upstairs were living quarters.

Walk across the street beneath the outstretched arms of the Kamehameha statue into the foyer of the Aliilolani Hale, Hawaii's first government building. A visit to the Judiciary History Center (open 10 A.M. to 3 P.M. Tuesday, Wednesday, and Thursday) reveals historical exhibits and a restored 1913 courtroom.

The royal pew still stands inside the gray coral rock walls of Kawaiahao Church at South King and Punchbowl streets. Next door is Mission Houses Museum, which served as headquarters for the first mission to Hawaii. Outstanding exhibits here offer not so much a royal perspective as a fascinating glimpse into life in Hawaii during the formative years of the Kamehameha dynasty.

A short side trip up the Pali Highway takes you to Queen Emma's Summer Palace (see page 51). The home of the widow of Kamehameha IV is filled with royal furnishings and gifts from other monarchs, including Queen Victoria.

Central Honolulu

Hawaii's major financial institutions and business firms are situated downtown between Richards Street and Nuuanu Avenue. Mingling with high-rises are a few structures dating from the mid-19th century, most with face-lifts and new roles.

A good place to start your tour is at the waterfront near Aloha Tower. Here, around the piers, you'll discover a busy world of ship repair, fishing sampans, tugboats, tour boats, and cruise liners. Anglers converge on the main piers, seemingly oblivious to the action around them, while downtown workers enjoy lunchtime picnics at Irwin Park and the grassy shoreline fringe between Piers 5 and 6.

Aloha Tower, Pier 9 at the foot of Fort Street. A downtown landmark since 1926 and now dwarfed by much taller buildings, the 164-foot white tower greets everyone who arrives or departs the harbor with a friendly "Aloha" inscribed on all of its four sides, which also show the faces of a bronze clock. The tower controls harbor traffic.

A 10th-floor observatory (open daily 8 A.M. to 9 P.M.) offers grand views of the city and harbor. A free museum on the ninth floor (open weekdays 8:30 A.M. to 4 P.M., Saturday 10 A.M. to 4 P.M.) traces the history of the harbor and its ships from 1792.

Hawaii Maritime Museum, Pier 7 at the foot of Alakea Street. Included within the museum are the world's only four-masted square-rigger, *Falls of Clyde,* and *Hokule'a,* a 60-foot, double-hulled canoe sailed to Tahiti by contemporary islanders to reproduce the remarkable voyages made by ancient Polynesian settlers. Inside Kalakaua Boat House are displays, exhibits, a theater, a children's "hands-on" museum, and a delightful open-air restaurant. One price admits you to the museum (open daily 9 A.M. to 5 P.M.) and the square-rigger.

Bishop and Alakea Streets. Central downtown's main thoroughfares, Bishop and Alakea streets, are lined with office structures. Four are island homes of the famous "Big Five"—Amfac, Alexander & Baldwin, Castle & Cooke, Theo. H. Davies, and C. Brewer and Company—sugar factors that once controlled Hawaii business. (All five have now branched into other fields and spread around the world.)

Amfac, Hawaii's largest corporation, is headquartered in one of the twin marble-and-glass towers of Amfac Center. The center's garage has a public, rooftop garden with trees, picnic pergolas, great views, and a jogging track. Amfac Plaza Exhibition Room (Monday through Friday 8:30 A.M. to 5 P.M.) hosts shows by major Hawaiian artists each month. Outside is Walker Park, a memorial to a former Amfac chief executive; it covers the *makai* block of Fort Street Mall and features an oval pool with four fountains surrounded by sculptural bollards.

At Grosvenor Center, you admire the Italian Renaissance features of the Dillingham Transportation Building. Named for Benjamin F. Dillingham, who founded early

Downtown

"HAWAII CALLS" REPRISE

The popular musical show "Hawaii Calls" has returned to Waikiki after an absence of 17 years. The original broadcasts, first aired in 1935, were picked up by radio stations on the mainland, Europe, and Asia for 40 years. The new program airs in 45 cities worldwide.

The show is performed from 12:30 to 1:30 P.M. at Hilton Hawaiian Village's Tropics Room on three Saturdays a month. On the fourth Saturday, it moves to a neighbor island. In addition to music, performances feature interviews with entertainers and other celebrities, and information on Hawaii.

To see the show you must buy the Hilton show package ($22 for adults, $14 for children under 12), which includes a buffet luncheon, tax, tip, and parking. Or you can pay $10 ($7 for children) for one drink, tax, tip, and parking.

railroads on Oahu and the Big Island, the 1929 building has rich ornamentation, arcades, and an elegant lobby.

The plaza of the Davies Pacific Center attracts a lunchtime crowd on the fourth Friday of each month for free beer and entertainment. Attractive anytime are its random-pattern brick paving, palm trees, and volcano-shaped fountain.

The 1929 Alexander & Baldwin Building stunningly combines Oriental and Mediterranean styles in its peaked and overhanging tile roof, terra cotta-faced walls, and Chinese-inspired ornamentation. Three buildings of different heights and shapes comprise the 1968 Financial Plaza of the Pacific, but all share a sculptural quality, volcanic aggregate facade, and tinted bronze windows. (Castle & Cooke has the projecting top floor of the 22-story tower.) The King-Bishop corner plaza has a geometric pool, fountains, and the mirror-polished bronze *Sun Disc*, movable though it stands 11 feet tall and weighs 5 tons.

The block-long, Neo-Classical S. M. Damon Building framed by high-rises is an attractive sight from Tamarind Park on the King-Bishop corner just opposite. Built in 1925 to house both the Bishop Bank and Bishop Trust Company started by Charles Reed Bishop (husband of Princess Bernice Pauahi, last of the Kamehamehas), it remains the home of Bishop Bank's descendant, First Hawaiian. Today, the Bishop Trust Building is catty-corner.

Tamarind Park is an acre of grass, trees, terraces, benches, and ledges. A pretty stream falls into reflecting pools; one has an arresting 11-foot bronze by noted sculptor Henry Moore entitled *Upright Motive No. 9*. This Bishop Square gathering place, created by landscape architect James C. Hubbard, is named for Charles and Bernice Bishop, whose nearby home was shaded by a tamarind tree—the park has two tamarinds. Follow the locals' lead and pick up lunch to eat in the park while enjoying a free musical concert, ranging from jazz to the Royal Hawaiian Band.

The 30-story, textured concrete Pacific Tower was built in 1972. Its 1983 companion is the stunning, 28-story Pauahi Tower of gleaming black glass with an elegant two-story lobby of Italian marble. Take the polished brass escalator to the mezzanine, scene of changing art exhibits mounted by the Honolulu Academy of Arts.

On Bishop Street *mauka* of Hotel Street, notice the white-columned Hawaiian Telephone Company tower; the Union Mall, an arc between Bishop and Hotel streets; and a mural depicting 19th century Honolulu in the lobby of the building at 1136 Union Mall.

Along Alakea Street are two prominent 1980s buildings. Central Pacific Plaza at the corner of King has *Mana-La* ("sun power"), a 12-foot-tall rectangle of granite topped by three stainless steel blocks; two have solar cells and move. In the bank lobby, a gallery (Monday through Thursday 8:30 A.M. to 3 P.M.; Friday 8:30 A.M. to 6 P.M.) shows the work of promising young local artists. Kauikeaouli Hale, home of the State District Court, is a fortress of coarsely textured concrete, recessed window slits, and

protruding stairwells; from the open-walled entrance plaza, big escalators rise almost to its high glass roof.

Fort Street Mall. Downtown's main shopping street and lively pedestrian way runs six blocks, from Beretania Street to Nimitz Highway, the approximate site of the fort that guarded the harbor from 1817 to 1857. It's lined with stores, eateries, refurbished old buildings, benches, trees, vine trellises, and speakers for music. An underpass beneath King Street has a waterfall and pool and a 70-foot wall of crushed *pahoehoe* lava incised with petroglyphs by contemporary artist Edward Stasack.

At Beretania, Damien Plaza's *padrao*—a tall, carved, masonry column with capital—memorializes Hawaii's first Portuguese immigrants who landed in 1878. Surrounding the plaza, noteworthy buildings include the Central Fire Station in 1930s Moderne style with Art Deco aluminum doors.

Our Lady of Peace Cathedral (open in daytime; masses several times each day) is the oldest remaining downtown building. Begun in 1843 as a coral block rectangle with steeple on the site of Hawaii's first Roman Catholic chapel, it has been enhanced over the years with new towers, columned lanai, tile roof, buttresses, and, inside, a vaulted, hand-painted ceiling, balconies, and choir loft. The tower contains French bells and a Chilean clock from the 1850s; in the courtyard stands the stump of Hawaii's parent *kiawe* tree, started from seed in 1828, and an 1893 statue of Mary, Our Lady of Peace.

Just across the mall is the restored 1898 Model/Progress Building, with dark, sturdy, rusticated walls and fortresslike parapet. A remodeled 1937 store next door houses Hawaii Pacific College, where nearly 4,000 students study for bachelor's degrees in liberal arts and business while working. All the rooms in the 1912 Blaisdell Hotel across Chaplain Lane have been converted to office suites, but they're served by a 1915 wrought-iron cage elevator (now enclosed in glass).

Walk over to the Bethel-Pauahi corner to see the classic Hawaii Theatre, built in 1922 for movies and stage shows and newly restored. Note its beaux arts styling and Art Deco ornamentation. Periodic concerts are given on its console organ.

Near the foot of the mall stands the haciendalike C. Brewer and Company Building, headquarters for the oldest of the "Big Five" (founded in 1826). The tiled, double-pitched hip roof, overhanging eaves, lanais, and garden courts make it a superb example of Hawaiian architecture. Built in 1930 of concrete and cut stone, its railings and grilles represent waving sugar cane; lights are shaped like sugar cubes.

Historic Merchant Street. Walk Merchant Street from the Capital District to Chinatown and, with a few jogs, you'll see the city's oldest remaining commercial buildings, most put to new uses, with their handsome detailing all restored. Just behind Hawaiian Electric on Palace Square stands an earlier (1901) home of the company at 222 Merchant Street, now The Croissanterie, a coffee house and gallery.

Buddhist and Taoist deities *grace Chinatown's Kwan Yin Temple. You'll usually see people engaged in the rituals of blessing.*

Chinatown's open-air markets *contain many wonders from the sea, are always crowded with neighborhood shoppers.*

PACIFIC RIM CUISINE—ISLAND STYLE

Gone are the days when island dining meant pretentious Continental dishes made with imported ingredients. Exotic fare now typical of the new Hawaiian cuisine includes lobster wonton ravioli with mustard cabbage-lemon grass sauce, ohelo berry-Maui onion compote, and red prawn and coconut curry with jasmine rice and crisp haupia.

Recognizing that today's savvy, well-traveled customers are interested in bolder flavors and regional specialties, Hawaii's chefs are setting aside formal rules in favor of greater reliance on local influences and the islands' multiethnic heritage.

Fresh fish may be the premier Hawaiian specialty. Menus present *ahi* and *ono* along with such tongue twisters as *opakapaka* and *mahimahi* (for identifications, turn to page 145). On some menus you'll encounter Kahua beef, Kahuku prawns, free-range chicken, Peking duck, and even wild boar loin.

The following restaurants feature chefs who are particularly innovative in the preparation and presentation of regional dishes:

Oahu

Orchids Restaurant, Halekulani Hotel, Honolulu. This open-air Waikiki beach- level restaurant looks out to Diamond Head and the passing parade. The cuisine is a combination of the fare from the Tropics, Asia, and southern Europe.

Roy's Restaurant, 6600 Kalanianaole Highway, Honolulu (also in west Maui). Chef Roy Yamaguchi, a major

Grilled Hawaiian fish with papaya relish

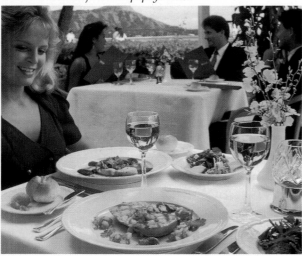

influence in Hawaiian cuisine, combines classic training and flavors from his native Japan, from California, and from other Pacific Rim countries to create deftly seasoned dishes. Savor them in the casual-chic suburban setting of Hawaii Kai; look out to Maunalua Bay and Diamond Head.

Keo's Thai Cuisine, 625 Kapahulu Avenue, Honolulu. Dine amid bowers of orchids as you sample exotic dishes like Evil Jungle Prince, a restaurant specialty concocted of chicken, cabbage, chilies, and coconut milk.

Maui

Prince Court Restaurant, Maui Prince Hotel, Makena (also in Waikiki). A leader in regional fare, chef Roger Dikon concocts unusual dishes that take advantage of local foods and cooking styles. The restaurant's second-floor setting overlooks the hotel's interior garden.

Avalon Restaurant & Bar, 844 Front Street, Lahaina. Kick back beneath an umbrella and enjoy this little oasis among the boutiques while the chef conjures up innovative entrees.

Hawaii

The CanoeHouse, Mauna Lani Bay Hotel, Kohala Coast. Decorated with petroglyphs and a koa canoe, this plantation style restaurant is the oceanfront stage for chef Alan Wong, a creative force in Hawaii's emerging cuisine. His touch is evident in all selections, from pupus to dessert.

Coast Grille, Hapuna Prince Hotel, Kohala Coast. Though billed as a seafood and steak house, Executive Chef Cory Waite, formerly with the Mauna Kea, makes sure that the hotel's signature restaurant serves some of the island's best fresh regional cuisine. A dramatic ocean view and five types of fresh oysters are a powerful combination.

The Grill, Ritz-Carlton Mauna Lani, Kohala Coast. Chef Amy Ferguson-Ota experiments with new techniques in preparing the islands' freshest ingredients. Chandeliers and candlelight cast a warm glow over the intimate room, where you might begin a meal with pohole fern salad with Maui onions and Kula tomatoes.

Merriman's Restaurant, Opelo Plaza, Waimea. A champion of area producers, chef Peter Merriman incorporates much of their bounty—goat cheese, fresh produce, and the local catch—in menus at his upcountry plantation house–restaurant.

Kauai

A Pacific Cafe, Kauai Village Shopping Center, Kapaa. Seafood and Kauai-grown produce are incorporated in dishes with Japanese, Thai, Chinese, and French influences. Chef Josselin's wife, who painted the plates, oversees a changing display of local art.

Chinatown and Lower Nuuanu Stream

Early in the 19th century, Chinese traders, shopkeepers, and businessmen began to settle near the outlet of Nuuanu Stream, mostly in the blocks bounded by Nimitz Highway, Nuuanu Avenue, Beretania Street, and Nuuanu Stream that are today's official Chinatown. The area is contiguous to old Merchant Street, and, similarly, on the National Register of Historic Places.

Though relatively few Chinese residents remain, the district is still the financial, commercial, cultural, and social center of Oahu's Chinese community. It has always been a first home in the city for immigrants; its current mix of Filipinos, Vietnamese, and other recent settlers support a concentration of dry-goods stores and ethnic restaurants found nowhere else.

Chinatown has twice burned down; most of its older buildings today sprang up soon after the 1900 fire. Typically, they are harmonious ensembles of two and three-story structures of brick, stone, or concrete with decorative cornices and window trim. Their almost-continuous corrugated iron awnings extend over narrow congested sidewalks often edged with wares bursting out of open-front shops.

Many buildings have been restored; some now have offices of architects, artists, and other professionals in their former upper-story living quarters and landscaped courtyards in back. But you still experience markets with exotic foods and pungent odors, cluttered drygoods and import stores, lei stands, Chinese noodle factories, bakeries, chop suey houses, and herb shops with the making of centuries-old medicines, a Japanese confectionary and some *okazu-ya* (delicatessens), signs in oriental calligraphy, and people chatting in native tongue. Expect, too, bars, night clubs, pool halls, and other miscellany that inhabit an area that has street people and entertains servicemen on the town.

Chinatown Visitor Center. Make your first stop the Chinatown Visitor Center on the second floor of Maunakea Marketplace (see below). Designed to duplicate a turn-of-the-century Chinese store, the center has self-guided tour maps and information on area shops, restaurants, and galleries. There's also a gift and souvenir shop. A 12-minute video (small charge) on the story of Chinatown is shown in the meeting hall. The center is open from 10 A.M. to 4 P.M. daily.

Maunakea Marketplace (Maunakea Street between Hotel and Pauahi streets). Enhanced by a handsome clock tower, Maunakea Marketplace contains a collection of shops and other businesses, including a food court with more than 20 vendors offering foods from around the Pacific Rim, along with a traditional open market. Note the engraved bricks in the courtyard; you can buy one at the visitor center to add your sentiments. Proceeds go to a nonprofit group that preserves historic buildings.

Tours. Chinatown Historical Society offers two free walking tours of colorful Chinatown and nearby Foster Botanic Garden (see page 47). The morning tour (10 A.M.

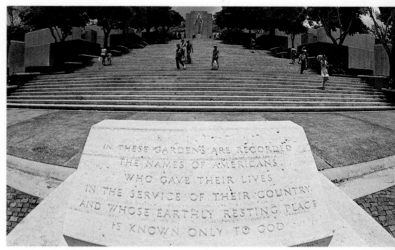

Punchbowl Crater's Columbia *watches over final resting place of war dead.*

weekdays) covers the heart of Chinatown's exotic and aromatic shops and historic buildings. The afternoon tour (1 P.M. weekdays) visits Chinese and Japanese temples and returns to the garden. Walking tours meet inside Asia Mall, 1250 Maunakea Street. Reservations are not necessary; for more information, call 521-3045.

Inexpensive guided tours are also offered by the Chinese Chamber of Commerce (9:30 A.M. Tuesday from 42 N. King Street, optional lunch; 533-3181) and the Hawaii Heritage Center (10:30 A.M. Friday from 1128 Smith Street; 521-2749). On the walks, you'll explore markets, import stores, Chinese bakeries, noodle factories, herb pharmacies, an acupuncture center, and temples along Nuuanu Stream.

Nuuanu Avenue. Known locally as Gallery Row, Nuuanu is the heart of the downtown art scene. Housed in historic buildings are galleries showcasing arts, crafts, and antiques. Among them are Gateway Gallery (Nuuanu Avenue and Hotel Street), Bakkus Gallery (928 Nuuanu Avenue, in the old Hawaii Times Building), and Pegge Hopper Gallery (1164 Nuuanu Avenue).

For more galleries, stroll Smith, Pauahi, and Maunakea streets. Ramsay Galleries (1128 Smith Street) has a cafe.

Maunakea Street. At the corner of Pauahi, a colorfully painted, three-story building houses Chinese community groups over the street-level noodle factory. Three of the groups are mutual aid societies formed by early immigrants; they have become perpetuators of traditional social and religious customs. Their meeting rooms contain carved altars, shrines, folk images in bronze and gold leaf, and Chinese carved furniture, often antique. Wo Fat on the corner of Hotel Street is a Chinatown landmark; Honolulu's oldest Chinese cafe, it dates back to 1882, though the present tile-roofed structure with unrestrained interior decor was built in 1936. Across Maunakea stands the Marketplace dining and shopping complex.

Protected, reef-filled waters *lure throngs of snorkelers to Hanauma Bay. Remnants of nature's volcanic handiwork outline the state's first underwater conservation park.*

Toothy grins *from wahine and false killer whales greet visitors at Sea Life Park's Whaler's Cove. Performing porpoises and sea birds show off in front of scenic Makapuu Point.*

King Street. The Oahu Market (Monday through Saturday 6 A.M. to 5 P.M.; Sunday 6 A.M. to noon) at King and Kekaulike bristles with shoppers drawn from all over the island by its wide selection of fresh fruits and vegetables, fish, and meat. Here you'll find ethnic favorites not available in supermarkets—red sweet pork and crispy duck, wing beans, pumpkin blossoms, taro and ti leaves, fish fresh from the morning's auction, every variety of local banana, lychees, mangoes, soursops, and cherimoyas in season. The stalls are family businesses, some now third generation; the 22 owners recently formed a corporation, bought the open-walled, iron-roofed, 1904 building, and restored it. "Oahu Market Island Recipes & Shopper's Guide," available inside, gives a history of the market and its families and recipes for foods from the stalls.

Markets and shops of the newest immigrant groups—Vietnamese, Laotian, Samoan—have opened in other rehabilitated buildings on King Street. Catty-corner from Oahu Market is the 1909 brick L. Ah Leong Building; its builder came to Hawaii as a cook and made a fortune in the wholesale-retail business. At King and River streets, two structures form an attractive gateway into Chinatown from Nuuanu Stream: the Armstrong Building, a 1905 bluestone, and the 1904 Chang Building, of exposed lava rock and plastered brick painted light blue and trimmed in red.

Nuuanu Stream. This picturesque watercourse offers a view up Nuuanu Valley to the Pali. Fishermen moor small boats under the arched bridges that connect River Street with College Walk—both largely pedestrian malls. Dotting the malls are arbors with tables for chess, checkers, or *mah jong* and abstract sculptures by E. M. Brownlee. At River and Beretania is a statue of Sun Yat-sen, founder of modern China, who lived and was educated in Hawaii before leading the overthrow of the Manchu dynasty in 1911. Across the bridge on College Walk stands a figure of Jose Rizal, Filipino hero who died in 1896 while leading the Philippines' fight for liberation from Spain.

Old Oahu Railway Station, North King and Iwilei streets. Now the Kalihi-Palama Multi-Service Community Center, its handsome, 1925 Spanish Mission-style porte cochere, arcades, patios, balconies, tile roofs, and four-sided clock tower are all restored. From this depot, trains ran around the island to Kahuku until 1948.

Aala Park. The triangle between North King, North Beretania, and Nuuanu Stream is a neighborhood gathering place. Here retired men play cards and "talk story" under the old banyans and monkeypods; young boys show off with acrobatics on wheels in the skateboard arena; and sumo amateurs wrestle in the *dohyo* (sumo ring) on Sunday afternoons (see "The Sporting Guide," page 27). The park also contains a fountain, bandstand—scene of frequent multiethnic festivities—and stream bank covered with the city's oldest bougainvillea, planted half a century ago.

Along College Walk. At the Beretania end of this mall is Town Square, roofed in striking blue tile and filled with specialty shops and restaurants. Toyo Theatre, 1230 College Walk, is a concern of preservationists now that its days as a cinema have ended. Built in 1938 for Japanese films and stage shows, its style recalls a Japanese shrine. In the entrance court, weathered balustrades surround a Japanese garden; entry and exit walks bridge fish ponds.

Izumo Taishakyo Mission, College Walk and Kukui Street (open all day; service the 10th of each month at 7 P.M.). A typical *torii* and hand-washing basin stand at its entrance; the roof ridge ends with protruding gable boards and barrel. The shrine was built without nails by a carpenter from Japan in 1923 and then moved to this site in 1968. The Taishakyo sect of Shinto, the ancient Japanese religion in which gods represent elements of nature, was started in Hawaii in 1906. On New Year's, from midnight on through the day, thousands line up to make offerings, ring the bell as the priest waves a wand over their head, drink sake, and take home packets of blessed rice.

Along River Street Mall. The low contemporary buildings of Chinatown Cultural Plaza fill a square block beside the stream from Beretania to Kukui streets. The plaza contains small shops, oriental restaurants, fish and produce market, exhibit hall and stage for ethnic shows, and four Chinese societies. At the two Chinese language schools—Sun Yat-sen School at Kukui and River, Mun Lun at 1290 Maunakea Street—you can look in on large groups of children learning Chinese, weekdays from 3:30 to 5 P.M. Lum Sai Ho Tong at River and Kukui (open mornings) is a Taoist temple of the Lum clan (including surnames Lam, Lim, and Lin).

Kwan Yin Temple, 170 North Vineyard Boulevard (open all day). Flamboyant with its green tile roof, red trim, and colorful interior, the temple is dominated by a ten-foot statue of Kwan Yin, Chinese Buddhist goddess of mercy. Worshippers come and go, leave offerings of fruit or flowers, consult a fortune teller, light joss sticks at altars, and burn heavenly money and symbolic paper clothing in incinerators on the terrace.

Foster Botanic Garden, 180 North Vineyard Boulevard (daily 9 A.M. to 4 P.M.; admission fee includes self-guided tour pamphlet or guided tour Monday, Tuesday, Wednesday at 1:30 P.M. by reservation). On 20 acres are excellent collections of palms, orchids, bromeliads, gingers, heliconias, and prehistoric plants; more than a score of the city's rare and unusual trees, such as Africa's sausage tree and the aromatic cigar box specimen; and a nursery with thousands of newly introduced plants. You may glimpse a mongoose sunning on a rock.

The garden is one of six sites comprising Honolulu Botanic Gardens, where attempts are being made to propagate plants and trees from around the world in appropriate island locations. This particular tropical oasis began in 1855 as the home garden of Dr. William Hillebrand, the first director of Queen's Medical Center. It was enlarged by the Thomas Fosters and was bequeathed to the city by Mrs. Foster when she died in 1930. In the gift shop you'll find books, plant and seed packets cleared for mainland entry, and plant-related handicrafts.

On the *Ewa* side of Nuuanu Stream are the old districts of Palama, Kapalama, and Kalihi, a mix of humble dwellings and small businesses and industries, and above them, residential Alewa Heights, Kapalama Heights, and Kalihi Valley. Farther out are vast new industrial and housing tracts and big military bases. Several routes to the airport, Pearl Harbor, and beyond cross this side of the city and open up some worthwhile sightseeing.

If you want to do a lot of stopping, drive on North King Street or North School Street, or near the sea on Nimitz Highway (92) or Dillingham Boulevard, which becomes Kamehameha Highway and merges with Nimitz at Keehi Lagoon. Highway 92 then travels under H-1 Freeway past Honolulu International Airport to Nimitz Gate at Pearl Harbor Naval Base. Kamehameha Highway continues (as Highway 99) past the entrance to the Arizona Memorial museum and boat dock (see page 62) and around Pearl Harbor.

H-1 Freeway has several off-ramps into the old districts and exits to the airport, Hickam Air Force Base, Nimitz Gate, and Kamehameha Highway where it starts around Pearl Harbor. From where H-1 turns *makai* at Middle Street, you can continue on an inland route on freewaylike Moanalua Road (78) which intersects with H-1 and Kamehameha Highway near Aloha Stadium.

Sand Island. Manmade protection for Honolulu Harbor, Sand Island houses busy industrial yards, coast guard bases, and unoccupied oceanfront spots popular for camping and fishing. Sand Island State Recreation Area covers 85 acres on the tip of the island, offering picnic areas, fine views of the city waterfront, and play places in old military structures.

Honolulu International Airport. Lei stands line the approach roads to the terminal, their fresh flower offerings providing the perfect aloha to travelers. The open-air terminal, with eating spots and a variety of shops, overlooks Chinese, Japanese, and Hawaiian gardens; the information centers offer guides to commissioned works of art scattered throughout the main lobbies and central concourse. *Wikiwiki* buses, which now provide free shuttle service between the main and interisland terminals, will be replaced by automated people-mover trains in the next few years.

Pacific Aerospace Museum, located in the central concourse, contains interesting aeronautical exhibits and a theater (see page 24).

Hickam Air Force Base. Adjacent to Honolulu International Airport is the chief military airfield in the Pacific. Its octagonal water tower, a local landmark, rises 171 feet.

Bishop Museum, 1525 Bernice Street (Monday through Saturday and first Sunday of the month; admission fee). This outstanding museum was founded in 1889 by Charles Bishop in memory of his wife, Princess Bernice Pauahi Bishop, last member of the Kamehameha dynasty. In the three-story Hawaiian Hall, images of ancient gods guard exhibits on Hawaii's peoples and cultures to 1900—everything from feather capes and royal jewels to Chinese ivory carvings and a missionary's diary. Polynesian Hall exhibits concentrate on Pacific Basin cultural history.

Recent additions include the Atherton Halau, where a daily music and dance performance augments the displays and demonstrations of Hawaiian arts and crafts (9 A.M. to 3 P.M.), and Ululani Jabulka Pavilion, the museum entrance, a gift and book shop, and restaurant. Other exhibits are found in the Hall of Hawaiian Natural History, the Hall of Discovery, and the Shell Room. The planetarium on the museum grounds has two different shows daily at 11 A.M. and 2 P.M. and an evening show Friday and Saturday at 8 P.M. Admission to the planetarium is included in the entrance fee.

Kamehameha Schools campus. Occupying 618 acres on Kapalama Heights, these prestigious schools for boys and girls of Hawaiian blood were founded in 1887 as the sole beneficiary of the estate of Princess Bernice Pauahi Bishop. You can pick up a map at the main entrance.

Moanalua Gardens. On Moanalua Road at the Tripler off ramp, this private estate with magnificent monkeypod trees, two streams, carp pond, and taro patch is open to the public for picnics and strolls. Notice two historic buildings moved here from a nearby site: the Victorian gingerbread cottage, built as a summer house by Kamehameha V, and Chinese Hall, a party pavilion. Admission to the gardens is free; for information on guided walks into Moanalua Valley, call 833-1944.

Tripler Army Medical Center. Built by the army in 1948 and used by all the services, Tripler is the world's largest military hospital. Its 560-bed capacity can be expanded to 1,500 during emergencies. The sprawling pink buildings are a mountainside landmark.

Temples and churches. Scattered throughout this district are temples and churches reflecting the diversity of Hawaii's religious organizations. Among them are the Korean Christian Church, 1832 Liliha Street (English-Korean services); Higashi Hongwanji Temple, 1685 Alaneo Street (Buddhist); Kaumakapili Church, 766 North King Street (Hawaiian hymns); and Kotohira Jinsha, 1045 Kama Lane (one of Oahu's four Shinto shrines).

Fascinating food stops. This area is dotted with small businesses and shops. Two of particular interest are located on North King Street.

Nisshodo Candy Store, 425 North King Street (Monday through Saturday 7 A.M. to 4 P.M.; Sunday 7 to 11 A.M.). This 70-year-old family enterprise manufactures Japanese rice and wheat flour confections (*mochi, manju, chi chi dango*) sold throughout Oahu and available here.

Tamashiro Market, 802 North King Street (Monday through Saturday 9 A.M. to 6 P.M.; Sunday 9:15 A.M. to 4 P.M.). Hawaii's largest retail fish market sells all fish and shellfish caught in local waters, many of them still live.

Two boulevards run from the downtown area to Waikiki: Ala Moana near the waterfront and Kapiolani several blocks inland. King and Beretania, two of downtown's parallel one-way streets, connect with Kalakaua Avenue at its *Ewa* end (King traffic moves toward Waikiki, Beretania toward downtown), and King Street and Kapiolani Boulevard meet in the Capital District.

The Kakaako District

From the Capital District to Ala Moana Center and the sea to Kapiolani Boulevard is Kakaako (*Waikiki* of Ward Avenue, strictly speaking, is Kewalo). It's a district of narrow, traffic-clogged streets shaded here and there by an aged mango tree; of auto repair shops, mom and pop groceries, hole-in-the-wall cafes, lunch wagons, fishing supply stores, antique dealers, and all sorts of other small businesses and industries.

There is much to see and visit. The Contemporary Arts Center of Hawaii, News Building, 605 Kapiolani Boulevard, exhibits new work of artists with an island connection. Kamaka Hawaii, 550 South Street (tours by arrangement) is Hawaii's only ukulele factory, in business since 1916. Blair, Ltd., 404A Ward Avenue, manufactures serving pieces, furniture, and decorative articles from local woods. Ala Moana Farmers Market, 1020 Auahi Street, includes about a dozen wholesalers and retailers of fruit and produce, fish, and Hawaiian and oriental food favorites. Eurasian Antiques, a warehouse with a mix of treasures, Indich Collection with oriental rugs, and Jade East, Ltd. with antique jade and Chinese porcelain, are all at 1108 Auahi Street.

Along Ala Moana

In this area you'll find a shopping complex, harbor, and an expansive ocean-front playground.

Ward Warehouse and Ward Centre. Between Ala Moana and Auahi and opposite Kewalo Basin, are low-rise complexes with shops, arts and crafts galleries, and a concentration of specialty restaurants to rival Waikiki's. Ward Warehouse was built of rough-sawn lumber to resemble a wharfside marketplace; Ward Centre has stucco buildings and two tiled interior malls.

Kewalo Basin. You'll find a jam of boats for sport-fishing charter, diving, glass-bottom and Pearl Harbor tours, and dinner cruises. Sampans and other commercial fishing craft unload for the fish auction (see page 26). It is held on the *Ewa* side of the basin, where you'll also find Fisherman's Wharf and John Dominis' seafood restaurants and access to Point Panic surfing grounds (take Ahui Street off Ala Moana).

Ala Moana Park. On the *Diamond Head* side of the harbor is a 76-acre expanse of grass, tree-shaded arbors, ponds, and a long sand beach bordering a swimming lagoon. This ocean-front playground is well used. On a typical weekend, you'll find park-goers participating in picnics, softball, lawn bowling, tennis, jogging, canoe paddling, fishing, or just sun-bathing. McCoy Pavilion includes a Balinese style courtyard with Indian banyans and reflecting pools.

Magic Island. Jutting out near the *Waikiki* end of Ala Moana Park is this landscaped, 32-acre, manmade peninsula completed in 1972 with a beach that continues as a seaward curve from Ala Moana's and a lagoon protected by a rock breakwater used by fishermen and surfing spectators.

Ala Moana Center. This enormous "shopping city," bordered by Ala Moana and Kapiolani boulevards, Piikoi Street, and Atkinson Drive, is a place to browse, shop, eat, and people-watch. Several levels contain a fantastic variety of shops; more than 150 stores and restaurants (with almost 8,000 parking stalls) make it one of the world's largest. Restaurants here feature an intriguing assortment of oriental and occidental foods. Malls display the works of some of the state's most famous artists; colorful carp (*koi*) share ponds with fanciful sculptures.

Between Kapiolani and H-1 Freeway

You'll discover Honolulu cultural centers (symphony and opera, and arts) in this region.

Neal S. Blaisdell Center, along Ward Avenue between Kapiolani Boulevard and South King Street, consists of a 2,158-seat concert hall, exhibition and assembly rooms, and a large sports arena in a park-like setting with coconut palms, lawns, and a large fishpond. The concert hall is the home of Honolulu's symphony and opera (see page 26) and is used by various performing groups.

Thomas Square, outlined by Ward Avenue and South Beretania, Victoria, and South King streets, has a central fountain and four Indian banyans, a bordering hedge, carpet of grass, and other large trees. The park honors British Admiral Richard Thomas who restored Hawaii's independence in 1843 a few months after a lower-ranking officer had unofficially seized the Islands for the Empire from King Kamehameha III.

Honolulu Academy of Arts, 900 South Beretania Street (Tuesday through Saturday, 10 A.M. to 4:30 P.M.; Sunday, 1 to 5 P.M.; free; a walk-in tour is given each day; check for time). A treasure of a building as well as a museum, the Academy has thick textured masonry walls, sloping tile roof with broad eaves, columned lanai and loggias, and many galleries opening to handsome courtyards.

The museum is noted for its Asian art pieces, has a part of the Kress Collection of Italian Renaissance paintings, shows good local work and changing, often traveling, exhibitions. Additions to the 1927 building include the Clare Boothe Luce Wing (with contemporary art)

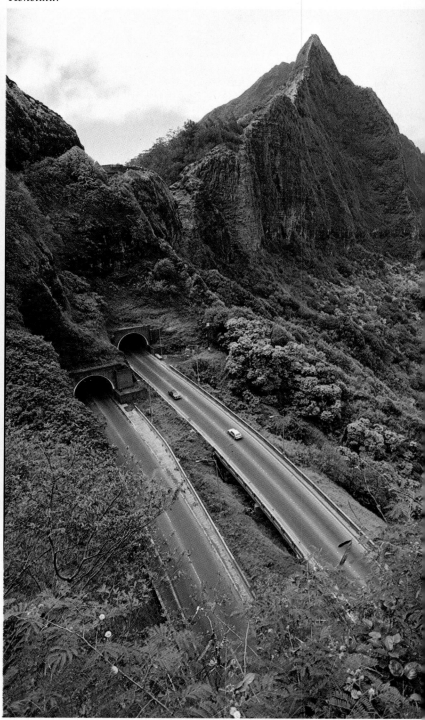

Twin tunnels *of Pali Highway pierce the Koolau Range. The 2,000-foot sheer cliffs separate Windward Oahu from Honolulu.*

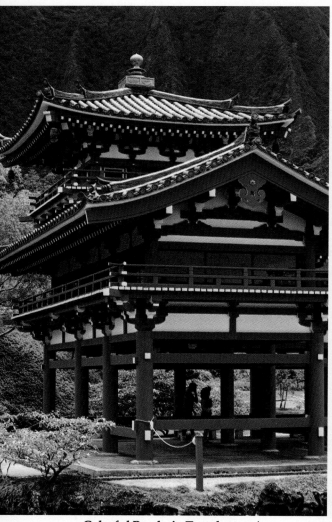

Colorful Byodo-in Temple *occupies striking setting against backdrop of fluted cliffs in Ahuimanu Valley.*

overlooking a sculpture garden and the Academy Theatre for films, concerts, and lectures (usually admission fee). The Academy has a shop and a popular Garden Cafe.

Kapiolani's business district, between Ala Moana Center, South King Street, and Kalakaua Avenue, is a clutter of stores, offices, apartments, restaurants, and oriental-style hostess lounges, art galleries, and antique shops.

Many interesting churches and temples lie along or just off the main streets between downtown and Waikiki.

Honolulu's Heights and Valleys

Mauka of H-1 Freeway are heights and valleys with many fine homes that overlook the central city. To see them, pick up a city map and drive the roads up to the heights named Alewa, Pacific, Makiki, Tantalus-Round Top, St. Louis, and Maunalani, and explore the valleys in between. You'll encounter interesting places:

Liliuokalani Garden, with entrances at the end of Waikahalulu Lane off North School Street and Kuakini Street, is a five-acre natural park on the banks of Nuuanu Stream with a large swimming hole fed by forceful Waikahulu Falls; it's a picnicker's delight.

Nuuanu—churches, temples, consulates. The built-up part of this valley you drive through on the way to Nuuanu Pali and Windward Oahu has become a "church row" and center for consulates and other institutions, some using former grand residences. Royal Mausoleum, 2261 Nuuanu Avenue, is the burial ground of the Kamehameha and Kalakaua dynasties.

Queen Emma Summer Palace, 2913 Pali Highway (daily 9 A.M. to 4 P.M.; admission fee). This mid-nineteenth century white frame house with classical features became Queen Emma's retreat after King Kamehameha IV's death in 1863. The Daughters of Hawaii, who administer the property, have preserved her home and furnishings, and have restored many of her personal possessions. Spending an hour among the artifacts offers a fascinating look at Hawaiian royalty.

Tantalus is the city's highest, coolest residential section (its summit is 2,013 feet). Homes here are almost hidden in magnificent rain forest. On a loop that combines Tantalus Drive and Round Top Drive you climb to 1,600 feet, pass view turnouts and the beginnings of many of the easy hiking trails in Tantalus State Recreation Area. The park's Puu Ualakaa unit, off Round Top Drive, has a picnic ground and spectacular views.

National Memorial Cemetery of the Pacific, Puowaina Drive, spreads over the vast bowl of Punchbowl Crater, which Hawaiians called Puowaina (Hill of Sacrifice). Tablets in seemingly endless rows mark more than 30,000 graves of war dead from World Wars I and II, the Korean War, the Vietnam War, and members of their families. A massive monument, "Courts of the Missing," gives the names of 28,745 missing servicemen on marble slabs leading up to a 30-foot statue of Columbia, that represents a mother looking over her lost children.

Tour buses only drive through this popular attraction; they're not allowed to park or drop off visitors. If you'd like a closer look, the Department of Veterans Affairs offer a free one-hour walking tour of the grounds daily from 1 to 5 P.M. for more information, call 541-1430.

Punahou School, 1601 Punahou Street, was founded in 1841 for children of missionaries and is now one of the nation's largest college preparatory schools. Its buildings range from the coral stone Old School Hall (1852) to a contemporary chapel built out over a lily pond.

Lyon Arboretum, 3860 Manoa Road, includes 124 acres of tropical trees and shrubs (4,000 species) and is a University of Hawaii teaching-research ground. You can walk through on your own or make reservations for a guided tour given periodically.

Mid-Pacific Institute, 2445 Kaala Street, a residential secondary school, occupies a 34-acre campus overlooking the University of Hawaii. Note Kawaiahao Hall, the original building (1908) of local lava stone; Juliette May Fraser's 92-foot mosaic mural on the auditorium facade; the outstanding rainbow shower tree.

University of Hawaii, lower Manoa Valley, has more than 20,000 students and a faculty of 2,100. It excels in geophysics, tropical agriculture, ocean engineering, Asian and Pacific studies, travel industry management, biomedical sciences, astronomy, and art. Columned entrances grace the original quadrangle buildings, of which Hawaii Hall was the first (1912). A public gallery in the Art Building (Monday through Friday 8 A.M. to 4 P.M.) features faculty and student art. For self-touring information, see page 26.

East-West Center, 1777 East-West Road, was established in 1960 to promote cultural and technical interchange among peoples of Asia, the Pacific, and the U.S.A. Students come from some 40 countries and territories.

St. Louis-Chaminade Education Center, 3140 Waialae Avenue, includes a picturesque cluster of Spanish Mission-inspired buildings that dates from 1928–1929 when an early Roman Catholic boys' school, St. Louis, re-established its campus here. The Administration Building serves two schools. To the left are the main buildings of St. Louis (with 1,200 boys, grades 7 through 12) and to the right, the halls of coeducational Chaminade University which has more than 2,400 students.

Waahila Ridge State Recreation Area, at the end of Ruth Place atop St. Louis Heights, is a 45-acre park in a setting of Norfolk pines and other trees, with hiking trails, picnic tables, and group camp shelters.

The city extends out to Makapuu, Oahu's easternmost point, and it's citylike all the way to Koko Head and Koko Crater as Honolulu's newer residential districts cover ridges, valleys, peninsulas, and shoreline along the way. For a scenic route between Waikiki and East Honolulu's main artery, Kalanianaole Highway (72), take Kalakaua Avenue, then Diamond Head Road along the coast and go through Kahala.

Kahala

Kahala Avenue, which starts from where Diamond Head Road turns inland, is shaded by splendid trees and lush shrubbery and lined with fine homes. Many, extensively remodeled during the 1980s real estate boom, are now for sale. It ends at the luxurious Kahala Hilton (closed until early 1996 for renovation).

The posh Kahala community is one of Honolulu's finest—and most expensive. The district has many amenities, including a climate tempered by sheltering peaks, and a long, narrow beach that affords excellent sites for surfing, snorkeling, and swimming.

Kahala also boasts the Waialae Country Club, home to the Hawaiian Open International Golf Country. Waialae is the island's most exclusive golf course; even Kahala Hilton guests are unwelcome unless invited by a member.

Kealaolu Avenue will take you from Kahala Avenue to Kalanianaole Highway, along the hibiscus border of Waialae Country Club's links. But first have a look at the rest of Kahala and Kahala Mall, its big shopping center. Take one of the roads to the left from Kealaolu over to Makaiwa Street or Pueo Street and follow it inland to Kilauea Avenue which passes the mall (you can wind about on other streets, but make Kilauea your goal). Kahala Mall has department stores, supermarkets, popular restaurants, and some fine boutiques and gift shops,

many opening to its air-conditioned mall. In addition to upscale stores, the mall also houses eight theaters for after-shopping enjoyment.

Koko Head and Koko Crater

Waialae Avenue, along one side of the mall, moves *Koko Head* right into Highway 72 which, with Koolau ridges and valleys to your left (many with houses) and alternating neighborhood and ocean views to the right, will convey you to Hawaii Kai. This vast development of houses, townhouses, high-rises, two golf courses, and shopping centers spreads over 6,000 acres of Koko Head and Koko Crater foothills, adjacent valleys, and Kuapa Pond (an ancient, 523-acre fishpond, now Hawaii Kai Marina).

The volcanic peak and crater are the centers of Koko Head Regional Park, consisting of natural areas, Hanauma Bay and Sandy Beach parks, and scenic lookouts. Koko Head rises to 642 feet, Koko Crater to 1,208 feet.

On the crest of Koko Head is a side road that leads to the parking area above sparkling, coconut-palm-fringed Hanauma Bay. Paths wind steeply down to the beach park (crowded on weekends). Trails along rock ledges about a foot above the sea go from the wide beach along both sides of the bay almost to the headlands, past tide pools and incredible rock formations. High tides and heavy surf can sweep across the ledges, so use caution.

Along the east shore, you scramble through an arch eroded by sea and wind from an old lava flow and end up at Toilet Bowl, a small cove named for the way incoming waves raise and lower its water level.

The bay is one in a line of craters formed during Oahu's last eruption. Over centuries, the elements opened it to the sea. Because of its great clarity and extensive underwater life, it has been made a marine preserve.

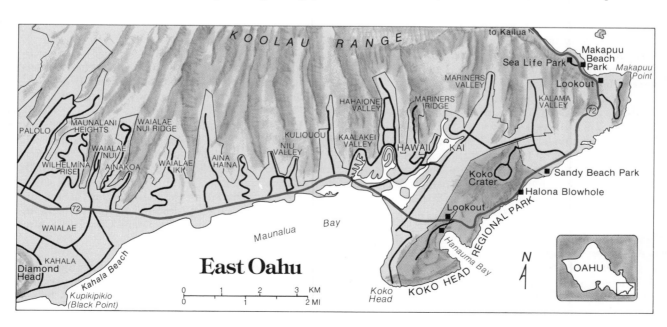

East Oahu

THE PERFECT WAVE

Though the origins of surfing are lost in prehistory, the ancient Hawaiians developed the sport to a degree unmatched anywhere in the world.

After surfing caught the imagination of *haoles* in the beginning of the 20th century, a drawback for many would-be surfers was the weight of the board (100 to 150 pounds); only the strong could surf. Experiments with reducing board weight began; the mid-1940s witnessed the birth of the modern board made of fiberglass covered with balsa. The front was scooped out and the skeg, a vertical "fin" that provides stability, was added.

Surfboards continued to evolve; modern boards have a foam core covered with fiberglass. Boards are now designed to suit every purpose, from learning on the gentle swells of south shore beaches to riding the big waves at the Banzai Pipeline. One common variation is the *paipo* board, or body board.

Surfers flock to Hawaii for the waves. With no continental shelf to slow down the swells, the velocity of a wave moving toward the beach is considerably greater in Hawaii than on the mainland. When these fast-moving swells come out of deep water and hit the shallow coral reefs, the result is an explosive wave, filled with unleashed power.

Surfers describe both the parts of the waves and the waves themselves. When speaking of the *lip*, they're referring to the leading edge of the breaking part of a wave. The *curl* is the lip of a wave when it's falling in an arc. A *hollow* wave is one in which the lip pitches out, creating a tube (a hollow curling wave or section of a wave). A *peeling* wave breaks with the curl moving across it diagonally.

The ideal shape the surfer looks for is a hollow, peeling wave. This type of wave breaks with the lip pitching out, hitting the flat water in front of the wave, and peeling left or right in a somewhat consistent manner. The place to ride is just in front of the falling lip, scribing a diagonal as the wave moves toward the beach.

No matter how many advances are made in equipment, in the end it's the wave that matters—the wave that hurls the surfer either toward the shore or under the water. Just as 15th century chiefs did, the surfer in Hawaii today waits in the water, hoping the next swell will be "the perfect wave."

Sandy swimming channels have been blasted out of the coral bottom, a favorite haunt of snorkelers. Note the coloring of the water: emerald green in the channels, purplish over coral, and deep blue beyond the reef.

Between Koko Head and Halona Blow Hole, the road snakes through a series of stratified cliffs of volcanic tuff—hardened remains of explosive showers of ash and mud once thrown out by Koko Crater and smaller vents.

From the highway, turn off to the lookout terrace above Halona Blow Hole. When waves are big, a geyser shoots up through a hole in the ceiling of a submerged lava tube. From the opposite side of the parking area, you look down upon Halona Cove, a narrow inlet between sheer cliffs with a nice beach for picnics.

Sandy Beach Park is a popular picnic and body surfing spot, but these waters are best left to experts as the very strong shore break (and resulting undertow) can be extremely dangerous.

Makapuu and Sea Life Park

The highway passes a fine windward overlook above Makapuu Beach Park, famous for its body surfing. Like neighboring Sandy Beach, Makapuu's waves and currents can be very strong. Flags advise beachgoers—red for very dangerous conditions, green for safe, and yellow for moderately rough. If you're unsure about water safety, try the surf at sheltered Kaupo Beach Park or sandy, calmer shores at Waimanalo.

Offshore is Manana Island, better known as Rabbit Island for the descendants of European hares taken there by a sugar planter in the 1880s. They live compatibly with shearwaters, noddies, and terns.

Sea Life Park. Opposite Makapuu, this fascinating park (open daily 9:30 A.M. to 5 P.M., and to 10 P.M. on Friday evening; moderate admission fee) is home to one of the greatest varieties of marine life on exhibit. Numerous shows star dolphins, penguins, sea lions, and whales. Trained dolphins and whales engage in a wider range of activities here than they do elsewhere in captivity. The 300,000-gallon Hawaiian Reef Tank has more than 2,000 species of marine life. Take the spiral ramp from the rim to three fathoms beneath the surface for an underwater view through large acrylic windows. The Rocky Shores exhibit includes a "wave zone," whose manmade black rock shelters are washed every 90 seconds by 600 gallons of seawater, and shallow tidepools, home to sea cucumbers, feather duster worms, and cowries. Other sections to visit are the Turtle Lagoon, where the endangered green sea turtle is bred; Sea Lion Feeding Pool, where you can buy fish the animals will jump up and take from your hand; Kaupo Falls, an arborarium with indigenous plants and island waterfowl; and Seabird Sanctuary, with a breeding, nesting colony of free-flying marine birds.

Just outside the entrance are a restaurant, gift shop, and the Pacific Whaling Museum (free) displaying one of the Pacific's most extensive private collections of whaling artifacts.

Depending on how much time and driving you want to devote to sightseeing, there's a loop trip from Honolulu to the windward side and back to fit your schedule. The shortest route to the north face of the Koolau Range is by way of Waimanalo, leaving Honolulu via Highway 72 and returning on Highway 61 (or Highway 63), or vice versa. For a longer loop, cross the Koolau mountains, then go northward up the Windward Coast, along the North Shore, and back over the Central Plateau.

Crossing the Pali

To make the big circle trip you can leave the city on either of two highways that cut across the rugged Koolau Range, Oahu's 37-mile-long (59-km) eastern spine. One route, Pali Highway (61), not only leads to Nuuanu Pali Lookout, a foremost scenic attraction, but it passes through a pair of tunnels beneath this natural break in the *pali* (a line of nearly vertical cliffs) and continues as Highway 61 through Maunawili Valley to Kailua. On its windward descent it intersects with Kamehameha Highway (83), which goes north past Pali Golf Course and Hawaii Loa College to Kaneohe, and with Highway 72 from the east.

The second route, Likelike Highway (63), conquers the Koolaus with the Wilson Tunnel and passes through banana groves at the windward base of the mountains before veering *makai*. On the windward side you can turn north onto Kahekili Highway (83), an inland drive that by-passes Kaneohe and joins coastal Kamehameha Highway in Kahaluu (the route continues north as 83). This is a convenient route if you're planning to visit Haiku Gardens or Byodo-In Temple. Or you can stay on Highway 63 until it intersects with Kamehameha Highway and go north through Kaneohe's downtown and past Heeia fishpond and park. Both cross-island highways intersect with H-1 Freeway in Honolulu.

Nuuanu Pali Lookout. Marking the center of Nuuanu Pali State Wayside, Pali Lookout lies at the end of a right-hand spur road off Pali Highway, 6½ miles/10½ km from downtown. On the way, you can get a more intimate view of Nuuanu Valley's rain forest by turning off and taking the two remaining stretches of two-lane, winding Nuuanu Pali Drive (they're well-marked and return you to the highway).

From the concrete viewing platform at the lookout, a breathtaking view confronts you—usually accompanied by great blasts of chilly wind. From the 1,186-foot-high site, your eye follows the fluted palisades for several miles northwest to Mokolii Island and then travels back to Mokapu Peninsula at the opposite end of Kaneohe Bay.

The lookout also conjures up a vista for your mind's eye. In the spring of 1795, the army of Kamehameha the Great landed on Oahu's southern shore, battling the island's defenders up the Nuuanu Valley to the pali where many fell or jumped to their deaths.

The abandoned old pali road, which you see below the lookout, was a Hawaiian footpath. Improved for a horse trail in 1845, it was later widened for carriages and then for cars. A footpath goes underneath the highway to Auloa Road.

The descent from the pali opens up new vistas, including a view of 1,643-foot Olomana Peak (a green Matterhorn), highest point on the ridge between Maunawili and Waimanalo and a favorite subject for local artists.

Ho'omaluhia. Part of the sweep of green you gaze upon from Pali Lookout is Ho'omaluhia (Thursday through Monday, 9 A.M. to 3 P.M.), a 400-acre botanic garden between Pali Golf Course and Likelike Highway. The entrance is at the end of Luluku Road off Kamehameha Highway; it's also accessible via Anoi Road off Likelike Highway to Luluku. The garden has a 32-acre lake, five camping areas, and several miles of trails. You can pick up a map at the visitor center. Guided walks are given on weekends, by reservation; call 235-6636.

The Waimanalo Plain

If you've come around the island's east end, you'll start up the Windward Coast at Waimanalo, guarded by the fortresslike cliffs of the southern Koolau Range. The Waimanalo Plain is a roughly triangular area beginning as a narrow coastal strip near Makapuu and gradually broadening towards Olomana Peak and the Lanikai shoreline.

The coast here is flat, with long strips of attractive sandy beach, a few rocky areas frequented by fishermen, and houses strung out over several miles. Parks along scenic Waimanalo Bay offer good beachcombing, surfcasting, board and body surfing, swimming, and snorkeling. Kaiona Beach Park also affords access to a remnant of early aquaculture—a rock-walled holding pond that probably once held turtles for exclusive consumption by a local chief.

Mostly planted in sugarcane until 1947, much of Waimanalo's land is now used to raise fruit, vegetables, flowers, horses, and cattle.

Waimanalo's modern lava-and-sandstone Catholic church, on the *makai* side of Kalanianaole (across the street from Waimanalo Elementary and Intermediate School), has a mosaic of its patron, St. George, over the door; sculptures, a mural, and frescoes, mostly by community members, ornament the interior.

Bellows Field Beach Park (access from Tinker Road). Popular for board and body surfing, swimming, surfcasting, and strolling, the 46 acres of coral sand, coconut palms, and ironwoods are open from Friday noon to midnight Sunday for camping, and weekends and national holidays for swimming and picnicking (see page 69 for details about permits).

Past the park turnoff, Highway 72 continues northwest before forming a junction with Kailua Road/Highway 61, which meets Pali Highway. The road provides fine views as it cuts east to Kailua through verdant foothills.

Lone boat *navigates waters of Kaneohe Bay. Kamehameha Highway provides scenic route between bay and encircling cliffs, links small towns of coastal plain.*

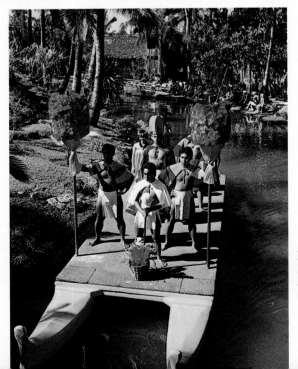

Pageantry enlivens daily events *at Laie's Polynesian Cultural Center. University students entertain with traditions from their native homelands.*

The Windward Coast

Kailua and Kaneohe

Neighboring Kailua and Kaneohe are the twin population centers of Windward Oahu. Elsewhere on this coast, small settlements and beach parks cluster alongside photogenic bays, and farms and pastures reach deep into lush valleys. Highway 83 strings these scenic pearls together en route to the North Shore.

Kailua now has high-rises and shopping centers on the fringes of its "small town" main streets. It also contains extremes of the architectural spectrum, juxtaposing an ancient temple with contemporary churches. Along Kailua Road's "church row" above town, turn off into the Windward YMCA parking area and visit Ulu Po Heiau. This temple, a state historic site, was probably built by captured warriors, but legend attributes it to *menehune,* the construction-minded little people. Walk the stone path across the huge platform and down the far side to a rock well at the edge of Kawainui Marsh, a moist, green bowl of 750 acres to be dredged and made into a park.

St. Anthony's, Kailua's largest church (114 Makawao Street), is shaped like a cross and has four patios and a massive red copper roof. Its impressive handwork includes pews made by Trappist monks and stained glass abstracts by Erica Karawina.

Kailua Bay has a sandy shoreline of several miles, from Lanikai to Mokapu Peninsula. It is lined with homes, but frequent rights of way provide beach access. Off Lanikai Beach, served by Mokulua Drive, are the Mokulua Islands seabird sanctuaries; the one shaped like a camel's back has a fine beach. Kailua Beach Park, at the ends of Kailua Road and South Kalaheo Avenue, is splendid. Popoia (Flat) Island, just offshore, is reachable by many swimmers. Kalama Beach Park, farther north along Kalaheo Avenue, is a favorite of body surfers.

Mokapu Peninsula, occupied by Kaneohe Marine Corps Air Station, juts out between Kailua and Kaneohe bays. It's separated from the rest of the island by two fishponds. Off the peninsula's Ulupau Crater tip is Moku Manu (Bird Island), a refuge for terns, boobies, and man-of-war birds.

Along Kaneohe Bay

Kaneohe Bay Drive continues from North Kalaheo Avenue and winds close to the shoreline of Kaneohe Bay out to the junctions of Kamehameha and Likelike highways. It offers many views of the bay as it passes Kaneohe Yacht Club, the YWCA's Camp Kokokahi, Bay View Golf Center, hillside homes, and homes with boat piers.

Kaneohe Bay is huge—8 miles/13 km long—and home for numerous recreational craft. In the south end is Moku O Loe (Coconut Island), a once luxurious private estate now partly the University of Hawaii's Hawaii Institute of Marine Biology. The bay's formerly extensive marine habitats have been greatly reduced by pollution largely from silty freshwater runoff.

Kamehameha Highway takes you past Heeia Fishpond, an ancient 88-acre fish pen with a 5,000-foot wall. Drive up on Kealohi Point in Heeia State Park for magnificent views of it against a mountainous backdrop. Glass bottom boats leave Heeia Kea Boat Harbor just north of the park to cruise over sections of an offshore coral reef.

On the Inland Road

To reach photogenic Haiku Gardens and Byodo-In Temple take Kahekili Highway (83). The gardens, a jungled estate at 46-336 Haiku Road (left turn off the highway), include a restaurant that overlooks grass houses, lily ponds, and bamboo groves.

Byodo-In Temple is the main feature of the Valley of the Temples, a memorial park in Ahuimanu Valley. A concrete replica of a classic Kyoto temple, it occupies a spectacular setting between the majestic pali and a reflecting lake enlivened by colorful carp. A small entrance fee allows you to visit the temple, open daily from 8 A.M. to 4:30 P.M.

In Kahuluu, 2 miles/3 km north of Byodo-In Temple, Senator Fong's Plantation and Gardens showcases the variety of products grown in Hawaii. Minibuses tour 725 acres of grounds named for the presidents under which Hawaii's first elected U.S. Senator served. There's a moderate entrance fee to visit the attraction, which is open daily from 9 A.M. to 4 P.M.

To Kahuku

Kamehameha Highway follows the shoreline closely all the way to Kahuku at the north end of the island. It passes a string of beach parks (crowded on weekends), beach cottages, modest motels or cottage resorts, a few restaurants, and some large condominiums.

Farms dot the Waiahole and Waikane valleys. Most of Oahu's sweet potatoes and almost a third of its papayas come from this area, which also produces bananas, beans, cucumbers, taro, and flowers. Scattered along the way are fruit and vegetable stands and a few souvenir stalls.

To the north, Kaneohe Bay ends at Kualoa Point, part of Kualoa Regional Park. Listed on the National Register of Historical Places, the area that includes the park was considered one of Oahu's most sacred. The point affords access to Apua and Molii fishponds (the latter is still used commercially) and a view of Mokolii (Little Dragon) Island (also known as Chinaman's Hat).

The rock formation on the cliff north of Makaua Beach Park is called the Crouching Lion. Below, a restaurant of the same name is a popular bus tour stop.

The road swings inland around magnificent Kahana Bay at the mouth of lush Kahana Valley, a 5,300-acre state park with a 5-mile/8-km trail that crosses a stream. From the beach park, shaded by false *kamani* and ironwoods, you can look across the water to the overgrown stone wall of Huilua, Oahu's oldest fishpond and a national historic landmark.

At Hauula, a marker points the way to Sacred Falls, which drop 80 feet from a 50-foot-wide gorge at the head of Kaliuwaa Valley. The falls form a deep swimming hole contained on three sides by plummeting, foliage-covered cliffs; it's a 2-mile/3-km walk from the parking area near the highway. Don't attempt the walk in bad weather; the last mile can be muddy. Hauula's expansive beach park has a large, walled-in swimming area. Visit charming Hauula Congregational Church and the ruins of large Lanakila Church, built in 1862 of local coral and timber.

Laie is largely a settlement of Hawaiian and other Polynesian Mormons. About 6,000 mountain-to-sea acres have been a church development project since 1864. They include the town, the impressive Polynesian Cultural Center, a lodge and restaurant, the campus of Brigham Young University-Hawaii, and the landmark Mormon Temple, set off by a formal garden. The Visitor Center is open daily from 9 A.M. to 8 P.M.

North of the BYU-H campus (just before the Laie Shopping Center) you'll notice a Hawaii Visitors Bureau warrior marker for nearby windswept, sea-battered Laie Point. The promontory offers views of the coast and two adjacent islands; the ocean surging through the hole in one of these islands adds to the drama of this "land's end" lookout.

Just north is the state's large and lovely beach park on Malaekahana Bay with fine swimming and lawns and woods for picnicking and camping (see page 69).

Polynesian Cultural Center

Condensing the vast span of Polynesia into walking distances, the Polynesian Cultural Center (open Monday through Saturday; admission fee) re-creates villages of Samoa, Tonga, Hawaii, Tahiti, Fiji, the Marquesas, and Maori New Zealand. Dedicated to preserving the cultural heritage of Polynesia, the center provides jobs and scholarships for students at the adjoining Brigham Young University branch campus.

You can tour the various regions in the complex by tram or in a double-hulled outrigger canoe. Activities include a 40-minute film in the 600-seat Imax theater, a band concert, a canoe pageant, and a song and dance festival. A dramatic, open-air Polynesian revue is performed at night against a cliff backdrop with fountains for a curtain.

The center opens at 12:30 P.M. daily except Sunday; activities start at 1 P.M. Dinner with a choice of buffet or luau is served between 4:30 P.M. and 7 P.M., and the show begins at 7:30 P.M. Several different ticket packages are available.

The center's villages are situated along the banks of a lagoon. At each you'll learn about the dwellings and culture and see—and even join in—demonstrations of crafts, songs, and dances. Attractions include a replica of a missionary settlement, scene of Hawaiian quilt demonstrations, and a typical plantation store. The center has a snack bar and a crafts shop.

Like pink islands *in a sea of green, crownlike water lilies grace pool in Waimea Valley, Home of Waimea Falls Park. Tour highlights ancient Hawaiian lifestyles and botanical preserves.*

Windward Oahu resident *presents impromptu serenade outside charming church near Hauula.*

K ahuku, the fertile plain across Oahu's north tip, has changed from sugar plantation to resort area with smaller-scale agriculture. Since the plantation's final harvest in 1971, some of the acreage has been replanted with feed and truck crops. At the heart of this plain is the former sugar mill town of Kahuku. At the restored, turn-of-the-century Kahuku Sugar Mill, you can take a free self-guided tour daily from 10 A.M. to 6 P.M. The mill also has gift shops and a restaurant.

On your way to the Turtle Bay resort area, you'll pass other newcomers to the North Shore—prawn ponds, windmills pumping water and generating electricity, and open markets selling the harvest of ponds and fields. The Turtle Bay development includes a large hotel, cottages, cabanas, an 18-hole golf course, riding stables, and lighted tennis courts. Next to the hotel and along the highway are two condominium villages.

Sunset Beach: Surf, Stables, and Satellites

The coast from Kawela to Waimea Bay has big winter surf (for seasoned experts only), including the famous Banzai Pipeline. Just to look at Sunset Beach waves when they run as high as 30 feet is a thrill. However, don't get more involved than being a spectator; even the currents of water swirling on the beach are too strong from about October to April.

On the *mauka* side of the highway near the beach, you'll pass the Waialee Livestock Research Farm, operated by the University of Hawaii. In the Paumalu section, you'll see Comsat—largest, most versatile earthstation for international commercial satellite transmissions; one dish antenna is 10 stories tall. Call a day in advance to visit on weekdays. To reach the facility, take Comsat Access Road from Highway 83.

As the highway continues southwest, you pass a marker that points to a cliff formation in the likeness of George Washington's head; legend says it's a prince turned to stone while chasing a lover to whom he had been unfaithful.

Puu O Mahuka. To reach Oahu's largest ancient temple, turn left from the highway onto Pupukea Road and take the right-hand spur road at the first junction. Inside the walls of this large heiau, human sacrifices were made. Here, too, a famous Hawaiian priest forecast that the islands would be overrun by strangers from a far-off land.

The view from here extends from Waimea Bay and Stream far below all the way to Kaena Point.

Wet and Wild Waimea

As you leave the Pupukea area behind, Highway 83 rounds a bend, providing your first glimpses of Waimea Bay. Rising above the last cluster of buildings on the left is the tower of an early rock-crushing facility. The tower and

other buildings were later renovated as Saints Peter and Paul Mission. On the cliffs to the left of the highway grow sisal plants, wild descendants of a 1907 attempt to commercially harvest the leaves and stalks for hemp and fencing.

Waimea Valley, Home of Waimea Falls Park (daily 10 A.M. to 5:30 P.M.; admission fee). A half-mile up the north side of the Waimea River from the highway is this unspoiled preserve. You can ride open-air minibuses or walk a 1-mile/1.6-km-long trail through the valley to the 45-foot waterfall for which the park was named. Bus drivers describe the arboretum and botanical garden along the way; plants and trees are labeled. Guided walking tours are given throughout the day.

The 1,800-acre park also is a Hawaiian games site where guides demonstrate and teach the sports of long ago; visitors are welcome to try the games themselves. You can tour a Hawaiian living site, a recently excavated ancient burial temple, and the appropriately lei-shaped Lei Garden. Traditional hulas are presented several times each afternoon. Cliff diving from 55 feet above the pool takes place at 11 A.M., 12:30, 2, and 3:30 P.M.

Hikers can explore 7½ miles/12 km of trails that burrow deep into an unspoiled valley where there are fern grottoes and koa, guava, orange, coffee, mountain apple, and mango trees. Peacocks, geese, ducks, and jungle fowl roam freely in the park. Near the park entrance, there's a restaurant, snack bar, and country store. Free moon walks are conducted two nights each month at 8:30 P.M. when the moon is full.

Waimea Bay Beach Park. Just south of Waimea River Bridge is Waimea Bay Beach Park with its generous stretch of sand. Usually calm during summer, the bay roars to life in winter. Often two or three stories tall, the waves attract expert surfers. Because of their height and accompanying rip current, these waters are extremely hazardous from October to April.

From Waimea Bay to Haleiwa, you feast on more views of the unprotected coast, see attractive beach homes around Kawailoa, additional surf breaks (Chun's Reef and Laniakea), and a modern dairy farm that has provided a thatch-roofed picnic shelter and children's animal farm for the public.

Haleiwa Ages with Charm

Explore Haleiwa, a mix of old plantation and fishing village, grown a little Bohemian. Though Haleiwa lost out as the Waialua District's main settlement when newer Waialua grew up around the mill, the village has bounced back yet preserved much of its charm, its character now given some permanence by a protective ordinance.

There are new houses; some old buildings with character have had face lifts; and Haleiwa Shopping Plaza has

The North Shore

been designed to harmonize with neighbors that have stood here more than half a century.

Haleiwa Beach Park. The highway skirts Haleiwa Beach Park. The park's generous expanses of grass, sand, and coconut palms fringe the head of Waialua Bay and face the Mokuleia shore and the head of the rugged Waianaes. As you cross the narrow, arched bridge over Anahulu Stream, look inland at a few small boats resting under a cover of trees or outward at many craft moored in the boat harbor.

You'll pass a couple of restaurants, pint-sized bank, restored old wooden courthouse, new shopping complex, and archaic buildings that house pool halls, souvenirs, art galleries, and small markets that do a whopping business in "shave ice"; Matsumoto's has an island-wide reputation.

Waialua Church. A Kamehameha Highway stop should be Waialua Protestant Church, also known as Liliuokalani Church, the fifth (built in 1961) sanctuary on the old mission site. It has the ancient bell, a memorial archway, and the clock the queen presented in 1890—the hours are the 12 letters of her name. Ancient gravestones date from the 1830s. The church was enhanced recently with 15 memorial stained glass windows by Erica Karawina that symbolize Biblical verses.

Haleiwa Road. You can turn off the highway just south of the Anahulu bridge and drive Haleiwa Road. A spur to the right, at the end of the boat harbor, leads to Alii Beach Park, at one end of a long, broad ribbon of sand bordering winter surfing ground. On the same spur, Waialua Bay's 800-foot rock breakwater is popular with surfer-watchers and fishermen who turn out in crowds for the *hahalalu* runs that occur between July and December.

Summer seas are calm at Alii Beach Park (best swimming is at the southern half) and farther along at the beach in front of Jodo Mission and the Japanese language school. Haleiwa Road also passes a charming little Hawaiian Protestant church, graceful fire station, and former elementary school that residents plan to restore for an arts center. Next to the school a spur road goes to Kaiaka State Recreation Area on Kaiaka Point where picnicking and fishing are popular; there's swimming just down the beach.

From Haleiwa Road, Paalaa Road will take you back to the main highway, past taro patches, banana groves, and the Shingon Mission (note its fine Japanese roof).

Waialua and Mokuleia

Take Haleiwa Road or Kamehameha Highway to Waialua Beach Road, then turn onto Goodale Avenue and drive past the Waialua recreation field to Waialua's tree-shaded center. Go west on Kealohanui Street past Waialua's mill to see Hongwanji Buddhist Temple. Turn *mauka* on Puuiki Street and drive through a plantation camp with tiny houses and bright gardens and a pretty wooden church to Farrington Highway (930).

Farrington goes west to a vacation house colony, Dillingham Field (private planes and gliders), a beach park for camping, and organization camps. The road then becomes a dirt road around Kaena Point (see page 65; tough going even for 4-wheel-drive vehicles). Farrington goes east to Thomson Corner, where routes 930 and 803 join.

In a cane field on the Haleiwa side of the junction, you'll see the stack of the old mill of 1880s vintage. Continue south on a cane road from the end of Highway 803 and look in another field for ruins of a large Catholic church and graves marked with crosses or oriental characters. The church's successor is the 1923 Spanish-style St. Michael's on Goodale Avenue.

ACROSS THE CENTRAL PLATEAU

The cool, 1,000-foot plateau between the Waianae and Koolau ranges contains some of the state's best farm land, still planted primarily with pineapple and some sugarcane. Hub of the area is Wahiawa, shopping center for approximately 40,000 agricultural workers, suburbanites, and service families from nearby Schofield Barracks and Wheeler Air Force Base.

Two routes cross the plateau from the North Shore. From Weed Circle at Haleiwa's edge, you can take highways 99 and then 80 (together called "Kamehameha Highway") through Wahiawa. Highway 803, from Thomson Corner near Waialua, passes Schofield Barracks, bypassing Wahiawa; it begins as Kaukonahua Road and then becomes Wilikina Drive. Kamananui Road (99) connects the two routes north of Schofield Barracks and Wahiawa. Both routes climb through cane, then pineapple fields, and provide good views of the Waianae Range's 4,020-foot Kaala, Oahu's highest peak; Kolekole Pass, the only break in the Waianae mountains; and the more distant Koolau Range.

As you drive uphill to Wahiawa or Schofield, you'll view Kolekole Pass on your right. It was here, on December 7, 1941, that two flights of Japanese planes flew through the Waianae Range to bomb Schofield and nearby Wheeler Air Force Base on their way to Pearl Harbor. The pass is 1,700 feet high.

Southbound on Kamehameha Highway

About 7 miles/11 km along Kamehameha Highway, you reach the newly expanded Dole Pineapple Pavilion, where you can sample fruit juice at the visitor center, take a tram ride through the fields, shop for souvenirs at the gift store, and eat in the restaurant. The pavilion is open from 9 A.M. to 6 P.M.

Next door is the modest Helemano Plantation, which sells fruit, vegetables, and flowers. A bakery, country store, and lunch room round out the facilities. Down the road is Del Monte's Pineapple Variety Garden, with some 30 species of the bromeliad family (pineapple is a member) on exhibit.

Kukaniloko Birth Stones. Just north of Wahiawa, in the middle of a pineapple field and surrounded by a grove of eucalyptus and coconuts, are the stones upon which royal children were once born. The spot is accessible from a dirt road off Kamehameha Highway; the turnoff is opposite Whitmore Avenue (Highway 804).

Wahaiwa

Once a quiet plantation town, Wahiawa is now a commercial center with little of interest for travelers. North Cane Street was the town's first main street and the location of its railroad depot. The pastel-painted wooden buildings, some with balconies, that still line it are vintage 1910.

At 108 California Avenue, a healing stone housed in a concrete shelter is usually laden with flowers, fruit, and votive candles placed there by local people who believe in the stone's curative powers. A few blocks away, at 1067 California Avenue, stands the Wahiawa Hongwanji Mission, which boasts an impressive wooden Buddha covered with gold leaf.

Wahiawa Botanical Gardens. Open daily from 9 A.M. to 4 P.M. (no fee), the gardens, at 1396 California Avenue, provide a shady retreat from the sun. The 27-acre site contains trees, shrubs, ferns, and other plants that thrive in cool, wet regions, including a collection of aroids (relatives of the calla lily and jack-in-the-pulpit). Paths lead to fine picnic spots.

Schofield Barracks

Home of the 25th Infantry Division, Schofield Barracks began in 1909 as a cavalry base and island fortification and was the army's largest post until World War II. The museum (see below) contains interesting military exhibits. To look around, drive in Macomb Gate from Wilikina Drive. (For your visitor pass, you'll need proof that you have automobile insurance for public liability and personal indemnity.)

On the base you'll drive tree-shaded roads past graceful, quadrangular-shaped, three-story barracks buildings in Second Renaissance Revival style. They were constructed between 1914 and 1933.

Tropic Lightning Museum. Exhibits in the base museum trace the history of Schofield and the 25th Division and include artifacts and weapons used in wars from 1812 through Vietnam. In front stand some representative American tanks and cannons from World War II and a 7-foot dragon statue, emblematic of the 14th Infantry's Peking assault during the 1900 Boxer Rebellion. The museum (no fee) is open to visitors Wednesday through Sunday.

Kolekole Pass. Early on December 7, 1941, Japanese planes flew through this pass west of Schofield before bombing the barracks. The pass is about 5 miles/8 km from Macomb Gate. You can drive almost up to it on a road that snakes through luxuriant forest.

Just below the sentry post at Kolekole Lookout, you can park and walk two short trails. The one to the right of the road leads to a white steel cross erected for Easter sunrise services. The trail above the parking area heads up to Kolekole Rock, which old-timers say represents the female guardian for which the pass was named. Lookouts on both paths offer grand views over the entire Central Plateau.

The road over the pass, which drops quickly around hairpin turns through Lualualei Valley to the Waianae Coast, is restricted because it passes Lualualei Naval Magazine.

...Across the Central Plateau

To Pearl Harbor through Mililani

South of Wahiawa, Kamehameha Highway changes its numbers back to Highway 99. It intersects Wilikina Drive (page 61), skirts Wheeler Air Force Base, cuts through forested hills, and sweeps past patches of new houses. Highway 99 then bridges deep Kipapa Gulch before it reaches continuous residential and commercial development near Pearl Harbor.

Wheeler Air Force Base. Wheeler, shared by both army and navy, is preserved in its parklike, pre-World War II form. Near the main gate stands a replica of a P-40, the aircraft in use on that fateful December 7th. You'll also find plaques commemorating two of the earliest mainland-to-Hawaii flights, both in 1927.

Mililani. The highway bisects Mililani, a comfortable suburban community built on 3,500 former pineapple

acres. Wide streets have islands of trees (mostly shower trees). Features of the planned community include a bike-path-walkway system, a continuous string of parks, recreation centers, a public golf course, and attractive shopping centers.

Modern Catholic Church of St. John, at 95-370 Kuahelani Street, is worth a look. Note particularly the sculptures along the Stations of the Cross, the bronze statues of the Virgin Mary and St. John, and the stark stone altar.

You'll have Pearl Harbor (see page 64) in view on the long downhill drive. Then the highway passes part of that huge navy base, meeting the H-1 Freeway between Waipahu and Pearl City. Pearl City Tavern, at the corner of Kamehameha Highway and Lehua Avenue, has been a landmark for some 40 years. Its huge menu includes Japanese dishes and seafood specialties. There's a fine bonsai collection on the roof.

An alternate route. If you've lost track of the time while touring the Central Plateau, you may want to take the fast H-2 Freeway south to the Waipahu/Pearl City area, where you can pick up the east-west corridors, H-1 Freeway or Kamehameha Highway (99). You can catch the six-lane H-2 from Wilikina Drive (Highway 99) or Kamehameha Highway (80 at this point) just south of Wahiawa.

Kunia Road

Another route from Schofield and Wahiawa to Waipahu is scenic Kunia Road (Highway 750), starting from Wilikina Drive (Highway 99). The road descends through pineapple fields and then sugarcane beneath the forested windward slopes of the Waianae Range on the right. It passes Del Monte's big shed where workers pack fresh pineapple into containers to be shipped to mainland markets, and Kunia village, noted for its highland gardens—a mix of temperate zone and tropical flowers—and for its annual spring show of orchids and the oriental arts of bonsai and ikebana.

Below Kunia, Highway 750 gradually winds to the southeast, joining the H-1 Freeway in Waipahu and then intersecting Farrington Highway.

Pearlridge and Aiea

Between Kamehameha Highway and Moanalua Road is Pearlridge Shopping Center, a huge, air-conditioned complex with department stores, specialty shops, and eating places common to several large island centers. A monorail connecting two sections of the shopping center runs at 5-minute intervals between the rooftop of the first mall and the third level of the second mall.

Below the shopping center, the swampy watercress fields of Sumida Farm are a welcome patch of green in the midst of all the urban congestion. From the parking lot at the shopping center, you can watch pickers in rubber boots and waterproof aprons working patches of the 11-

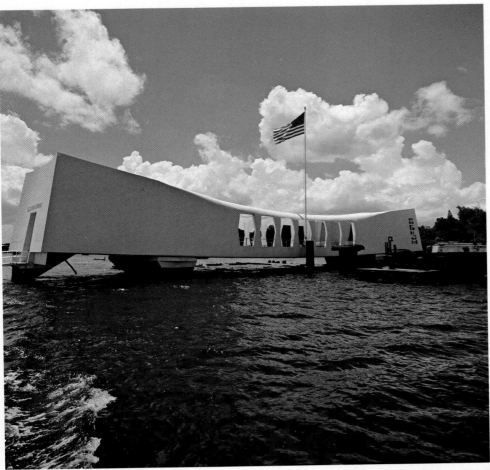

Pearl Harbor's *U.S.S. Arizona Memorial spans the hulk of the ship in which 1,102 men were entombed; boats ferry visitors from shore. Nearby attractions include the U.S.S. Utah, a submarine museum, and a plaque honoring the Apollo 11 splashdown.*

Pineapple *and neighboring sugarcane fields dominate the Central Plateau. For a close look at the plant and its family tree, stop by Pineapple Variety Garden. You can sip the juice at the Dole Pineapple Pavilion.*

...Across the Central Plateau

acre family farm started in 1928. Workers walk on tiles that divide the flooded fields. One-third of the state's watercress crop (1½ tons a day) is grown here. Island watercress is taller and milder than its mainland counterpart.

Take Moanalua Road from Pearlridge to Aiea's center and drive uphill on Aiea Heights Drive, past Hawaii's only sugar refinery. All island-grown sugar consumed locally is processed here; all other raw sugar goes to Crockett, California, for processing.

At the top of the road, about 3 miles/5 km up, a lovely state park contains the ruins of Keaiwa Heiau, an ancient healing temple. The park has picnic and camp grounds, magnificent groves of Norfolk pines, and plants grown by the early Hawaiians for medicinal uses. An easy 5-mile/8-km trail loops through the area.

To reach Honolulu from Aiea, you can stay on Moanalua Road (Highway 78), which becomes freewaylike from Halawa Interchange to Middle Street and then becomes H-1. Or you can return to the city on Kamehameha Highway; it passes Pearl Harbor's gates, joins with Nimitz Highway, and passes the airport under H-1.

Aloha Stadium. The 50,000-seat Aloha Stadium, built in 1975, converts from baseball to football configurations; movable grandstand sections ride on a cushion of air. Home teams include the AAA baseball Hawaii Islanders and Western Athletic Conference-member University of Hawaii Rainbow Warriors.

The facility also hosts all-star football games (NFL Pro Bowl and collegiate Hula Bowl), the Aloha Bowl, high school gridiron contests, and rock concerts. Exits to the stadium from H-1 Freeway and Moanalua Road (Highway 78) are well marked.

Aloha Flea Market. For a true island experience, stop by the tree-shaded Aloha Stadium parking lot on Wednesday, Saturday, or Sunday between 6 A.M. and 3 P.M. for the Aloha Flea Market. This large gathering draws secondhand merchandise of every description, all reasonably priced. In addition, you'll find a huge assortment of flowers, produce, and handicrafts.

A shuttle bus picks up guests at major hotels; for information, call 955-4050.

Pearl Harbor

The December 7, 1941, attack on Pearl Harbor by the Japanese propelled the United States into World War II and the Hawaiian port into the American consciousness. Today, the harbor's U.S.S. *Arizona* Memorial draws more visitors than any other attraction on Oahu. But long before the "day of infamy" and the battle cry "Remember Pearl Harbor," this area was well known to military strategists and to the Hawaiian population.

A strategic harbor. Competing powers in the islands, particularly the United States, viewed the former Pearl River lagoon as the most significant natural port in the North Pacific; the region became a major issue of negotiation in a series of 19th century treaties increasingly favorable to American interests.

Sacred home of sharks. Hawaiians believed that the site was the home of a beneficent shark queen and her subjects, so they viewed with apprehension the initial dredging of the harbor channel. This occurred without mishap, despite destruction of a fishpond and fish god shrine, because navy workers ceremoniously buried the image stones. But in 1913, offended sharks had their revenge; the first drydock collapsed before completion, an event attributed by some to the dock's construction over the home of the shark queen's son.

Arizona Memorial. Best known of the vessels sunk or severely damaged in the 1941 attack, the U.S.S. *Arizona* is the final resting place for 1,102 servicemen. The 1962 memorial, a white concrete bridge, seems to float above the water-shrouded battleship; oil still seeps from the ship's holds.

Visitor center. An onshore visitor center and museum (open daily 7:30 A.M. to 5 P.M.; free) houses materials on World War II naval history and wartime Hawaii. At the information desk, you'll receive a number (first come, first served) for a free shuttle-boat ride to the memorial, preceded by a film on the attack.

The boats operate from 8 A.M. to 3 P.M. daily. Shuttles may be canceled during inclement weather; call the center (422-0561) for information. Children must be 45 inches tall; those under 12 must be accompanied by an adult. Bare feet and bathing suits are not allowed. (Boat cruises from Waikiki do not stop at the Arizona Memorial.)

You can reach the center from Kamehameha Highway (Highway 99); turn west onto Arizona Memorial Place.

Other historical attractions. While waiting for your shuttle to the Arizona, walk over to Bowfin Park. Here, you can tour the U.S.S. *Bowfin*, a storied World War II diesel submarine credited with sinking 44 enemy ships, and visit the expansive Pacific Submarine Museum. The museum contains "hands-on" exhibits of undersea vessels, from Revolutionary days to the future.

The park is open from 8 A.M. to 5 P.M. daily; be there by 4 P.M. to tour the submarine. There's a small admission fee. Call 423-1341 for more information. A nearby restaurant overlooks the harbor.

On Ford Island, beyond the Arizona Memorial, stand monuments to a disparate pair of events. One honors the dead aboard nearby U.S.S. *Utah,* another victim of the Pearl Harbor attack (civilians must be guided by an armed forces member or dependent); the other monument acknowledges the return to *terra firma* of Apollo 11's astronauts following the dramatic first moonwalk mission in July 1969.

THE WAIANAE COAST

To the west of the Waianae Range, amid large plains, deep valleys, and steep ridges, lies leeward Oahu's scenic and historic Waianae Coast. Ancient ruins, remains of plantation communities, military and industrial sites, and Ko Olina Resort (hotel, condominiums, and golf courses) all call this coastline home. To reach the coast from Honolulu, take the H-1 Freeway.

The road passes Waipahu (see map on page 62), where Hawaii's Plantation Village, the centerpiece of Waipahu Cultural Park (94-695 Waipahu Street), is located. The outdoor museum contains dozens of replicas of homes and buildings once used by sugar plantation workers; included are a Chinese cook house, a Japanese bathhouse, and a Filipino men's dormitory. A small admission fee is charged to tour the village and plantation museum, open from 8 A.M. to 4 P.M. Monday through Saturday. On the hill above stands the Oahu Sugar Company's mill, which dates from 1896.

You can visit Ewa, as compact and pretty a plantation town as you'll find, by taking Fort Weaver Road (Highway 76) south from Farrington or from the Kunia turnoff from H-1 and turning west into Renton Road. Part of Oahu Sugar now, Ewa and its camps were built in the 1920s and 1930s by Ewa Sugar Company, whose abandoned mill is still a landmark. Renton Road is divided by trees, passes graceful houses, pretty churches, handsome company buildings, and ends at the working yard of the Hawaiian Railway Society with 40 pieces of rolling stock including the restored Waialua No. 6, a plantation engine built around 1918 from spare parts.

As H-1 rounds the Waianaes to merge into Farrington Highway, you'll see the large refineries on the coast that mark Campbell Industrial Park and the new deep draft harbor for the largest ships afloat.

In Waianae Shopping Mall is E'ala, a native Hawaiian cultural center and gift shop with exhibits on the coast's historic sites (call or stop in and ask about guided tours). E'ala's double-hulled voyaging canoe is berthed at Pokai Bay at the entrance ot Ku'ili'o'loa Heiau, a temple 200 feet long, 50 to 70 feet wide.

Along the highway shore at Makaha, you can see the attractive homes and apartments, a shopping center, and two beach parks—Mauna Lahilahi, and Makaha (the great winter surfing mecca). Inland is one of Oahu's largest tourist and residential developments outside Waikiki, the Sheraton-Makaha Resort and Country Club. Makaha Valley's deeper recesses are being left in their natural state for hiking and riding. Ask permission at Sheraton Makaha to visit Kaneaki Heiau, restored to the way it looked in the 18th century, when it was used as a war temple. The platform atop its dry-laid rock walls has grass houses, prayer towers, and a sacrificial altar.

At Makua is dramatic Kaneana Cave, whose inner reaches are blocked by cave-ins. Hawaiians of long ago believed the cave led to spirit dwellings of dead chiefs. Farrington Highway ends at Yokohama Bay, and no vehicles are permitted between here and Kaena Point on Oahu's northwestern tip.

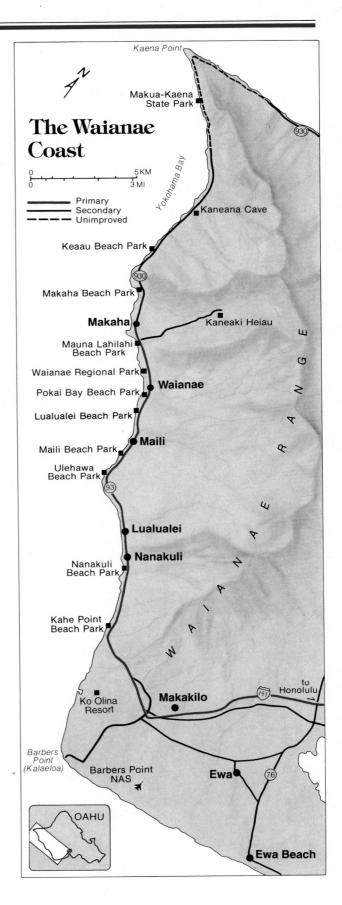

Silhouettes *of kiawe trees break the wide expanse of sea in this view from Keaau Beach Park.*

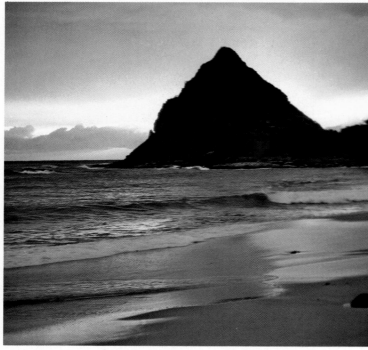

Pink glow *lights up sky and water as sun sets beyond Mauna Lahilahi at Mauna Lahilahi Beach Park.*

OAHU RECREATION GUIDE

 Oahu, the most populous island, provides a wealth of recreation activities for visitors. For further details on any activity listed below, consult your travel agent or the Hawaii Visitors Bureau, 2270 Kalakaua Avenue, Honolulu, HI 96815; 923-1811. The local area code is 808.

Most large hotels also offer an activities desk for their guests where you can arrange tee times, reserve tennis courts, and make arrangements for snorkeling or scuba diving expeditions. Transportation may be provided to some of these activities, either by the hotel or by the company.

Jogging. Bring your running shoes to Oahu. Hardly a month goes by without an organized run somewhere on the island. From March through November, you can take part in the free Honolulu Marathon Jogging Clinic. Just show up at the Kapiolani Park Bandstand Sunday morning at 7:30 A.M. Best jogging sites around Waikiki are Kapiolani and Ala Moana parks, Diamond Head Crater, and Alai Wai Canal.

Parasailing. Skyriding excursions are offered along Waikiki and in east Honolulu's Maunalua Bay. Flights generally last about 10 minutes; the boat ride and flight time together take a little more than an hour. Trips cost about $40. Aloha, Seabreeze, Skyrider, and Hawaii Kai are some of the parasail companies you'll find along the beaches.

Golf. Oahu boasts 30 golf courses, more than half of which are open to the public, with more in the offing. Six are private courses, including Waialae Country Club in Kahala, site of the United Hawaiian Open. Make tee times as far in advance as possible. Unless noted, all are 18-hole courses; most offer restaurants, pro shops, and cart and club rentals. Yardages are from the regular tees.

Public/municipal courses. Alai Wai Golf Course, Honolulu, 296-4653, par 70, 5,817 yards; Hawaii Country Club, Wahiawa, 621-5654, par 72, 5,761 yards; Hawaii Kai Golf Course (36 holes), Honolulu, 395-2358: Championship Course, par 72, 6,350 yards, Executive Course, par 55, 2,433 yards; Kahuku Golf Course (9 holes), Kahuku, 293-5842, par 35, 2,699 yards; Makaha Valley Country Club, Waianae, 695-9578, par 71, 6,091 yards; Mililani Golf Club, Mililani, 623-2254, par 72, 6,360 yards; Olomana Golf Links, Waimanalo, 259-7926, par 72, 5,856 yards; Pali Golf Course, Kaneohe, 296-7254, par 72, 6,494 yards; Pearl Country Club, Aiea, 487-3802, par 72, 6,230 yards; Ted Makalena Golf Course, Waipahu, 296-7888, par 71, 5,946 yards; West Loch Golf Course, Ewa Beach, 671-2292, par 72, 6,070 yards.

Resort courses. Hawaii Prince Golf Club (27 holes), Ewa Beach, 956-1111: Hibiscus Course (9 holes), par 36, 3,579 yards, Ilima Course (9 holes), par 36, 3,537 yards, Plumeria Course (9 holes), par 36, 3,437 yards; Ko Olina Golf Club, Ewa Beach, 676-5309, par 72, 7,252 yards; Links at Kuilima, Kahuku, 293-8811, par 72, 7,084 yards; Moanalua Golf Club (9 holes), Honolulu, 839-2411, par 36, 2,972 yards; Sheraton Makaha Resort & Country Club, Waianae,

695-9544, par 72, 6,398 yards; Turtle Bay Country Club, Kahuku, 293-8574, par 72, 6,366 yards.

Military courses. Active and retired members of the armed forces, their families, and civilian guests accompanied by a military sponsor may play at eight military courses on Oahu: Barbers Point Golf Course, Barbers Point NAS, 682-3088, par 72, 6,394 yards; Hickam Golf Course, Hickam AFB, 449-6490, par 72, 6,419 yards; Kalakaua Golf Course, Schofield Barracks, 655-9833, par 72, 6,186 yards; Kaneohe Klipper Golf Course, Kaneohe MCAS, 254-2107, par 72, 6,269 yards; Leilehua Golf Course, Schofield Barracks, 622-1776, par 72, 6,521 yards; Navy Marine Golf Course, Honolulu, 471-0142, par 72, 6,561 yards; Walter Nagorski Golf Club, (9 holes), Fort Shafter, 438-9587, par 34, 2,837 yards.

Tennis. In addition to the public and resort or commercial courts listed below, many condominiums have courts for guest use. The big military bases have a generous supply of courts for active, reserve, and retired servicemen, their families, and civilian guests.

Public courts. These facilities are available for use at no cost. More than 150 courts are located in parks and playgrounds around the island; more than half are within Honolulu's city limits. The Parks and Recreation Department, 523-4525, can give you information about facilities and clinics or other instruction. Listed here are courts close to Waikiki: Kapiolani Park has 4 lighted courts at Kapiolani Tennis Courts on Kalakaua Avenue and 9 unlighted courts at Diamond Head Tennis Center on Paki Avenue; Ala Moana Park has 10 lighted courts.

Resort/commercial courts. Honolulu: Hawaiian Regent Hotel, 1 court; Honolulu Tennis Club, 4 lighted courts; Hawaii Prince Hotel, 2 courts at golf club in Ewa Beach; Pacific Beach Hotel, 2 courts; Oahu Club, 6 lighted courts; Outrigger Malia, 1 court; Ilikai Hotel, 7 courts (1 lighted). Kahuku: Turtle Bay Hilton & Country Club, Kuilima Tennis Club, 20 courts. Waianae: Sheraton Makaha Resort & Country Club, 4 lighted courts.

Swimming. Swimming is generally safe in reef-protected areas. Beaches aren't necessarily marked as unsafe, though, so check before entering the water in any area where you are unsure of currents.

Ocean swimming. The beaches listed here, most of them beach parks, are usually safe for swimming: Ala Moana and Magic Island, all sections of Waikiki from Duke Kahanamoku Beach to Diamond Head, Kaalawai, Waialae and Kahala Hilton, the close-to-shore areas of Hanauma Bay, Kaiona, Waimanalo, Bellows Field, Lanikai shore, Kailua, Kalama, Kualoa, Kaaawa, Kahana, Punaluu, Hauula, Malaekahana, Kuilima Cove (at Turtle Bay Hilton), Kawela Bay, Haleiwa, Mauna Lahilahi, Pokai Bay, Kahe (Tracks Beach), Nimitz, Oneula, and Ewa.

Spots that look inviting but are hazardous are Halona Cove (rocks), Koko Head Sandy Beach (treacherous waves and currents), Makapuu (powerful waves, some undertow), Waimea Bay, and Sunset Beach (dangerous riptides and very strong undertow except when absolutely placid). Except for Kawela and Pokai, any of the north and west side beaches from Kahuku to Barbers Point can become dangerous when the sea is agitated.

Freshwater swimming. For a quiet paddle or a brisk workout when the beach looks bad, there are many swimming pools open free to the public in city parks.

Surfing. Oahu has the highest surf in the world—30-foot swells at Waimea Bay and Sunset Beach that challenge the most experienced surfers. But for beginners, there are excellent surfing beaches with calmer conditions. You should be a strong swimmer since you will spend more time paddling in the water than riding on it. Private lessons are available along Waikiki Beach.

Board surfing. Beginners can learn at Waikiki (though summer waves sometimes reach 8 feet), the Kalama shore, Chun's Reef, Nimitz, and Oneula Park.

Point Panic, Ala Moana, Magic Island, Diamond Head, Black Point, and Koko Head have higher summer surf. Challenging winter surf is found at Sunset Beach, Banzai Pipeline near Ehukai Beach Park, Waimea Bay, Haleiwa, Yokohama Bay, Makaha, and Maili (for experts only).

Body surfing. For gentle waves, try Kuhio Beach Pier at Waikiki, Waimanalo, Bellows Field, and Kalama. When the waves are small, you can switch from board to body surfing at Black Point, Koko Head, Ehukai Beach Park, Makaha, and Nimitz. For body surfing in big waves, head to Makapuu.

Windsurfing. Kailua and Lanikai are excellent grounds for all windsurfers, beginners to advanced. Tricky Diamond Head and "Backyards" at Kawailoa Beach are for the skilled. Aloha Windsurfing in Waikiki, Kailua Sailboard Co. and Naish Windsurfing Hawaii in Kailua, and Surf N Sea in Haleiwa offer lessons and rent equipment.

Beachcombing, tidepooling, and reef walking. To see Oahu's marine life without putting on diving gear, wait until the tide goes out and walk on lava rocks or coral reefs. Wear tennis shoes and remember gloves if you handle any rocks. Leave the rocks and reef as you found them and turn back any rocks that you may move (exposure to light can kill marine life).

Low-tide walking. Areas of Fort Kamehameha near the airport, Waialae Beach Park, Kaneohe Bay, Kualoa Point, Kaaawa Beach Park, Punaluu Beach Park, Chun's Reef, Kaiaka Bay, Mokuleia Beach Park, and Ewa Beach Park. The Waikiki Aquarium offers periodic beach walks.

Skin and scuba diving. Explore Oahu's underwater world of brilliantly colored fish and beautiful coral reefs. Snorkeling and diving equipment can be rented in Honolulu and other major beach areas; several diving companies offer skin and scuba diving excursions. Some also offer instruction, certification courses for scuba diving, and night diving excursions.

Diving spots. Good diving spots lie along the Waianae Coast beaches, the North Shore beaches in summer (par-ticularly Shark's Cove at Pupukea), off Rabbit Island and Magic Island, Maunalua Bay, and Hanauma Bay, a marine life conservation district (see the interpretive display in the beach pavilion).

Diving companies. Some 20 diving companies are listed in the Oahu *Yellow Pages* under "Skin Diving—Equipment, instruction, tours."

Military personnel or dependents may rent from the Special Services departments on the bases.

Boating. From beach service stands at several places along the Waikiki strip you can take off on an hour-long sail offshore aboard a small speedy catamaran or take an outrigger canoe ride—you'll surf in on three waves and likely do some of the paddling. All of the beach stands have surfboards for rent and offer surfing lessons, and some may also rent *paipo* (belly) boards, air mattresses, kayaks, and surf skis.

The *Yellow Pages,* under "Boats," lists companies that rent catamarans and other craft you can sail yourself. The Honolulu Sailing Co. in Kaneohe is a major concern that offers bareboat or skippered charters, instruction, and boats from 20-foot day sailers to 90-foot yachts.

Popular water skiing spots are Keehi Lagoon and Hawaii Kai Marina, and the *Yellow Pages* (under "Water Skiing") lists companies that can supply equipment or take you out.

Mainland yacht club members are welcomed at the Hawaii Yacht Club and Waikiki Yacht Club at Ala Wai Yacht Harbor (see page 29), and Kaneohe Yacht Club on Kaneohe Bay. Active or retired military personnel can look to the Pearl Harbor Yacht Club on the U.S. Naval Base, the Pacific Yacht Club at Hickam Harbor, or the Kaneohe Marine Corps Air Station Marina; they have sailboats of various sizes available for rent.

See also Boat Tours, page 25, and Fishing and Skin Diving in this section.

Fishing. Fishing areas abound on Oahu. No matter what type of fishing you prefer, you're sure to find something to suit your fancy. No license is required for saltwater fishing. For more information, call (800) 888-4376 to get a copy of the monthly publication *Hawaiian Charter Fishing Guide.*

Fishing locations. Most charters will take you trolling off the Waianae Coast, off Koko Head's choppy water, around the Penguin Banks near Molokai, or along the Windward Coast, notably in the open sea off Kaneohe Bay.

Waianae's deep and inshore waters are excellent for spearfishing. North Shore areas are good in some summer months. Best spots for spin fishing, surfcasting, and poling from lava ledges are the rocky coast beyond Koko Head, Koko Head Sandy Beach, Waimanalo Beach, some parts of Kaneohe Bay, and selected spots along the entire north and Waianae coasts.

In late summer *'oama, moi-li'i,* and *hahalalu* (baby goat fish, threadfin, and scad respectively) come into shallow sandy beaches to spawn—at Waikiki, Ala Moana, Waimea Bay, Pokai Bay, Ewa Beach. People wade in up to their hips and catch dozens with a simple bamboo pole and line. Some fish like mullet and *moi* favor the brackish water near the mouths of streams. You can fish for them and net crabs from highway bridges near the ocean at Haleiwa and Waialua and the banks of the Ala Wai and Kahaluu canals and Nuuanu Stream.

For freshwater fishing on Oahu, Lake Wilson (Wahiawa Public Fishing Area) is well stocked with bass, bluegill, sunfish, tilapia, and tucunare. Nuuanu Reservoir Number 4 has channel catfish, Chinese catfish, and tilapia, and is open for fishing on a limited basis. Check with the Division of Aquatic Resources, 1151 Punchbowl Street, Honolulu, for the freshwater fishing seasons.

Charter companies. Most fishing charters leave from Kewalo Basin, a few from Waianae Boat Harbor. You can get a list from "Fishing Parties" in the *Yellow Pages.*

Horseback riding. Three stables give visitors the opportunity to see some of Oahu's hidden beauty on horseback. Kualoa Ranch, 237-8515, offers 2½ and 3½-hour guided rides on a working cattle ranch. Trails extend from the mountains to the sea. Outings include lunch and transportation from Waikiki. Sheraton Makaha Lio Stables, 695-9511, ext. 7646, feature 1-hour guided trail rides through coffee trees, across a stream, and into the old Makaha Valley Plantation on the leeward coast. Turtle Bay Hilton & Country Club stables, 293-8811, ext. 36, offer 1-hour escorted rides along the North Shore coast.

Cycling. Rental bikes (the majority are 10-speeds) are plentiful in Waikiki; look under "Bicycles" in the *Yellow Pages.* Hawaii Bicycling League, 988-7175, schedules many guided weekend outings. Honolulu has a number of bike routes that ease riding through traffic-congested areas and help you explore quiet residential streets. One word of warning: As in other vacation areas, vandalism and thefts are on the rise. Lock your bike and take along a companion when riding in less-populated areas.

Oahu has a number of good destinations for cyclists. A day trip up Nuuanu Valley to Pali Lookout offers forest scenery and good views; the round trip from downtown is 12 miles/19 km. You can detour twice into the luxuriant jungle on two ½-mile meandering segments of the old road, Nuuanu Pali Drive.

Ride from Waikiki to Hanauma Bay for great snorkeling and swimming; round trip from Waikiki is about 23 miles/37 km.

A good ride of two days or more is to circle all or part of Oahu. Continue past Hanauma Bay, up the Windward Coast, and along the North Shore. From Haleiwa, turn inland and uphill to Wahiawa; then head down to Pearl City, Aiea, and Honolulu. This trip is just over 100 miles. If you start this ride on the Pali Highway out of Honolulu, you can cut about 15 miles/24 km off the trip. Reversing the direction of the round-the-island trip allows you to avoid riding into the wind over the long Windward Coast,

but either way it's a long climb through the island center to Wahiawa. Along the entire coast are camping areas and occasional hotels, condos, and tourist cottages.

Hiking, camping, off-road touring. Oahu's mild weather tempts all out-of-doors enthusiasts, and the hiking and camping are plentiful.

Hiking trails. Both the Koolaus and the Waianaes are crisscrossed by trails, many of which are described on a map available free from the State Division of Forestry and Wildlife, 1151 Punchbowl Street, Honolulu. Many trails cross private or restricted areas and are off-limits; check with the Division of Forestry, 548-8850, for the latest conditions and for permits. Better still, join organized hikes with Hawaiian Trail and Mountain Club, 247-3922, Hawaii Nature Center, 973-0100, or Sierra Club, 538-6616.

Here are a few trails easy and safe enough to do on your own: Judd Trail, a short loop trail to Nuuanu Valley past Jackass Ginger Pool; the interconnecting trails (about a dozen) in the Tantalus State Recreation Area through forested land from Manoa to Nuuanu valleys (the Makiki Environmental Education Center, 2131 Makiki Heights Drive, Honolulu, has a good map and interpretive booklets); Diamond Head summit trail; and the Moanalua Valley trail; call Moanalua Gardens, 833-1944, for information and to make reservations for their periodic guided hikes.

Other state parks and recreation areas with good hiking are Waahila Ridge State Recreation Area, Keaiwa Heiau State Park (it has the Aiea Loop Trail), Sacred Falls State Park, Kaena Point State Park, and Kahana Valley State Park (for which a permit is required from the division office at 1151 Punchbowl Street).

Camping. Camping is permitted at these city and county beach parks for a maximum of five consecutive days—they're closed on Wednesday and Thursday: Makapuu, Kaiona, Waimanalo, Kualoa, Kaaawa, Kahana Bay, Punaluu, Hauula, Haleiwa, Mokuleia, Keeau, Lualualei, Nanakuli, and Kahe Point. Camping is permitted on weekends at Bellows Field and Swanzy. You'll need to get a permit to camp from Honolulu's Department of Parks and Recreation, 650 South King Street.

Two state parks offer beach camping, Malaekahana State Recreation Area and Sand Island State Park; Keaiwa Heiau State Park campgrounds enjoy cool mountain air. Camping at all three is by permit from the Division of State Parks and is limited to five consecutive days (they're closed Wednesday and Thursday). Ho'omaluhia Botanic Garden offers camping to participants in its outdoor education programs. Call 548-7455 for reservations.

Family camping is permitted at some of Oahu's private camps (see Yellow Pages), including Camp Kailani at Kailua Beach, operated by the United Methodists; Mokuleia Episcopal Church Camp; Camp Puu Kahea at Waianae, run by the Southern Baptists; the YWCA's Camp Kokokahi on Kaneohe Bay; and Camp Hauula, run by the Catholic Youth Organization.

KAUAI

• LUSH, GREEN, QUIET ... BUT THIS COMPACT ISLE CONTAINS SURPRISES •

With 1992 Hurricane Iniki only a distant, if unpleasant, memory, Kauai once again welcomes vacationers. And first-timers will find little evidence of the hurricane's wrath, though it caused several deaths and countless injuries, uprooted trees and crops, denuded famed botanic gardens, smashed coral reefs, and started landslides along the Na Pali Coast.

Kauai had previously survived another hurricane in 1982, an experience which fostered a unique sense of community and made it easier for the island to rebound so rapidly this time. Regular airline flights and boat and helicopter tours resumed only a few months after the hurricane. Other than pockets of new construction and a few shuttered hotels, all of the island's tourist operations are back in full operation.

Quickly reclaiming its title as the "Garden Isle," lush Kauai offers a formidable range of attractions, activities, and visitor experiences packed into a verdant scenic area half the size of Rhode Island.

Land of Contrast

Kauai, Hawaii's oldest island, was created by an ancient volcano, Waialeale, which rises to 5,243 feet at its highest peak, Kawaikini. Once volcanic activity stopped here thousands of years ago, other forces of nature softened and changed the land. Torrential rains totaling 400 to 600 inches a year falling on Waialeale eroded gorges up to 3,000 feet deep along its flanks and sent streams large enough to be called rivers flowing to the sea.

Rain, wind, and powerful wave action have sculptured Kauai's northwest coast into a series of bold precipices that drop off steeply to the ocean and into verdant valleys worn between them. The deep gulches of the Na Pali Coast and Waimea Canyon border the Kokee Plateau (3,000 to 4,000 feet high) and its huge Alakai Swamp—so nearly level that heavy rains drain off slowly and drop over the tableland cliffs in the form of high waterfalls. Most of this vast, nearly inviolate region is protected in state parks.

You'll see striking contrasts by following the shore of this small (550 square miles/1,430 square km) circular island, Hawaii's fourth in size. The long stretch of windward coast from Na Pali around to Wailua is damper, cooler, and greener than the lee side from Koloa to Polihale. Rainfall varies from over 50 inches a year on the north shore to about 20 inches at Kekaha in the southwest.

Past, Present, and Future

The waves of Polynesian immigrants came early to Kauai, and this was the first island visited by Captain Cook in 1778. It was the only one of the islands not conquered by King Kamehameha. After Kamehameha's two attempts to reach the island had been thwarted, Kauai's King Kaumualii voluntarily submitted to the all-island rule in 1810. A few years later, a Russian emissary almost persuaded him to break away from Kamehameha and put his island under Russian protection. The remains of a Russian fort at Waimea Bay are a reminder of the 19th-century rivalry between the United States, Great Britain, France, and Russia for control of the islands—a rivalry that was largely responsible for Hawaii's remaining independent until 1898.

Hawaii's first successful sugar plantation was started at Koloa in 1835. Today, sugar defers to tourism as Kauai's leading income producer, and some cane fields have been taken out of production in favor of other crops such as papaya and guavas, now cultivated in the stretch from Moloaa to Kilauea. Bananas, macadamia nuts, and more than half the state's crop of taro are grown on Kauai, too.

Most of Kauai's 52,000 residents live in small towns with charming lanes of old, wooden buildings. Principal tourist enclaves lie around Poipu, Wailua, and Hanalei.

Everywhere on Kauai you'll hear tales of *menehune*, the legendary little people who were skilled workers in stone and who completed each job in a single night or never returned to it. The island is dotted with temples, dams, ditches, and trails supposedly built by the industrious race.

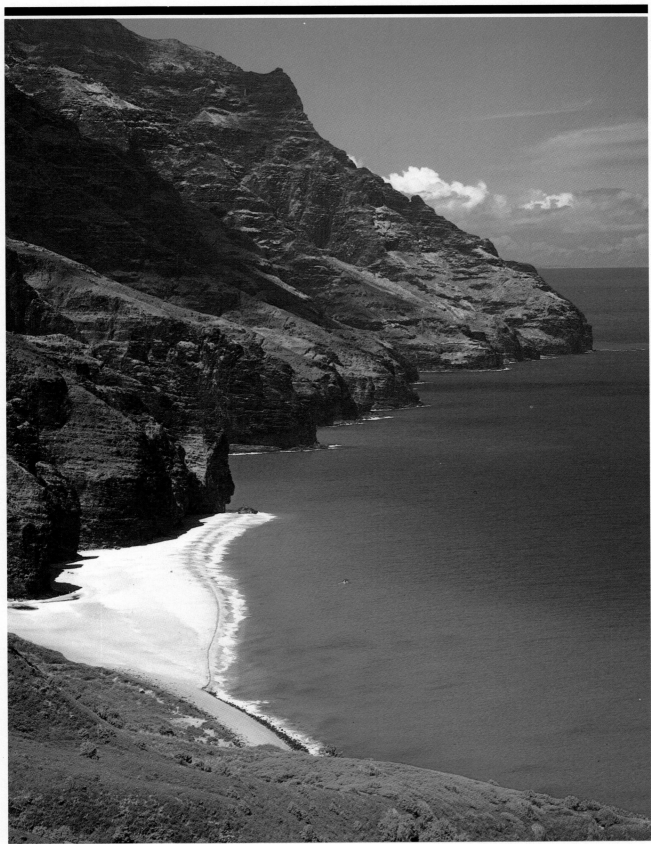

Pristine pocket beach along rugged Na Pali Coast

Kauai lies 72 miles/115 km northwest of Oahu. It's a 27-minute flight between Honolulu and Lihue airports via Aloha or Hawaiian airlines. Aloha IslandAir flies regularly between Honolulu, other island cities, and Princeville on Kauai's north shore. Travelers whose schedules prohibit a more lengthy stay can visit Kauai on one-day flightseeing tours from Honolulu. The island is also a stop on American Hawaii Cruises.

Getting Around

Formidable cliffs—Na Pali, on the northwest side of Kauai—prevent a circle trip completely around the island by car. Most visitors break Kauai sightseeing into two main excursions: the coast from Lihue north to the road's end near Haena (80 miles/128 km round-trip from Lihue); and the south shore, including a side trip to Kokee Park and the lookouts above Waimea Canyon and Kalalau Valley (100 miles/160 km round-trip from Lihue).

Tour companies visit all of these areas. If you drive these trips yourself, plan a day for each to allow time to stop often, tour a garden or museum, have a swim and picnic, and take side trips—to Koloa and Poipu (if you're staying elsewhere), Lawai Valley, Kukuiolono Park, the Wailua Homesteads, or a boat trip up the Wailua River to Fern Grotto.

Cars, mopeds, bikes, and 4-wheel-drives. The best way to explore Kauai is in a rental car. Most rental agencies have offices at Lihue Airport terminal. In addition, discounted rates may be available through local companies located at the airport, in Lihue town, or at resort areas. It's wise to reserve vehicles in advance during busy seasons. Mountain bikes and mopeds can be rented by the day in resort areas.

Shuttle, taxi, and limo services. No public buses serve the entire island. Prices for Shoppe Hopper shuttle vans, which connect the airport and major hotels, depend on distances; call 332-7272 for information. Some hotels provide pickups; taxis and limos are also available.

Where To Stay

Kauai has four main resort areas: the Lihue-Nawiliwili region, Wailua-Kapaa just to the north, Hanalei at the north shore, and the Poipu Beach area along the south shore.

In Lihue, you'll find several small apartment and motel facilities. At nearby Nawiliwili, accommodations include condominiums and a motel. The Westin Kauai, part of the 800-acre Kauai Lagoons development on the north shore of Nawiliwili Bay, has been replaced by the Kauai Marriott, which offers wildlife tours, carriage and horseback rides, and golf courses.

A cluster of resorts, hotels, condomiums, and motel units stretch along the east coast between Hanamaulu and Kapaa. Most are within walking distance of shops

and restaurants. Among the largest are Coconut Plantation, Coconut Beach Hotel, Lae Nani, Islander on the Beach, Kauai Beach Boy, Kauai Resort (at Wailua River), Kauai Sands, and Kauai Beach Villas (north of Hanamaulu). Though most of its century-old coconut palms were unhurt by Iniki, Coco Palms remains closed.

Along the north shore, accommodations include the Sheraton Princeville Hotel, Hanalei Bay Resort, Hanalei Bay Villas, Hanalei Colony Resort (on the beach beyond Princeville), The Cliffs at Princeville, and Pali Ke Kua. The area offers 45 holes of golf.

In the sunny Poipu Beach area the prestigious Waiohai and neighboring Poipu Beach Hotel fell victim to Iniki. As of early 1995, they were not rebuilt. The area's largest hotels and condominiums include the luxurious Hyatt Regency Kauai, the completely rebuilt Kiahuna Plantation, the new Pointe at Poipu, upscale Whaler's Cove, Sheraton's Garden Hotel (beach hotel still shut), and Colony's Poipu Beach Resort. A handful of smaller properties also line the coast. Most large properties include such amenities as pools, tennis courts, and respected restaurants. Poipu's two 18-hole golf courses are open to the public.

In Kokee State Park, you can stay in individual cottages or you can camp (tent and trailer spaces). For cabin reservations, write Kokee Lodge, Box 819, Waimea, HI 96796; to get camping permits, stop by state park offices in Lihue (see page 89 for address).

Camping permits are also required for overnight stays in Polihale State Park and for all county parks. For more information, turn to page 89.

Many of Kauai's bed and breakfasts can be reserved through Bed and Breakfast Hawaii, (800) 733-1632.

Touring the Island

You can explore Kauai by land, sea, and air. Popular activities include horseback rides, Na Pali Coast boat tours, and helicopter sightseeing. Tours can be booked through your hotel activities desk. For more information, turn to the recreation guide on page 88. Riverboating excursions up the Wailua River to Fern Grotto are discussed on page 77. Hyatt Regency Kauai sponsors free archeology tours, coastal dune walks, and dance and craft exhibits. Activities are open to the public.

The Shopping Experience

Though Kauai lacks the wide range of stores you'd find on Oahu, it does offer some intriguing small shops in such historic towns as Hanamaulu, Hanapepe, Koloa, and Lihue, as well as a few interesting shopping complexes: The Market Place at Coconut Plantation (Wailua River region), where machinery and relics remind you of its former sugar mill existence; Ching Young Village Shopping Center (Hanalei), a center that encompasses the Native Hawaiian Trading and Cultural Center; Kilohana (Lihue), a shopping complex/museum on a 1935 sugar-cane estate; and Kukui Grove Center (Lihue), a

KAUAI

0 4 8 12 KM
0   4   8 MILES

——— Primary
——— Secondary

modern mall. You'll also find shops in most major resort hotels. Souvenir shopping and bargain hunting is perhaps best among the vendors' tables at Spouting Horn.

Probably the best craft shopping is for the delicate Niihau shell leis. These exquisite shells are collected, hand-sorted, and fashioned into leis by the residents of the privately owned island off Kauai's coast (see right).

Dining and Entertainment

Kauai's restaurants offer a wide variety of cuisine, ranging from fast food, such as Mustard's Last Stand on Highway 50 in Lawai, to gourmet dining, à la Kapaa's Pacific Cafe. Try Prince Billy (Westin Kauai) and Terrace (Waiohai) for Sunday brunch. J.J.'s Broiler, Nawiliwili Bay, features "Slavonic steak," and Green Garden in Hanapepe has a lavish menu with low prices. Hanamaulu Cafe & Tea House, a local favorite for both Japanese and Chinese cuisine.

Most entertainment centers around resort lounges, but Smith's Tropical Paradise has a luau three or four times a week. For late night activity, residents head to Club Jetty on the wharf at Nawiliwili Harbor.

On pages 88–89, we've included a guide to the island's recreational facilities. For information and addresses of specific accommodations, excursions, and attractions, contact the Hawaii Visitors Bureau, 3016 Umi Street, Lihue, HI 96766.

KAUAI'S INTRIGUING NEIGHBOR

Because Niihau, the small island off Kauai's leeward coast, was off limits to tourists until recently, it has acquired an air of mystery. Today, Niihau Helicopters, 335-3500, reaches the island on tours from Kauai, even making two stops on lonely beaches.

The Sinclair family bought the island from King Kamehameha V in 1864 and established a cattle and sheep ranch. Descendants of the family still operate the estate; only relatives of the some 200 Hawaiian workers are permitted lengthy island visits. Life remains much as it was in the 19th century: no electricity (except at the ranch house and school), television, telephones, shops, or restaurants. Employees supplement the staples provided by the ranch with fish and home-grown vegetables.

In October the entire population combs the beaches for tiny shells from which they carefully sort and fashion their famous leis. The shells are fashioned into complex designs that can take weeks to string. Look for them in some of Kauai's better gift stores.

LIHUE & NAWILIWILI BAY

One of the state's oldest plantation towns, Lihue is the business center of Kauai and the seat of Kauai County, which includes the privately owned island of Niihau off Kauai's southwest coast (see page 73). It's also the first place most visitors see after landing at the airport, 2 miles/3 km from downtown.

Nawiliwili Harbor, 2 miles/3 km downhill, is Kauai's chief port. Down in a gulley in another direction stands the Lihue Plantation Company mill, one of the state's largest (and last) sugar mills.

Around Town

Lihue still exudes a small-village atmosphere. Here you'll find the handsome state and county office buildings, Courthouse, and Hawaii Visitors Bureau office (3016 Umi Street). Though now eclipsed by Kukui Grove Center at Puhi, Lihue Shopping Center on Rice Street has a mall and eating spots. The Haleko Shops section across Rice Street on Haleko Road reflects the architectural preferences of the Germans who owned Lihue Plantation until World War I. The four restored two-story, concrete duplexes house stores and a restaurant. Shrines and sculpture dot the garden—including the Lihue Horse Trough, a marble fountain bought in Italy and shipped around Cape Horn in 1909 by Pastor Hans Isenberg, a German immigrant and brother of a plantation founder.

On a hill overlooking the mill, Lihue Cemetery's rows of simple tombstones contrast sharply with a stately white marble monument erected in 1911 in honor of the Rice family, island pioneers. The monument was exhibited at Bremen and Paris art galleries before it was shipped.

Back of nearby Lihue Union Church rests a little Hawaiian cemetery nestled in a grove of plumeria trees. On a neighboring hill perches Lihue Lutheran Church, built in 1883 with an ornate altar and pulpit like a church of old Germany.

Kauai Museum. A visit to the two-building museum complex at 4428 Rice Street will help you get your bearings before further island exploration. In the William Hyde Rice Building a 6-minute film gives a bird's-eye view of areas seldom seen by the average visitor. You'll see an elaborate display of island history from its volcanic genesis some 60 million years ago up to the end of the 19th century, when Hawaii was annexed by the United States.

The Albert Spencer Wilcox Building (handsome historic landmark and former town library) houses changing exhibits of Hawaiiana and Hawaii's ethnic heritage. Its shop sells outstanding imports from the South Pacific, as well as Kauai and Niihau handcrafts.

Kauai Museum is open weekdays from 9 A.M. to 4:30 P.M., Saturdays until 1 P.M. There's an admission charge.

Grove Farm Homestead Museum. Time seems to stand still when you enter Grove Farm Homestead's 80-acre grounds. It's one of Hawaii's earliest sugar plantations and a living memorial to the Wilcox family who lived here from 1864 to 1978. Descendants of missionaries, the family also restored the Waioli Mission House in Hanalei.

Unhurried, 2-hour, guided tours offer visitors a look at carefully preserved buildings and grounds. In addition to viewing a vast repository of Hawaiiana, you'll learn how a sugar plantation operated. The tour covers the

Reached by boat, *Fern Grotto provides natural setting for Hawaiian serenade.*

well-furnished main house, outbuildings, Kaipu Camp (one of the last collection of workers' dwellings on the island), gardens, orchards, and groves of grand trees dating back to the days of Kalakaua. Along the way, you'll hear fascinating family tales, sip mint tea, and eat the traditional sugar cookies that the family cook prepared for more than four decades.

Tours begin promptly at 10 A.M. and 1:15 P.M. Monday, Wednesday, and Thursday. Because the sizes of the groups are limited, reservations must be made well in advance of your visit. For information and reservations, write to Grove Farm Homestead, P.O. Box 1631, Lihue, HI 96766, or call (808) 245-3202. Upon confirmation of your reservation, you'll be given directions to reach the homestead. A modest admission is charged. One tip: Wear shoes that slip off easily; you'll be removing them indoors.

Kilohana. On Highway 50 south of Lihue lies Kilohana, a former sugar plantation that has now become a 35-acre shopping, dining, and exhibition center. Specialty shops and arts and crafts galleries fill the former Wilcox home; Gaylord's restaurant looks onto a courtyard. Clydesdale horses pull carriages on tours of the outbuildings and beautiful grounds.

Nawiliwili Bay

As with any deep-water port, Nawiliwili's business centers around ships, docks, and wharves. But there's a lot of activity and local color. If a freighter is being loaded, you can watch raw sugar moving by conveyor from a bulk plant into the hold. Harborside Club Jetty is a good spot to watch the flotilla of fishing and pleasure craft. You get a fine harbor view from Niumalu Beach Park.

Kauai Lagoons. At the ocean end of the harbor, Kauai Marriott and its two 18-hole golf courses overlook Kalapaki Beach and Nawiliwili Bay to the Hoary Head Mountains. Horse-drawn carriages, outrigger canoes, and motor launches reach lagoonside restaurants, shops, and a fitness facility. The water tour gives guests and visitors a good look at island zoos.

Alakoko (Menehune) Fishpond. There's not much to see from the roadside lookout on Niumalu Road off Highway 58; it's the lore surrounding the serene pond that attracts visitors.

According to legend, the pond was built for a princess and her brother by menehune under their usual conditions—that no mortals watch them and that they complete the wall in a single night. But the royal pair could not restrain their curiosity. By the light of the moon, they watched the little people, lined up in a double row as far as they could see, passing rocks from hand to hand to workers at the dam. But they watched a little too long and were discovered by the menehune, who turned them into the twin pillars of stone you see on the mountainside

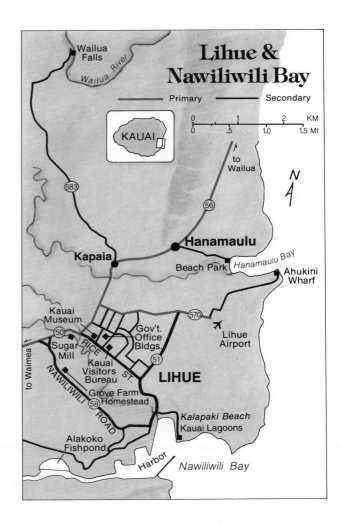

above. Having used up their time, the menehune had to leave two gaps in the wall. Chinese mullet raisers later filled these in, and the resulting pond is still in use.

North to Hanamaulu Bay

Two routes lead to Hanamaulu Bay. Highway 570 continues for another mile past Lihue Airport to Ahukini Landing. From the remains of the extensive wharf, you'll see fishers and get a look at the windswept eastern coast. Highway 56 leads to the bay through Kapaia, the turnoff for a 4-mile/6-km drive inland to Wailua Falls, where about a half dozen white ribbons of water plunge over a high canyon wall in the river's upper reaches. A trail descends the steep bank below the falls to a pool.

At Kapaia, also note the picturesque stores (former plantation houses), modern Hongwanji Buddhist temple, and Spanish-style Immaculate Conception Catholic church. Kapaia Stitchery, south of town, is the best place to find traditional Hawaiian quilt patterns and fabrics.

Hanamaulu, another plantation village, presents classic false-front facades on its post office and store; inside the latter is a free museum.

WAILUA RIVER REGION

Midway along Kauai's east coast lies Wailua, former home for Hawaii's royalty, the *alii*. In those days no visitors were allowed without specific invitation, and royal children had to be born here to be recognized as high chiefs. Today, it's a favorite tourist destination.

The mouth of the Wailua River marks the supposed landing site of Tahiti's first migrants. Seven sacred heiau once lined the river from its mouth to its source, the slopes of Waialeale. You'll hear stories of the royal years during the popular boat ride upriver to Fern Grotto.

Wailua River State Park

Several recreational and historic areas comprise Wailua River State Park. The Lydgate area of the park complex contains picnic sites and campgrounds, a beach, lava-rimmed ocean pool, and remains of a temple of refuge that once sheltered fugitives. Shore boulders with petroglyphs are sometimes exposed on the ocean side of the highway bridge.

On the north side of the river, Highway 580 heads inland. This route was the ancient Highway of the Kings; commoners were forbidden to use it, and rulers were carried over it because their feet were considered too sacred to touch the ground.

Kaumualii Park, alongside the river in a coconut grove, is a pleasant spot for a picnic.

The Poliahu area of Wailua River State Park is about 2 miles/3 km inland along this road. Here you'll find Holo-Holo-Ku, one of Kauai's oldest heiau, which bears a remarkable resemblance to a Tahitian temple. Partially restored, it contains reproductions of idols and a priest's grass house, a sacrificial rock, and royal birthstones. A trail up the hillside leads to an interesting Japanese graveyard.

At the top of the hill, stop at the site of Poliahu Heiau and the king's home. A trail goes down to the Bell Stone, which resounds musically when struck with a rock. This method was once used to signal Malae Heiau and to herald the birth of royal children. Just beyond is a view point over magnificent Opaekaa Falls and, across the road from it, a good view of the river far below.

The road continues into Wailua Homesteads, a region of small farms, ranches, and fruit and macadamia nut orchards. Stop at Alexander's Nursery, a mile from the falls—it's a fascinating, disorganized collection of just about everything that grows in Kauai's home gardens. Call ahead to visit the University of Hawaii Agricultural Experiment Station, which contains early Hawaiian medicinal plants and other varieties.

Roads crisscross the hills back of Kapaa and Kealia. Instead of reversing course, you can continue through this pastoral countryside, returning to the main route along Highway 581.

HAWAII'S WILD GARDENS

Hawaii's botanical gardens inspire hikers, photographers, and nature lovers. They also nurture unique and diverse species, including tropicals from other parts of the world, that are endangered in the wild. To help you plan a botanical foray, we suggest one wild garden on each major island. Others are mentioned elsewhere in the text.

National Tropical Botanical Garden, Lawai, Kauai; 332-7361; open daily; guided tours; admission fee. A verdant valley near Poipu cradles this impressive 186-acre research garden, which includes the world's largest collection of Hawaiian natives and other rare and endangered species. The 1992 hurricane did $5 million damage to the garden and the adjoining 100-acre Allerton Estate gardens, but trees and plants are being replaced and tours are resuming. The nation's only congressionally chartered tropical botanical garden also maintains three satellite properties: Kahanu Gardens on Maui (see below), a preserve in Limahuli Valley on Kauai's northern coast, and The Kampong, at Coconut Grove, Florida.

Kahanu Gardens, 3 miles northwest of Hana, Maui; 248-8912; open from 10 A.M. to 2 P.M. Tuesday through Saturday; self-guided tours; admission fee. This branch of the National Tropical Botanical Garden sprawls over 126 acres of pandanus-fringed black lava on Maui's eastern shore. It features native plants and Polynesian imports. The grounds also embrace remains of an ancient *heiau*. From the entrance, drive past breadfruit trees and grassy fields fringed with coconut trees to the visitor center. Park here; plant displays are to the left.

Hawaii Tropical Botanical Garden, north of Hilo, Hawaii; 964-5233; open daily; guided tours; admission fee. Edging Onomea Bay north of Hilo, this garden mostly displays introduced tropicals, such as orchids and gingers. The short Cook Pine Trail leads past a small collection of native plants.

Ho'omaluhia Botanical Garden, end of Luluku Road, Kaneohe, Oahu; 235-6636; open daily; guided hikes 10 A.M. Saturday, 1 P.M. Sunday; free. Tucked against Oahu's windward cliffs, this 400-acre botanic garden hugs a 32-acre man-made lake and looks more like a scenic park. It presents trees and shrubs from many tropical countries. Bring light rain gear, walking shoes, and mosquito repellent. Picnic facilities are available.

Smith's Tropical Paradise. Ethnic villages located on 31 acres of tropical gardens and lagoons behind the Wailua Marina feature life styles from Japan, the Philippines, Portugal, Korea, China, and Polynesia. You can walk through, if you wish, or take a narrated tour by tram. The admission fee includes the tram ride. Smith's Tropical Paradise is open daily from 9:30 A.M. to 4:30 P.M.

Fern Grotto. The road inland along the river's south bank goes to Wailua Marina and ends at Smith's Tropical Paradise. Boats leave the marina daily between 9 A.M. and 4 P.M. for the short trip upriver to the Fern Grotto. As you glide between river banks covered with *hala* (pandanus), *hau* (jungle trees with hibiscuslike flowers), and rare *pili* grass that was once used for Hawaiian houses, boat captains entertain with fascinating legends about the area. Caves in the bluffs were royal burial grounds.

At the upstream landing, a short trail leads through dense jungle growth to the Fern Grotto, a cool, damp, 40-foot cavern trimmed with a trickling waterfall and lush, feathery ferns. The grotto forms a natural amphitheater and provides fine acoustics for the Hawaiian chorus serenade. Night excursions up the river include dinner and special pageantry.

Boats operate about every half hour. Both tour operators offer similar programs. A restaurant, shops, and other attractions allow you to linger at the marina before or after your trip. More than a half-million people visit the grotto each year; if you're allergic to crowds, plan to take the earliest trip.

North of the river. Just north of Wailua River, the century-old lagoon of Kauai's last queen and a large coconut grove planted in 1896 are part of the grounds of the Coco Palms Hotel. The elaborate torch-lighting ceremony that takes place nightly among the lagoons is well worth watching.

Kamokila Hawaiian Village, 2 miles/3 km east on Highway 580, is a re-creation of a Polynesian grass-hut village that stood on this site centuries ago. Tours include Hawaiian quilting and lei-making demonstrations.

The East Shore

Between the Wailua River and Kapaa, the highway skirts Wailua Bay and bisects a large coconut grove in the midst of the Coconut Plantation development, an 80-acre site with hotels, restaurants, and a shopping complex called The Market Place. Shops are set amid waterways, pools, fountains, trees, flowers, and the relics of a sugar mill.

Kapaa. Modern architecture combined with intriguing 19th-century balconied wooden stores—Kapaa is well worth a walking tour. Notice the restored Seto Building and the venerable Kauai General Store. The small plantation town's churches and temples represent a wide range of faith: Buddhist, Church of Christ, Episcopal, Mormon, and Seventh-Day Adventist.

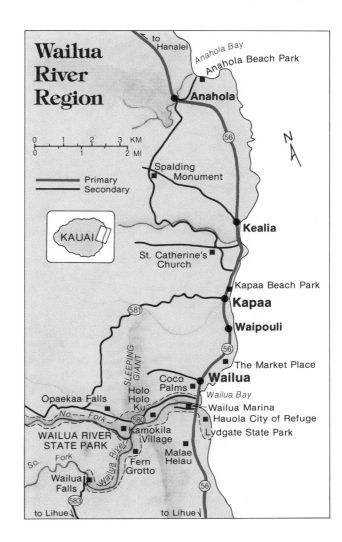

Between Kapaa and Anahola. The highway to Anahola bypasses wonderful scenery; to reach it, take stretches of the old winding road, spurs down to the sea, or the several roads that go inland from Kapaa and Kealia. The road uphill south of Kapaa Stream bridge goes to St. Catherine's Catholic Church, a square structure with ceramic murals and frescoes by Jean Charlot, Tseng Yu-ho, and Juliette May Fraser. The view back should cause you to reach for your camera.

You can continue from the church into Wailua Homesteads. Or turn right just past the building, go down into Kealia Valley, and follow the stream—and perhaps picnic on its bank under a monkeypod tree. The good road ends at the University of Hawaii agricultural station.

Just north of Kapaa the Hawaii Visitors Bureau marker indicates the fruit stand where you'll find papaya, guava, and other island delicacies.

Anahola. People still gossip and snooze on front porches in Anahola, a traditional Hawaiian homestead area. There's a pretty red-roofed church on the hillside and an inviting park alongside the tree-lined bay.

Deterred by rumors about wet weather and the quiet pace, many tourists plan only a day's outing to Kauai's North Shore. This doesn't bother residents and repeat vacationers. They prefer to keep the area secluded. They're delighted to have horses available at nearby stables and are pleased that Hanalei Valley's one-way bridges stop the tour buses.

But clear, sparkling days do occur. When first-time visitors see postcard-pretty valleys and cliffs halted only by the sea, stroll through bucolic Hanalei town, snorkel at Ke'e Beach, play a round of golf at Princeville, or watch the sun set over Hanalei Bay—the secret is out.

Between Anahola and Kilauea, rerouted Highway 56 bridges gulches and streams; the old road winds down through Moloaa Valley. From it, a turnoff leads to the remains of a little village virtually wiped out in the 1946 tidal wave. Much of this region's former pineapple and sugarcane land now grows papayas, guavas, and seed corn.

The old town of Kilauea contains some handsomely restored houses, unusual stores located in old plantation buildings, a historic schoolhouse, and a couple of intriguing churches. St. Sylvester's Catholic Church is an octagon with an interior designed as a "church in the round" that contains Jean Charlot frescoes. Rugged Christ Memorial Church is built of stone with a craggy lava rock facade and glowing stained glass windows.

Kilauea Lighthouse, now automated, sits on a peninsular bluff high above the sea, commanding rugged seascape views in both directions. The tower, on the state's northernmost point, contains the first light sighted by ships heading east from the Orient. Its clamshell lens is the world's largest.

The peninsula, known as Kilauea Point, is now a wildlife refuge for endangered seabirds. It's also the spring and summer resting place for red-footed boobies. These amusing birds are quite unafraid of people, so you can photograph at close range. Hordes of shearwaters and frigate birds with their impressive 7-foot wing spans make the point their home. An information center and a 20-minute self-guided walking tour introduce visitors to this national refuge. Several days a week, 2-hour guided hikes trace the rugged coastline; call 828-1520 for details.

Beyond Kilauea, you can reach Kalihiwai Bay and Anini Beach by turning back onto the old road after you cross the main highway bridge across Kalihiwai Valley. Stop on the Kilauea side for a valley view that takes in some sparkling waterfalls.

Anini Beach, down a side road from the old coastal route, is a little like Tahiti: some tumbledown shacks and comfortable summer cottages line a long ribbon of sand with a backdrop of cliffs festooned with mangoes, *hau*, hala, palms, bamboo, and parasitic vines. The water is shallow out to a protecting reef popular for torch fishing.

Princeville Resort

The main highway passes Princeville Resort at Hanalei. This resort community contains cliff-hugging Princeville Hotel, single-family homes, condominiums, cottages, and two championship golf courses perched on a bluff overlooking the ocean. A small shopping center fronts the highway. The airport sits inland.

The entire resort property maintains a low profile, in compliance with the island height restriction of "no building taller than a coconut palm." Consequently, most accommodations and restaurants offer good views of both Hanalei Bay and inland mountains.

Prestigious Princeville's 11,000 acres were once part of Kauai's oldest ranch. Princeville Ranch, established in 1853 by British minister R. C. Wyllie, once provided much of the island's beef.

The North Shore

Muumuus brighten *Sunday scene at Hanalei's Waioli Hui'ia Church; Social Hall next door was the original mission church.*

… The North Shore/Na Pali Coast

Hanalei Valley

Just past Princeville, you'll catch your first view of Hanalei Valley. From the lookout, you gaze down on taro patches bisected by the silvery Hanalei River and rimmed with precipitous green mountains. The backdrop of neighboring Waioli Valley is often laced with waterfalls. As the highway starts its winding descent, you'll get a different view—across the valley to crescent-shaped Hanalei Bay, bounded by a green headland. Soon you'll cross the first of many historic bridges between Hanalei town and the end of the road. Though you may have to wait for oncoming traffic, these crossings enhance the area's appeal.

From the bridge where the highway reaches the valley floor, you can follow a spur road along the river bank for several miles into the valley. Yellow ginger, purple ground orchids, guavas, and pomelo now abound in an area once cultivated for oranges.

Hanalei is still quiet and peaceful, but change is coming. Though the Ching Young Store, a landmark since 1906, has been replaced by the modern Native Hawaiian Trading & Cultural Center, much of the past remains.

Hanalei has humble bungalows, comfortable summer homes, some tourist apartments, a courthouse, post office, two general stores, eating places, a photogenic lily pond, museum, and five churches. It's also the headquarters for the inflatable boat tours of the Na Pali Coast. Note Waioli Social Hall, the original mission church, built in 1841; it's an example of the best in Hawaiian architecture. Pretty, pale green Waioli Hui'ia Church next door dates from 1912. Behind is the mission home, a two-story, white building with verandas; built in 1836, it has been restored and contains many original furnishings (tours conducted Tuesday, Thursday, and Saturday from 9 A.M. to 3 P.M. The half-hour tours are free, but donations are welcome.

Modern St. William's Catholic Church across the road has a Hawaiian longhouse shape and tile murals by Jean Charlot. Hanalei Museum, in a plantation cottage (open daily in summer; check hours for other seasons), features turn-of-the-century furniture, agricultural tools, and artifacts of various ethnic groups. A snack bar with tropical fruit juices and ice creams is located right behind the museum.

Hanalei also has a splendid beach—but because of treacherous currents, swim only by the pier, past the beach park near the end of the shore road.

To Road's End

One of the most photographed bays in the islands is Waikoko, at the eastern end of the Lumahai shore. From the marked view point on the highway, a trail descends the hala-laden cliffs to a small, rock-edged cove where you can picnic (swimming is not recommended). The Lumahai sands (sift through them for olivines) stretch west a long way.

At Wainiha Bay, take the road that climbs above the river to the powerhouse for a sampling of heavily wooded Wainiha Valley, strung with perpetual waterfalls that begin in Alakai Swamp.

The Wainiha General Store is your last chance to pick up picnic supplies before road's end. At the Hanalei Colony Resort, just beyond, you'll find a restaurant, bar, and art gallery.

The Haena region, once heavily settled, is now sprinkled thinly with old-timers' ramshackle homes and vacationers' cottages—old and new. Every rock, cave, and cliff speaks a legend; beaches are little roamed; mountain peaks are jagged but clothed in foliage and softly overhung with clouds. You will pass Maniniholo Dry Cave, which legend says was made by menehune as they dug seeking a supernatural being who had stolen their fish. Waikapalae and Waikanaloa Wet Caves are said to have

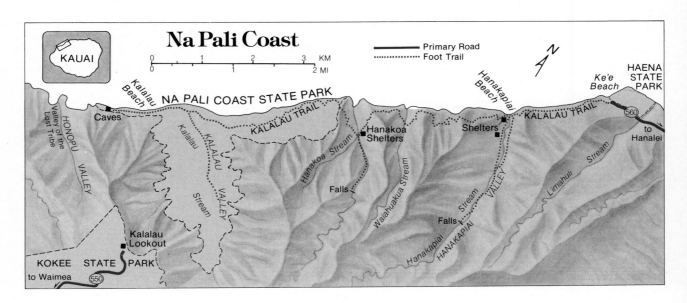

been dug by the fire goddess Pele while she was trying to find herself a home on this verdant island.

Even though it's not usually safe to swim off Haena Beach Park, idyllic Ke'e Beach at the end of the road (location for the movie *Thorn Birds*) is placid most of the year. Just east of it there's a tiny roadside pool in Limahuli Stream. At low tide you can walk a mile from Haena State Park to Ke'e along the sandy shore (take shoes because of a few rocky spots). Ke'e's backdrop is the triangular Makana (Fireworks Cliff).

Above the sandy cove you can hike up to ruins of the Hula Heiau, a platform from which the traditional dance was performed centuries ago.

The Na Pali Coast

From the northern end of Ke'e Beach, you can glimpse the spectacular Na Pali Coast. Ridges of cliffs rising 2,000 to 3,000 feet from the sea embrace a series of deep, jungled valleys from here all the way to Mana.

Until helicopter excursions began (see page 82), few people had viewed these uninhabited valleys, some accessible only from the sea in fair weather. Although the flights over the valleys are exciting, they show only a small sampling of what these valleys—from Hanakapiai west to Milolii—hold. Some of the scenery may look familiar; parts of *Fantasy Island* and *King Kong* were filmed along this coastline.

You can view Na Pali from an inflatable boat any time when the weather is favorable. Because sandy beaches disappear when big swells pound the shore, landing on this coast is usually impossible in winter. For boat trips, see page 89. A few valleys are accessible by hiking over the 11-mile/18-km Kalalau Trail. To camp in any of the Na Pali valleys, permits are required and camping limits are in effect (see page 89 for camping information).

Hanakapiai, the first valley, is a steep but easy 2-mile/ 3-km walk. If you go just ¼ mile along the trail that starts from the end of Highway 56, you will be rewarded with a splendid view back down upon Ke'e Beach and the Haena reefs. The trail on to Hanakapiai is resplendent with hala, ti, kukui, guavas, and wild orchids, has spectacular Na Pali overlooks, and reaches a broad beach. A 1¼-mile/2-km loop, a spur off the main trail, goes into the valley across ancient taro terraces, through a mango grove, and past ruins of a coffee mill where there's a shelter.

Out of Hanakapiai the trail climbs steeply and does not drop to sea level again until it reaches Kalalau Beach. Footing is good, but the going is either up or down (no level places to ease leg work) and the weather is hot. About 6 miles/10 km along is Hanakoa, a good rest stop or a destination in itself. A path leads from a rustic cabin to a wonderful swimming pool with waterfall in Hanakoa Stream. From across the stream, a short spur goes up to Hanakoa Falls, a cascade at the rear of a fork of the valley.

From Hanakoa on, the country gets drier. You encounter sisal, lantana, and cattle. The trail enters Kalalau, the largest valley, near the main stream. At this point,

you're more than a mile from the favored campsite on its mile-long beach—near a small stream with waterfall "shower" and bathing pool. As you cross the valley, note the branch trail that climbs inland near Kalalau Stream and offers good valley exploring. You can follow the main stream all the way to Davis Falls. Some like the beach dry caves for sleeping; everyone wades and splashes in the wet caves. In summer, you can partly swim, partly wade to neighboring Honopu, the legendary "Valley of the Lost Tribe," where remains have been found of an ancient Polynesian settlement that unaccountably vanished.

With ice cream cone in hand, *barefoot boy isn't distracted by ancient surfboard propped against the Hanalei museum wall.*

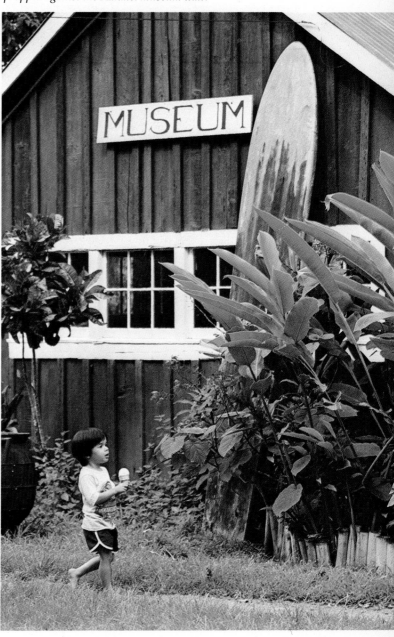

FLIGHTSEEING BY HELICOPTER —
A VIEW FROM ALL SIDES

A bird's-eye glimpse of a plummeting waterfall, a finger-tip pass over a jungle-clad mountain slope, a leisurely look at wave-sculptured lava cliffs, a peek into a desolate crater—these are all part of flightseeing Hawaii by helicopter.

You'll glide, whirl, and swoop through hidden canyons and over inaccessible beaches, flit across sugar, taro, and pineapple fields, and soar by tiny hamlets of civilization that punctuate the verdant landscape. The view from a helicopter is one of the best ways to see the islands' dramatic topography.

Service and destination. Helicopter flights are available on five islands: Oahu, Kauai, Maui, Molokai, and Hawaii. Kauai is certainly the capital with nearly a dozen companies offering flights ranging from 30-minute overviews of coastline and canyons to circle-island tours that might include a touchdown on a deserted beach or a sunset flight. There's even a helicopter trip to mysterious Niihau, Kauai's island neighbor generally off limits to tourists. Companies operate from the Poipu, Lihue, and Hanalei areas.

On Oahu, you can view sprawling Honolulu from the air, put Pearl Harbor into perspective, climb above Diamond Head and into the Punchbowl, and skim across the Pali on a circle-island itinerary. Service is provided by several companies from a Waikiki helipad.

A look at the Maui countryside might include a flight across the channel to neighboring Molokai or Lanai, sunrise over Haleakala, or a spin across the island for a picnic lunch in Hana. Eight companies offer a choice of flights; sunset tours are popular. On Molokai, you can fly over Kalaupapa and along the Pali Coast, which has the world's highest sea cliffs as measured from the ocean floor.

The diversity and size of the Big Island is better grasped from the air. Helicopters sweep along the Kona and Kohala coasts, peer into steaming craters, venture into the mountains, and peek into sheltered Waipio Valley. Flights leave from Hilo and Kona Coast airports and Waikoloa Heliport on the Kohala Coast.

Cost. How much you'll pay to hover over Hawaii depends on the length of the flights, itinerary, and number of people. Though extensive flightseeing is not inexpensive, you may receive extras such as champagne, snacks, or meals. Some companies provide free hotel pickup and delivery.

Additional information. Some helicopter companies are listed in island recreation guides. To get reservations and more details, check with your hotel activities desk or call companies directly; phone numbers are listed in island Yellow Pages.

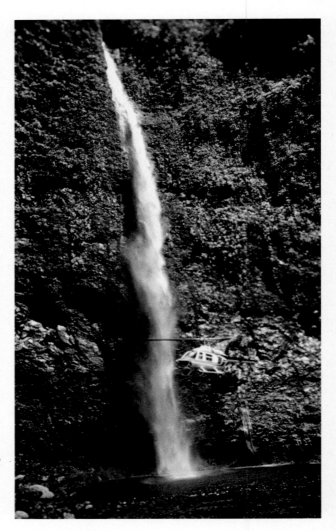

Helicopter hovers *near base of waterfall on Kauai's rugged Na Pali Coast. You can swoop, glide, and dip into the state's hidden scenic treasures on all major islands.*

THE SOUTH SHORE

Today, the South Shore is the destination for vacationers who seek plentiful sunshine, broad beaches, calm seas, and riotous plant life. In earlier days, the southern region played host to King Sugar. Some of the picturesque old plantation communities and mills still stand among the cane fields, but luxurious resorts, restaurants, shops, golf courses, and tennis courts have blossomed, turning the area into a site from which it's hard to wander.

To reach the South Shore from Lihue, follow Highway 50. Highway 520 branches off to historic Koloa and the resort areas around Poipu Beach. A network of roads between Poipu and Hanapepe takes you through a number of places of interest in the region south of the main highway.

En Route to Koloa

Within the first 8 miles/13 km out of Lihue, look for these attractions: wild ginger along the roadside, a marvelous old post office–store, a modern community college, Kukui Grove Center at Puhi, Kilohana estate, Halfway Bridge over the Huleia River, and Knudsen Gap (between the Hoary Head Mountains and Kahili peak at the end of the island's central mountain mass). The magnificent grove of fragrant eucalyptus that marked the beginning of Highway 520 to Koloa was devastated by Hurricane Iniki.

Koloa—Site of the First Sugar Mill

Stretch your legs in Koloa, Hawaii's first bona fide plantation town, 3 miles/5 km from the junction of highways 50 and 520. The stone mill stack is all that remains of the sugar mill. The town's charming wooden buildings have been renovated and now house shops and restaurants.

Visit three quaint-but-thriving temples (Hongwanji, Jodo, and Odaishi) and the restored church of Koloa Mission (1834), and ask the way to St. Raphael's Church south of town. Kauai's oldest Catholic mission (1841) has an impressive 1856 masonry church, coral stone houses, graveyard, outdoor altar, and tiny lava rock chapel seating eight.

In and Around Poipu

As you drive downhill to the sunny coast, you may encounter some confusing road forks. To reach Poipu beaches, resorts, golf courses, and restaurants, take Poipu Road to the left. The road passes Poipu Beach Park, Brennecke's Beach (popular with bodysurfers), and photogenic Shipwreck Beach. It ends at Makahuena Point, site of the crater where Kauai's last eruption occurred.

Damaged by the 1982 and 1992 storms, Poipu's beaches, magnets for swimmers and surfers, are on the mend. The offshore coral, a mecca for divers, will take longer to regenerate.

Following Hoonani Road from Highway 530 brings you to Koloa Landing, departure point for diving and snorkeling tours. Whalers—as many as 50 at a time—used to winter at Koloa Landing; hotel buildings now sit on the cove's west bluff.

There's plenty to do in the Poipu area if you tire of water sports: golf at Kiahuna or Poipu golf courses, tennis, cycling, horseback riding, whale watching (December through April), or browsing through shops in hotels or at Kiahuna Shopping Village.

Kukuiula Bay and Spouting Horn

Turn right at Lawai Road to reach Spouting Horn and the Kukuiula shore. The road to Kukuiula Bay passes Prince Kuhio Park, where a monument marks the birthplace of Hawaii's long-time delegate to Congress.

Beyond Kukuiula Bay, a photogenic sampan harbor, the road ends at Spouting Horn, where the sea pushes up like a geyser through a shoreline lava tube. The moaning sound that comes from beneath the lava is said to be the cries of a legendary lizard, Lehu, who crawled into the tube long ago and became entrapped.

From Spouting Horn's lookout you can gaze across the water to the south shore of Niihau, just 17 miles/27 km away. This private island is the home for some 200 pure Hawaiians.

En Route to Hanapepe

To continue along the southwest coast, you'll need to return to Koloa. Highway 530 meanders through the pastoral Lawai Valley in the few miles between Koloa and Highway 50. Lawai, site of the National Tropical Botanical Garden (see page 76), is a horticultural research center and botanical delight.

From Kalaheo, drive up to Kukuiolono Park, formerly the estate of the founder of McBryde Sugar Plantation. A favorite of picnickers, the park also provides a 9-hole hillside golf course, Japanese garden, display of Hawaiian legendary boulders, and inspiring views out over Lawai to the sea.

Beyond Kalaheo, a sign directs you inland to Olu Pua Gardens, previously a plantation manager's estate. Visitors receive a printed map with a suggested walk through the eight gardens that make up the complex: jungle path to native and orchid areas, hibiscus garden, oriental garden, palm garden, sunken garden, succulent garden, blue garden, and kau kau (food) garden. All plants are identified. The garden is open from 8:30 A.M. to 5 P. M. daily; there's a moderate charge.

The Charm of Hanapepe

From Hanapepe Canyon Lookout, you can scan the green valley nestled between red cliffs. You view taro patches and farm plots at the lush canyon's mouth.

A side road loops through the town, reminiscent of the Old West, which follows the winding Hanapepe River.

...The South Shore

Intriguing wooden buildings overhang the river bank; a narrow old bridge crosses the stream. A drive through the farms on the dead-end road back of town gives you the feeling of old rural Hawaii.

Turn off on Highway 543 to Salt Pond Park, a clean crescent of sand beside a reef-protected bay. Before reaching the park, you pass the ponds where coarse luau salt is still made in dry weather by evaporating sea water. Salt obtained in this way was used by early Hawaiians to preserve meat and fish and by traders to cure furs.

The drive to Kaumakani, a model plantation village, rewards curious visitors with a quaint post office nearby and the Kaumakani Methodist Church, uphill of the highway northeast of town.

Historic Waimea

Despite its small population (around 1,500 people), Waimea is west Kauai's center for commercial activity. This role isn't unexpected given the region's history; it was a seasonal court of chiefs in pre-Western times and the setting for exploration, trade, and missionary settlement by the English, Americans, and Russians.

Much of the town's attraction stems from an intriguing cultural mix, most readily apparent in architectural diversity. A site on Tsuchiya Road is the location of Kauai's first mission, established in 1820. The Waimea Foreign Church, constructed in 1853 of coral and sandstone, stands nearby between mission and Oriental cemeteries. A third house of worship was built by Reverend George Rowell, who also initiated the Waimea Hawaiian Church on Highway 50.

Other historic buildings include the old Ako Store (a general store across from the Hawaiian Church), the Mervin Kaohi house (circa 1880), and the island's oldest home, the Gulick-Rowell House on Huakai Road. The latter, a New England-style structure with limestone walls and gable roof, was started in the early 1830s by missionary Peter Gulick.

Well-preserved remains of Fort Elizabeth, built by the Russians in 1817, cover the bluff above Waimea River and Bay. Waimea was Captain Cook's first Hawaiian landing place. Both the fort and landing site are national historic landmarks. The fort, built in an irregular star shape about 400 feet across, flew the Russian flag briefly, mostly as a trading post. Hawaiian troops then occupied it until 1853. The state has reconstructed the fort trappings and added parking and rest room facilities.

Drive the narrow river road through town for 1½ miles/2 km to Menehune Ditch, once a long watercourse allegedly built by the little people. You pass taro and farm plots, a poi factory, and an unusual Shingon temple. The temple's 88 bullet-shaped outdoor shrines honor soldiers killed in World War II.

Polihale State Park

The sleepy town of Kekaha has a beach park for picnicking (swimming is dangerous along this shore). Offshore, you'll see privately owned Niihau.

From highway's end at Mana you can follow signs along several miles of cane roads to 140-acre Polihale State Park at the south end of Na Pali. This is a developed park (rest rooms, showers, picnic shelters) where you can camp, hike across dunes or along the base of the bluffs, and swim in summer—in the sea if it's calm or, if not, in Queen's Pond, an often-exposed brackish water channel in the beach.

THE NEW WORDS YOU'LL HEAR

As you might expect, the English spoken in the islands has been augmented with words and expressions from languages native to Hawaii's various ethnic groups. You'll hear people pronounce vowel sounds in English words as they would in Hawaiian, Japanese, or one of the Romance languages.

You'll also hear pidgin English—shortcut communicating that may be unintelligible. Most islanders can and usually do speak good English; they just enliven their talk with Hawaiian words and occasionally interject pidgin vocabulary.

Since names of most places and streets are Hawaiian, some knowledge of the pronunciation rules of this language will prove helpful. The Hawaiian alphabet contains only 12 letters: the 5 vowels plus 7 consonants (h, k, l, m, n, p, and w). Words seem to overflow with vowels, but pronunciation is not difficult if you remember to pronounce every letter separately. The vowel sounds are *a* as in "arm," *e* as in "end," *i* as in "machine," *o* as in "old," and *u* as in "rude." Consonants have the same sounds as in English except for the *w*. Some Hawaiians always pronounce it as a *v* unless it is preceded by an *o* or *u*; others do so only when it is the next to last letter in a word. In diphthongs (*ei, eu, oi, ou, ai, ae, ao, au*), stress the first member (*lei*).

If you see a glottal stop mark, or hamza, it indicates, in the Polynesian language, that the letter *k* has been omitted; there is a definite break in sound between the letters it separates.

Here are some frequently used words and phrases. Gourmets and anglers will also find helpful the list on page 145.

'ae	yes
ahui ho	until we meet again
ahupua'a	land division
aikane	friend (slang)
'aina	land, earth
akamai	wise, smart
ala	road, path
ali'i	royalty, a chief
aloha	greetings, welcome, farewell, love
aloha nui loa	much love
'a'ole	no
auwe	alas! ouch
ha'ina	end of song
hale	house
hana	work
hana hou	encore
haole	Caucasian
hapa	half, part
hapai	to carry, be pregnant
Hauoli la Hanau	Happy Birthday
Hauoli Makahiki Hou	Happy New Year
heiau	temple
hele mai	come here
hikie'e	large couch
holoku	fitted ankle-length dress with train
holomu'u	fitted ankle-length dress
ho'olaule'a	celebration
huhu	angry
hui	club, association
hukilau	to fish with a seine
iki	small, little
ipo	sweetheart, lover
kahili	feather standard
kahuna	priest, expert
kai	sea
kala	money
kama'aina	native born
kanaka	person, man
kanalua	doubtful, hesitant
kane	male, husband
kapakahi	crooked, lopsided
kapu	forbidden, keep out
kaukau	food (slang)
keiki	child
kokua	help
kona	lee side
kuleana	right, property, responsibility
kumu	teacher
lanai	porch, veranda
lei	garland, wreath
lomi (or *lomilomi*)	rub, press, massage
lua	toilet
mahalo	thanks
maika'i	good, fine
makai	toward the sea
make	dead
malihini	stranger, newcomer
malo	a loin cloth
manu	bird
manuahi	free, gratis
mauka	inland
mauna	mountain
mele	song
Mele Kalikimaka	Merry Christmas
menehune	dwarf, legendary race of dwarfs
moana	ocean
moemoe	sleep (slang)
momona	fat
mu'umu'u	long or short loose-fitting dress
nani	beautiful
ne'i	this place
nui	big, large, great
ohana	family
'okolehao	ti-root liquor
'okole maluna	bottoms up
'ono	delicious, tasty
'opu	belly, stomach
Pake	Chinese (slang)
pali	cliff, precipice
paniolo	cowboy
pau	finished
pa'u	wrap-around skirt
pehea'oe	how are you?
pikake	jasmine
pilau	putrid
pilikia	trouble
pohaku	rock, stone
popoki	cat
pua	flower, blossom
pua'a	pig, pork
puka	hole, door
pupu	shell, hors d'oeuvre
pupule	crazy, insane
tutu	grandmother
tutu kane	grandfather
wahine	female, wife
wai	fresh water
wikiwiki	fast, hurry

Y ou can combine visits to the "Grand Canyon" and a crisp mountain plateau in one trip to Waimea Canyon and Kokee state parks. It's a year-round destination by tour bus or on your own. In summer months, many people stay to enjoy the outdoor life—to camp, fish streams, pick plums, and hike luxuriant forest trails among such native flora as the *iliau* tree (a member of the sunflower family), *mokihana* berry, and lobelias found only in Kauai.

You reach this wilderness on Kokee Road from Kekaha, or by Highway 550 (Waimea Canyon Road) from Waimea. Highway 550 travels the canyon rim, where it is joined by Kokee Road. The highway then climbs arid, scrub-covered hills above Waimea Canyon for 12 miles/19 km to the main lookout.

If you're driving, check your gas gauge; the last station is in Kekaha. Bring a light wrap, since temperatures are lower in the higher elevations.

Waimea Canyon's Chasm

From Waimea Canyon Lookout at 3,400 feet, you can see most of the 2,857-foot-deep gorge that cuts into the Kokee Plateau. The canyon has a monumental quality as unexpected on a tropical island as the crisp, invigorating mountain air. It resembles the Grand Canyon in character, if not in size, with the addition of the blues and mossy greens of lush vegetation to complement the reds and browns of exposed volcanic rock walls. Clouds usually hang over the rim, their moving shadows heightening the impression of vastness.

About 1½ miles/2 km beyond the entrance to 1,866-acre Waimea Canyon State Park, there's a small parking area at the start of the Kukui Trail, which drops in switchbacks down the west wall of Waimea Canyon and ends at the Waimea River (a drop of over 2,000 feet in 2½ miles/4 km). At the start of the Kukui Trail is the Iliau Loop Trail, an easy, ¼-mile nature walk. Twenty native plants are identified, including the iliau, which blooms in June and July. The loop offers excellent vistas of the canyon and distant Waialae Falls.

From Puu Hinahina Lookout, farther up, your eyes can follow the canyon out to the coast and pick up Niihau across the sea to the west. Just above the lookout, you pass a paved spur that goes 4½ miles/7 km down Makaha Ridge, through typical reforested country, to views of the Na Pali Coast.

Kokee State Park

The highway climbs 8 scenic miles/13 km past several waterfalls and streams on its way to 4,345-acre Kokee State Park, a center for camping and hiking.

Around the park headquarters, you'll find Kokee Lodge, with restaurant, cabins, shops, and camp and picnic grounds. Adjacent Kokee Museum features exhibits of flora and fauna, geology, and petroglyphs.

Kokee is the starting point for about 45 miles/72 km of hiking trails, some of which go into the surrounding

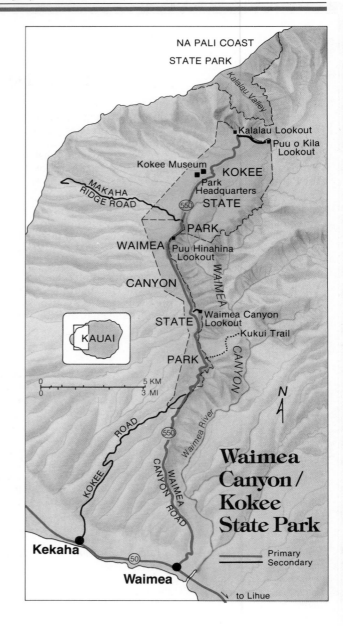

Waimea Canyon / Kokee State Park

forest reserve. Many of the trails are under a mile, making them popular picnic sites. Some of the longer trails include treks into the Alakai Swamp between Kokee and Mt. Waialeale, and over ridges separating valleys of the Na Pali Coast. When the hurricanes of 1982 and 1992 hit Kauai, many park trails were damaged by high winds. Hikers can inquire about conditions when they register at park headquarters. In dry weather, dirt roads that provide access to trail heads are open to all vehicles.

Past the park headquarters, Kokee Road becomes Kalalau Road on its climb to Kalalau Lookout, a 4,000-foot-high view point over broad, green-carpeted Kalalau Valley and the shimmering blue sea at its mouth. If a cloud obscures the view, as it often does, wait a while—it may lift. (Caution: No hiking is permitted from the lookout into the valley.)

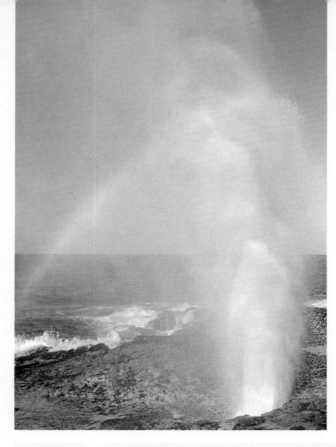

Spouting Horn *shows off. Geyserlike spray is accompanied by sorrowful moaning of a legendary lizard said to be trapped in the lava tube below.*

Visitor overlook *offers grand views of Waimea Canyon. Shifting cloud shadows constantly change colors of the lava slopes.*

Scenic distractions *make it difficult to keep your eyes on the ball at Princeville's tennis courts.*

 It's been said that the only flaw in Kauai's reputation is a lack of activities. Nothing can be further from the truth—Kauai is much, much more than an island-sized arboretum. The following listing offers a general look at Kauai's recreational attractions. For further details on any activity, consult your hotel activities desk or the Hawaii Visitors Bureau, 3016 Umi Street, Lihue; 245-3971.

Flightseeing. One of the best views of Kauai's dramatic topography, particularly the almost inaccessible Na Pali Coast and central island peaks and valleys, is from the air. More than a dozen helicopter, fixed-wing plane, and glider companies transport visitors aloft. Flights take off from Lihue, Princeville, or Port Allen to the south. Book flights through your hotel's activities desk.

Golf. Kauai boasts some of the state's most scenic golf courses, several of them sites of nationally televised annual tournaments. The links listed below are open to the public. Unless noted, all are 18-hole courses, with most offering restaurants, pro shops, and cart and club rentals. Yardages are from the regular tees.

Public/municipal courses. Kukuiolono Golf Club (9 holes), Kalaheo, 332-9151, par 36, 3,173 yards; Wailua Municipal Golf Course, Kapaa, 245-8092, par 72, 6,585 yards.

Resort courses. Kiahuna Golf Club, Koloa, 742-9595, par 70, 5,631 yards; Poipu Bay Resort Golf Course, Poipu Beach, 742-9489, par 72, 6,914 yards; Kauai Lagoons Resort, Kalapaki Beach, 245-5050: Kiele Course, par 72, 6,637 yards, Lagoons Course, par 72, 6,545 yards; Prince Golf & Country Club, Princeville, 826-5000, par 72, 6,521 yards; Makai Golf Course (27 holes), Princeville, 826-3580: Ocean Nine, par 36, 3,460 yards; Woods Nine, par 36, 3,460 yards; Lake Nine, par 36, 3,488 yards.

Windsurfing. Hanalei Surf Co., 826-9000, offers lessons for beginners and more advanced board sailors.

Waterskiing. Kauai Water Ski & Surf, 822-3574, pulls skiers down the Wailua River.

Tennis. Public and resort or commercial courts are listed below. Many condominiums also have courts for guest use. Check with your travel or rental agent.

Public courts. Waimea, next to Waimea High School; Hanapepe, near Hanapepe Pavilion; Kalaheo, Kalaheo School; Koloa, next to the fire station (near Highway 52); Lihue, next to Convention Hall; Kapaa, next to Kapaa Ball Park. All public facilities have 2 lighted courts.

Resort courts. Poipu: Kiahuna Tennis Club, 10 (7 with lights); Poipu Beach Resort, 6; Poipu Kai, 8; Sheraton Kauai, 3 (2 with lights); Hyatt Regency, 4. Nawiliwili: Westin Kauai, 8, stadium court. Wailua: Aston Kauai, 2; Coco Palms, 9 ((2 with lights); Kauai Beach Boy, 1; Coconut Beach, 3. Princeville: Hanalei Bay Resort, 11 (3 with lights); Princeville Tennis Center, 6.

Swimming. The most difficult aspect of swimming on Kauai may be choosing which beach.

Ocean swimming. Salt Pond, Kukuiula, Poipu, Kalapaki (Nawiliwili), Hanamaulu, Lydgate (in man-made ocean pool), Wailua (at Kapaa end), Anahola, Anini, Hanalei (at pier), Ke'e.

Freshwater swimming. Hanakoa Valley pool, Kokee's Kawaikoi Stream, Limahuli Pool, Wailua River.

Surfing. Check water conditions with residents, companies renting surfing gear, or your hotel's activities desk.

Board surfing. Poipu shore, Nawiliwili (Kalapaki Beach), Wailua Bay, Hanalei Bay.

Body surfing. Poipu shore, Kalapaki Beach, Wailua Bay, Hanalei Bay, Ke'e Beach.

Beachcombing, tidepooling, and reef walking. You can see a lot of the island's marine diversity without even donning mask and snorkel.

Low-tide walking sites. Polihale, Salt Pond, Poipu, Hanamaulu, Anahola, Moloaa, Anini, Lumahai, Haena.

Skin and scuba diving. Not all of Kauai's gardens are above sea level. For the underwater world, you'll find everything from classes to interisland dive trips.

Diving spots. Divers concentrate on Koloa Landing, Sheraton Caves, and Palama in the south; Anahola and Moloaa on the east; and Anini and Ke'e in Haena State Park to the north. For the very experienced, waters off neighboring Niihau offer the most pristine diving, as well as a home for the endangered monk seal.

Diving companies. Dive shops at Koloa, Poipu Beach, Wailua, Kapaa, and Hanalei rent snorkel and scuba equipment, offer instruction and certification, and arrange for boat and shore dives.

Kayaking. Over the past few years, kayaking has grown in popularity. The best-known experience is the ambitious ocean trip along the Na Pali Coast. But the Wailua, Huleia, and Hanalei rivers offer boaters tranquil settings that have been featured in many a film. Outfitters lead guided tours or can supply craft to experienced kayakers.

River trips. Island Adventures, 245-9662, lets you paddle up the Hulei River into a national wildlife refuge. The excursion starts at Nawiliwili Harbor. Luana of Hawaii, 826-9195, takes kayakers up the Hanalei River.

Ocean tours. Outfitters Kauai, Poipu Beach, 742-9667, conducts year-round tours along the south shore. A half-day trip departs from Kukuiula Harbor for a 1-mile/2-km introductory skim past Spouting Horn blowhole, which includes a 2-hour beach stop at scenic Lawai Bay. A longer, and more challenging, run is a day trip along the wave-pounded wilderness of the Na Pali Coast.

Kayak Kauai, Hanalei, 826-9844, has a basic day trip along the Na Pali Coast. From October through April, when seas are too rough on this stretch of coast, a day trip from Kalapaki Beach heads around Kauai's southeast corner to Koloa Landing near Poipu Beach. The company also offers tours up the Hanalei and Wailua rivers.

Raft trips. A handful of companies show visitors the Na Pali Coast from a rubber raft. Check your hotel activities desk for reservations. Because of high winter seas, trips around the more scenic northwest corner of the island run only from late spring through summer. Captain Zodiac, 826-9371, which started the adventure, has a fleet of 23-foot rubber rafts that run along the rugged coast on a day trip to a deserted beach for lunch and snorkeling.

Fishing. Kauai offers all types of fishing, from freshwater to deep-sea. Contact the State Parks Division of the Department of Land and Natural Resources (3060 Eiwa St., Lihue, HI 96766) for spearfishing regulations and freshwater licensing and limits; there are no saltwater licenses or limits.

Saltwater fishing locations. Spearfishing: reefs off Poipu and Kukuiula, Nualolo and Milolii valleys, and from Hanalei to Kalihiwai. Surfcasting: good all around Kauai. Pole fishing: along harbor piers to catch *'aweoweo* (red bigeye) and *hahalalu* (young bigeye scad) in late summer.

Freshwater fishing locations. Kokee: Choose from 13 miles of fishable streams and a 15-acre reservoir. Trout fishing requires an additional permit (free at park headquarters). Many ponds and reservoirs have bass, bluegill, tilapia, catfish, and carp. Lihue: contact Bass Guides of Kauai. Wailua: sites include a 30-acre reservoir and smallmouth bass fishing in Wailua River tributaries.

Horseback riding. Sightseeing from the saddle can range from hour-long rides to overnight events. In the north, Pooku Stables, Hanalei, 826-6777, offers waterfall-viewing valley rides and treks along the shore. CJM Stables, Koloa, 245-6666, explores the south shore on breakfast rides or beachside canters.

Hiking, camping, and mountain touring. You can experience Kauai in a variety of ways.

Hiking information. For maps, guides, and other information, contact Hawaiian Geographic Society, 217 S. King St., Honolulu, HI 96813; Hawaii Trail and Mountain Club, Box 5032, Honolulu, HI 96814; Hawaii Sierra Club, Box 22879, Honolulu, HI 96822; Department of Land and Natural Resources, Box 1671, Lihue, HI 96766.

Camping information. For campsite specifics and permits, contact the State Parks Division, 3060 Eiwa St., Lihue, HI 96766; for county parks, Kauai County War Memorial Convention Hall, 4191 Hardy St., Lihue, HI 96766.

Mountain touring and camping. Kauai Mountain Tours, Poipu, conducts 4-wheel drive trips through Waimea Canyon and Kokee State Park; call 245-7224 for details. Jungle Bob's, 826-6664, rents camping equipment.

Poipu's sunny shores *invite watery sports—swimming, snorkeling, surfing, diving, and boating.*

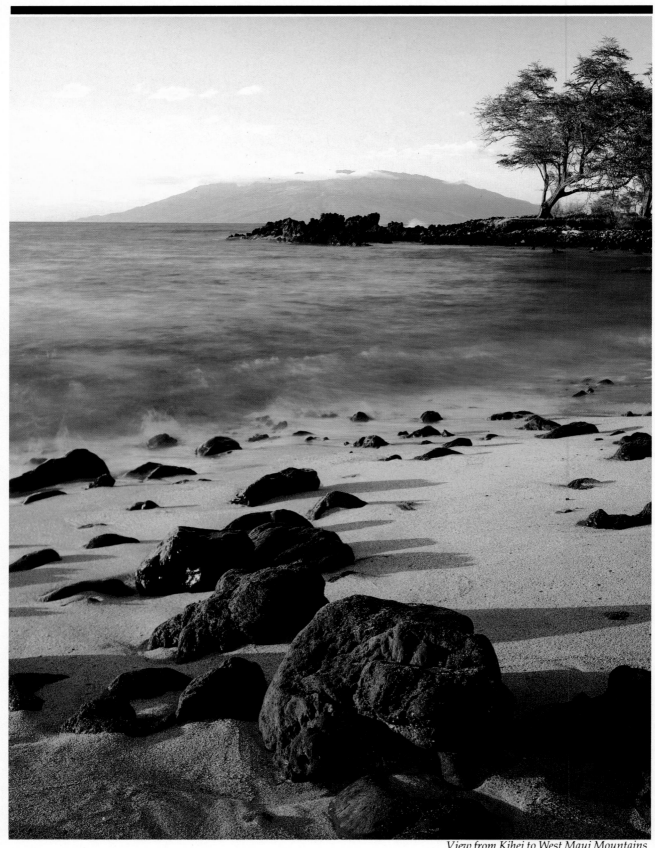

View from Kihei to West Maui Mountains

MAUI

- WHAT'S YOUR PLEASURE ?

JUST NAME IT … THE VALLEY ISLAND

CAN PROVIDE IT •

The minute you get off the plane at the airport, Maui introduces itself to you through one of its more subtle specialties—breezes, from sea and valley, that somehow are different in certain indefinable ways from those of any other place. Varying from gentle morning breezes to brisk afternoon tradewinds, they frequently carry the delicate fragrances of the tropics. Chances are that you'll notice and appreciate them throughout your stay—and remember them always.

"Maui No Ka Oi"

Hospitable Maui has a slogan, *Maui No Ka Oi*, "Maui is the best." Certainly few destinations rival the island's warm, friendly atmosphere, and it is a place of almost endless discovery. An increasing number of visitors return year after year.

Hawaii's second largest island (729 square miles/ 1,888 square km) offers superb beaches, fine golf and tennis facilities, and a world of family activity. There is plenty for hikers, bikers, joggers, horseback riders, garden enthusiasts, whale watchers, shoppers, bird lovers, gourmets, or just plain tired-out visitors wanting to relax and "unwind."

Sightseeing ranges from the heights of Haleakala to the scenic and invigorating upcountry ranchlands to the historic former whaling town of Lahaina—attractions so different from one another that the visitor may wonder "Can this be the same island?"

Until the late 1960s, Maui was known primarily for its agriculture, despite the fact that Kaanapali, on the west Maui coast, was already beginning to develop into the island's first major resort area. In recent years several other resort areas have been developed, increasing tourism dramatically. Agriculture, though still strong, has declined to some extent; many island residents (the permanent population numbers more than 90,000) whose forebears worked in the pineapple and cane fields now find employment in resorts, restaurants, and retail stores.

How Two Islands Became One

Maui began existence as two separate land masses. Centuries of erosion from their slopes formed the isthmus that joins them today. From that isthmus Maui gained its nickname, the "Valley Island." Cane fields now blanket the irrigated plain between the mountains, and sugarcane and pineapple cover the foothills. And spread out from where the plain meets the ocean to the north are Maui's two largest towns, Wailuku and Kahului.

On the 5,788-foot summit of the West Maui Mountains, Puu Kukui, more than 400 inches of rain falls annually, making it second to Kauai's Waialeale as Hawaii's rainiest peak.

On the other side of the isthmus, the great mass of the dormant volcano Haleakala rises to 10,023 feet. Its cool, grassy slopes provide grazing for cattle and other livestock, and vegetables and flowers are grown here for commercial markets.

At the foot of Haleakala's eastern slope, standing in contrast to the changing picture throughout most of Maui, is gentle old Hana—where an always-easy pace combines with geographical remoteness to make the area seem almost like an island in itself.

THE ESSENTIALS

Maui has three airports. Flights from the mainland arrive at Kahului in northcentral Maui; West Maui Airport (handy for Kapalua, Napili, and Kaanapali visitors) and a smaller field at Hana offer interisland service. United Airlines has nonstop flights from the mainland; American's Maui flights stop in Honolulu. Continental, Delta, and Northwest offer connections to Maui. Aloha Airlines, Hawaiian Airlines, Aloha IslandAir, and Air Molokai have scheduled interisland flights.

Getting Around

A quick glance at a map might lead you to believe that a circle trip around the island is possible. It's not advisable, though, since certain stretches of road on the northern and southeastern extremities of the island are unimproved and can be dangerous, particularly during and after heavy rains.

It takes at least 3 days to travel Maui's main roads and visit principal attractions. But you're in for some long hours of driving if you try to cover everything from one hotel base.

From Kahului, it's about 40 miles/64 km to the top of Haleakala and about 50 miles/80 km to Hana; these trips take longer than the distances indicate, though, because part of the route is over narrow, winding roads. Minibus tours to these two destinations are particularly popular.

Most of Maui's highways are excellent; auto exploring or simply getting from one place to another is pleasant and relatively easy—except for early morning and late afternoon commute hours. Four-wheel-drive vehicles are good choices for exploring the upcountry and driving on roads where rental cars are not allowed.

Car rental. More than 30 national, regional (Roberts), and local rental agencies are found at or near Kahului Airport; others maintain offices in west Maui. Most hotels also have car rental desks. You'll usually have a choice of models, including 4-wheel drives and minivans, and prices. Reserve ahead for busy holidays.

Shuttle services. Trans Hawaiian Services, (808) 877-7308, runs shuttles (moderate charge) from Kahului to Lahaina and Kaanapali; reservations are suggested. Besides circulating between Kaanapali and Lahaina, the Kaanapali Trolley meets flights (small fee) at West Maui Airport. Kapalua and Wailea resorts offer complimentary airport shuttles. Taxi and limousine service is also available. Lahaina Kaanapali & Pacific Railroad (see page 102) runs for 6 miles/10 km between Kaanapali and Lahaina.

Where to Stay

Most Maui vacationers head for one of three regional bases: the Lahaina-Kaanapali area on the west coast, Napili Bay and Kapalua on the northwest coast, or the southwest oceanfront area from Kihei to Makena. Few visitors stay in the industrial and commercial cities of Kahului and Wailuku in northcentral Maui, though they are conveniently located for upcountry sightseeing. Kahului has a couple of modest hotels.

In west Maui, the resort region extends from Lahaina town's intimate hostelries (Plantation and Lahaina Hotel) north to the plush Kapalua Bay and Ritz-Carlton hotels. Kaanapali Beach Resort has seven deluxe hotels strung along sandy swimming beaches: Hyatt Regency, Maui Marriott, Westin Maui, Kaanapali Beach, Sheraton Maui, Royal Lahaina, and Embassy Suites. Beachside condominium complexes include well-located Kaanapali Alii.

Less expensive apartments, condos, and cottages crowd the Honokowai shore between Napili and Kaanapali. Napili Kai is one of the best known of the small informal resorts clustered around Napili Bay to the north.

Maui's southwest coast, on the leeward side of Haleakala, is lined with resorts, hotels, and condominiums from Maalaea Bay south to Wailea. Kihei choices include its first hotel, beachfront Maui Lu, and its latest, Maui Sun, near Silversword Golf Course. Farther south Wailea boasts five resort hotels—Stouffer Wailea Beach, Maui Inter-Continental, Grand Wailea, Four Seasons, and Kea Lani—and several deluxe condominium projects.

South of Wailea, at Makena, two 18-hole golf courses and a condomium complex front the road to the secluded Maui Prince Hotel.

Elsewhere around the island lie such charmers as prestigious Hotel Hana-Maui; also in Hana are Hana Kai-Maui, Heavenly Hana, and Hana Plantation Houses. On Haleakala's slopes, in cool upcountry Kula, accommodations include rustic Kula Lodge.

SUN & SURF SAFETY

Visitors to Hawaii will have a safe and more enjoyable stay if a few simple rules are heeded:

• To avoid wrecking your vacation with a sunburn, expose yourself gradually to Hawaii's tropical sun. An hour at midday may be too much for fair-skinned people. Protect your skin with a good suntan lotion.

• Inquire locally about safety of a beach—currents, tides, drop-offs—before entering water.

• Duck or dive *beneath* breaking waves just before they reach you.

• Coral cuts are easily infected. Avoid swimming or snorkeling near coral in shallow water. Protect your feet with sneakers or similar gear when walking on reefs.

• Don't get mesmerized when snorkeling—you may suddenly find yourself far offshore.

• If you find yourself in trouble in the water, don't waste your breath with pointless yelling; remain calm and stay afloat until help arrives.

• Never turn your back on the ocean when you're near the shoreline.

• Never swim alone.

Touring the Island

A number of companies offer tours of Hana, Haleakala and upcountry towns, and Iao Valley; information is available at hotel activities desks. Amateur astronomers, art lovers, boaters, cyclists, horseback riders, snorkelers, and whale watchers will all find special-interest tours.

Shopping—Almost a Recreation

Shopping opportunities abound in the myriad of small stores lining Lahaina's Front Street and in resort hotel boutiques. For unique souvenirs, look for the label that signifies products are made locally. Maui's best buys include artwork, coral jewelry, seashells, scrimshaw, protea flowers, potato chips, and sweet Kula onions.

The three largest shopping malls are Kaahumanu Center in Kahului, Lahaina Cannery Shopping Center, and Lahaina Center (includes Hilo Hattie). Other major centers around the island include Kahului Shopping Center and Maui Mall in Kahului; Lahaina Shopping Center, Lahaina Square, Mariner's Alley, Lahaina Market Place, Wharf Cinema Center, and 505 Front Street in Lahaina; Whalers Village in Kaanapali; Azeka Place, Kamaole Shopping Center, and Rainbow Mall in Kihei; and Wailea Shopping Village in Wailea.

Kapalua Resort's collection of stores ranks high among resort shopping experiences. Small, off-the-beaten-path towns like Makawao and Paia also reward shoppers.

Dining and Entertainment

Maui's cuisine runs the gamut from fast food to Pacific Rim. Dining is casual, with only the fanciest places requiring men to wear a jacket. Late-night activity centers around resort hotels and Lahaina's bustling waterfront. The following restaurants currently receive accolades:

Lahaina: Alex's Hole in the Wall, Avalon, Chart House, Chez Paul (Olowalu), Gerard's, Kimo's, La Bretagne, and Lahaina Broiler.

Kaanapali-Kapalua: El Crab Catcher (Whalers Village), Erik's Seafood Grotto (Kahana Villas), Kapalua Bay Club, Grill & Bar (on Kapalua's Bay Course), Nikko (Maui Marriott), Roy's Kahana Bar and Grill, Sound of the Falls (Westin Maui), and Swan Court (Hyatt Regency Maui).

Kihei-Makena: Kihei Prime Rib, La Bahia, Hula Moon (Maui Inter-Continental), Prince Court (Maui Prince), and Raffles (Stouffer Wailea Beach).

Kahului-Upcountry: Bullock's (Moonburgers and shakes), Casanova, Haliimaile General Store, Mama's Fish House, Ming Yuen, and Siam Thai.

See pages 120–121 for a guide to Maui's recreational facilities. For information and addresses of specific accommodations, excursions, and attractions, contact the Maui Visitors Bureau, P.O. Box 1738, Kahului, Maui, HI 96732; (808) 871-8691.

Maui's business and commerce centers around Wailuku and Kahului, adjoining towns at the northern end of the isthmus separating the West Maui Mountains from Haleakala.

Wailuku, older of the two towns, is charmingly situated on the slopes of the West Maui Mountains at the mouth of Iao Valley. Narrow, hilly streets, wooden shops, tree-shaded residential lanes, and the handsome buildings in its historic district give the town a look of the past in spite of a growing number of modern office buildings. Wailuku is the seat of Maui County (which includes Lanai and Molokai). You can't miss seeing Kalana O Maui, the 9-story county office building that towers over its older neighbors in the government complex.

Kahului, 3 miles/5 km downhill alongside Kahului Bay, is Maui's deep-water port. Several hotels and three shopping centers face Kaahumanu Avenue, the main thoroughfare. Kahului Airport is just east of town.

A few minutes drive northwest of Wailuku is Waiehu Golf Course, a scenic and challenging 18-hole layout with an ocean setting. Just beyond is Waihee, a small plantation settlement. From here, the road winds through and around the West Maui Mountains (see page 104); many stretches are unimproved.

Three routes cross the isthmus from the island hub to Maalaea Bay at the south. From Wailuku, Honoapiilani Highway (Highway 30) skirts the West Maui Mountains and leads to Lahaina, Kaanapali, and the other west Maui

resort areas. Monkeypod-lined Puunene Avenue (Highway 350) goes to Puunene Mill (headquarters of Hawaiian Commercial & Sugar Company). Alexander & Baldwin Sugar Museum, in the mill's plantation office, is open Monday through Saturday; there is a small admission fee. Highway 350 then continues south to Kihei and Maui's southwest shore. Highway 380 runs southwest from Puunene to Highway 30, and then heads to Maalaea Bay and on up to Lahaina and points north.

Kahului...Port City

Kahului, Maui's port city, attracts few visitors to its workaday world. It's the island's business and commercial center and home to many island residents. Its main street, Kaahumanu Avenue, becomes Wailuku's Main Street.

Kanaha Beach Park runs along the beach just above the airport. You can picnic here beneath large shade trees and enjoy a panoramic view across the water. To reach the park, turn off the airport road at the Department of Water Supply baseyard near the terminal, then turn right on Alahao Street.

Kanaha Pond, between the airport and Kahului, was an ancient royal fishpond. Now it's Hawaii's most important native and migratory waterfowl bird refuge, particularly for the Hawaiian stilt. Its low water levels also attract a variety of migratory shorebirds.

Kahului Harbor, Maui's deep-water port, has the state's first bulk sugar plant and acts as a fueling base for several hundred Japanese fishing boats each year. Adjacent Hoaloha Park is a pleasant picnic spot.

Three shopping complexes, Kahului Shopping Center, Maui Mall, and Kaahumanu Center front a half-mile stretch of Kaahumanu Avenue. Kahului Shopping Center, oldest of the three, is gradually giving way to newer Maui Mall and Kaahumanu Center, but its well-worn benches in the cool shade of burgeoning old monkeypod trees are still a favorite gathering place for local residents. The three centers offer an assortment of shops, ranging from small boutiques and specialty stores to department stores and supermarkets. Here, too, are several restaurants, snack bars, and take-out counters featuring local foods. Special entertainment is staged frequently at all three centers; check local papers for events and times.

Maui Community College, part of the University of Hawaii, occupies a 78-acre site along Kaahumanu Avenue midway between Kahului and Wailuku. About 2,100 students are enrolled.

Maui Zoological and Botanical Gardens on Kanaloa Avenue is a good destination for families with small children. The gardens boast a modest display of native plants; the children's zoo will enchant youngsters with its array of birds and animals, including Hawaii's endangered *nene*

Central Maui

Primary
Secondary

goose, *pueo* owls, and other local species. The free zoo is open from 9 A.M. to 4 P.M. daily.

Halekii and Pihana Heiau State Monument is reached from Waiehu Beach Road about 2 miles/3 km from Kahului; turn off on Kuhio Place, just past the bridge over Iao Stream, and follow the markers to the hilltop site. From the parking area, there's a good view down over central Maui and Kahului Harbor. Halekii, a 150 by 300-foot temple of worship, was used during the reign of Kahekili (1765–1795). A diagram at the site explains its partially restored stone walls, terraces, and post holes. Pihana, 300 feet farther up at the end of a path, was a sacrificial temple consecrated in 1779.

Maui Jinsha, in Paukukalo off Highway 34, is a beautiful and fascinating Shinto shrine. Sacred objects are located in a separate little building; both it and the shrine have traditional roof symbols—protruding horns and a barrel-shaped ridge piece.

Wailuku...a mix of old and new

The best way to explore Wailuku's narrow, hilly streets is on foot. Many of the interesting new and old buildings are clustered in a compact area along High Street, between Main and Aupini streets. The Wailuku Historic District is on the west side of High Street. Walk some of the side streets to see older residential areas with small, tidy homes and colorful gardens. To view handsome homes on nicely landscaped hillside lots, drive up to Wailuku Heights; the road to it branches off the Iao Valley Road.

Government buildings line High Street. Most conspicuous is 9-story Kalana O Maui, the county office building. Adjacent to it, at the corner of High and Wells streets, sits the venerable 1907 Court House. Federal offices occupy the building on the opposite corner of Wells Street; just beyond, at High and Main streets, is the state office building.

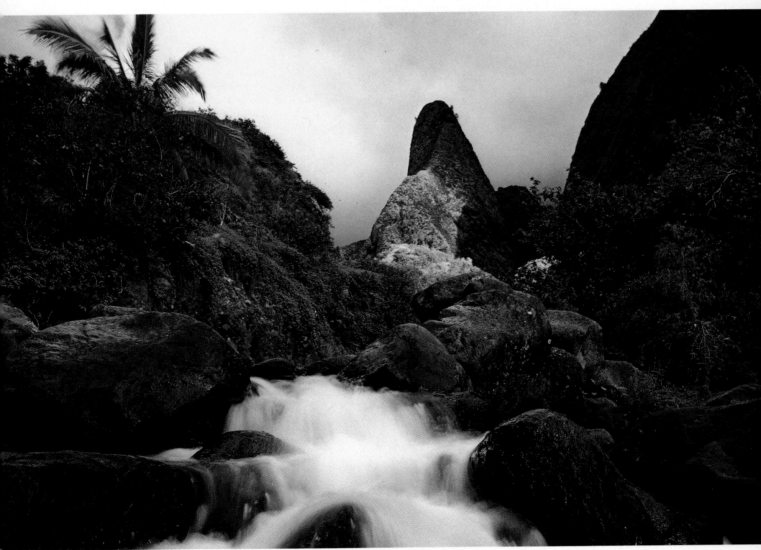

Iao Needle, *a Maui landmark, juts up from floor of verdant valley. Iao Stream cascades in foreground.*

Kaahumanu Church *was Maui's first Christian congregation (1832). Present church building was constructed in 1876.*

Happy Valley on Highway 33, a part of old Wailuku reached by driving north on Market Street, has balconied living quarters above open-front shops and taverns.

The Wailuku Library, housed in an attractive, low, white stucco building on High Street across from the county office building, contains an excellent Hawaiiana room.

Kaahumanu Church, built on High Street in 1876 of plastered stone, is third church building of Maui's first Christian congregation (1832). Its handsome spire, set off against a dramatic mountain backdrop, is a much-photographed subject. The church's name honors Hana-born Queen Kaahumanu, favorite wife of Kamehameha I.

Early Hawaiian Christian Cemetery, just above High Street on the Iao Valley Road, has been restored and landscaped. It contains the graves of a number of early Hawaiian Christians, including that of the first ordained Hawaiian minister to serve Kaahumanu Church.

Hale Hoikeike, off Iao Valley Road, is a museum consisting of two buildings: the home built in 1841 by Edward Bailey, head instructor of the Wailuku Female Seminary; and the kitchen–dining room of the school, an 1838–39 addition to its original building (now gone). The Bailey home has beams of hand-hewn sandalwood and 20-inch-thick stone walls covered with a mixture of plaster and goat hair. It contains historical exhibits, changing ethnic displays, and an exhibit of the 19th-century paintings of Edward Bailey.

The Church of the Good Shepherd, 2140 Main Street, is a 1911 Episcopal sanctuary of stone, with interior details of native woods and an unusual stained glass window behind the altar.

Wailuku Union Church, a small Gothic-style church on High Street, was built in 1911 to replace its 1867 predecessor.

Ka Lima O Maui, 95 Mahalani Street, is a rehabilitation center where you can buy Hawaiian craft products and nursery plants.

Iao Valley

From Wailuku you can drive for 3 miles/5 km into Iao Valley, never straying far from Iao Stream. The road (Highway 32) is a continuation of Wailuku's Main Street. Two miles/3 km from Wailuku, it passes Kepaniwai Heritage Gardens, a Maui County park with formal gardens and pavilions representing cultures that were instrumental to the growth of Hawaii. The name recalls a bloody battle fought here in 1790 in which Kamehameha I defeated the forces of the king of Maui. So many warriors were killed, says the legend, that their bodies choked the stream. This gave the park its name—Kepaniwai—which means "damming of the waters."

The road ends in Iao Valley State Park, dominated by 2,250-foot Iao Needle, a green-mantled remnant of erosion that rises sharply for 1,200 feet from the north valley wall. From the parking lot at the end of the road, you can follow well-marked paths through an impressive collection of exotic plants and trees down to the stream, up to a shelter view spot for a look farther into the hushed ravine, and to the top of the ridge for a commanding vista of the Needle, the valley floor, and, in the distance, Kahului Bay.

Maui Tropical Plantation

At Waikapu, 3 miles/5 km south of Wailuku on Highway 30, this 60-acre plantation presents the story of Hawaiian agriculture in a unique and fascinating way. A tram takes you through acres of tropical crops—coffee, pineapple, guava, mango, and macadamia nuts. In the market and restaurant, you have a chance to touch, sniff, and sample the plantation's harvest. The plantation is open daily from 9 A.M. to 5 P.M. Admission is free; there is a fee for the tram and for the lively country barbecue on Monday, Wednesday, and Friday at 5 P.M. (reservations suggested).

WEST MAUI: LAHAINA / KAANAPALI

This stretch of west Maui has for years been one of the most popular vacation destinations on the island. Devotees point out, quite rightfully, its scenic beauty and excellent beaches. Of at least equal importance are the well-preserved historical attractions which acquaint the visitor with the region's sometimes brawling and always fascinating past. Many vacationers (especially repeat ones) find everything they need or want right here and never stray far from this concentration of resort facilities.

Kahului to Lahaina

From Kahului Airport, you'll drive about 6 miles/9 km on Highway 380 to its junction with Highway 30; from there, it's another 17 miles/27 km to Lahaina.

Shortly after you join Highway 30, a road veers left toward Maalaea, a settlement with several condominiums, stores, restaurants, and a wharf and boat harbor. There's a sweeping view across Maalea Bay.

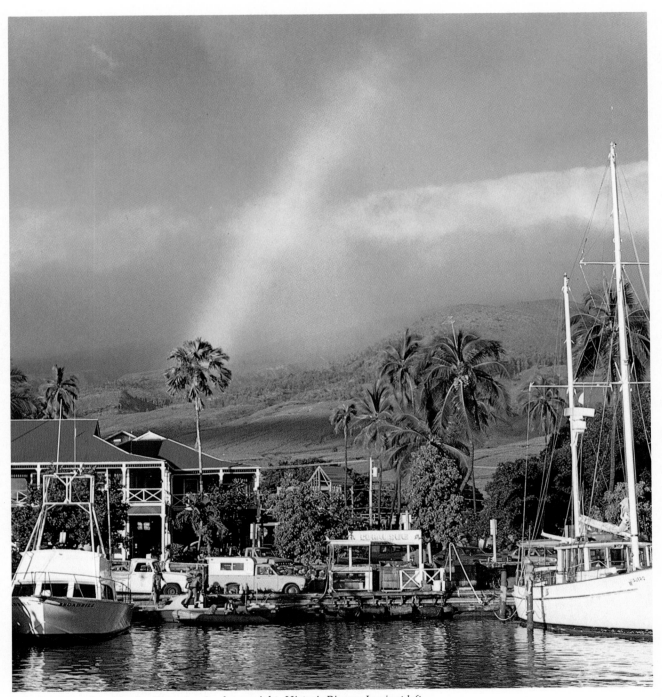

Lahaina waterfront *is a bustling place by day or night. Historic Pioneer Inn is at left.*

Giant bronze Buddha, *at Jodo Mission near Mala wharf, was erected to mark hundredth anniversary of the arrival of first Japanese plantation laborers in 1868.*

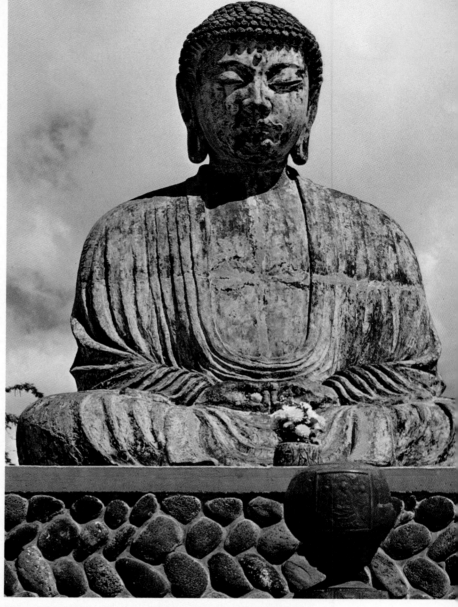

Sugar Cane Train *(see page 102) puffs merrily along, transporting rail fans and sightseers between Kaanapali and Lahaina town. Trip offers scenery ranging from oceanscapes to cane fields to golf fairways; a singing conductor helps keep things lively.*

...West Maui: Lahaina/Kaanapali

Highway 30 follows a picturesque route along the tops of seashore cliffs; at a scenic lookout, a plaque features information on the humpback whale. The highway then descends to the narrow Olowalu plain, where cane fields slope up to mile-high mountains broken by Ukumehame Gulch and other deep gashes.

Monkeypod trees shade quiet Olowalu, a small community with a few homes, a French restaurant (Chez Paul), and a little general store that seems typically Hawaiian. A half mile to the north lies a good hunting ground for "Hawaiian diamonds" (high-grade quality). Surfing waves boom offshore here and also farther north at Launiupoko State Park.

Between Maalaea and Lahaina, Ukumehame and Puamana county parks and Papalaua and Launiupoko state parks are good places for a picnic.

Lahaina...Historic Waterfront Town

Modern Hawaiian history has its roots deeply embedded in Lahaina ("*cruel sun,*" as translated from early-day terminology). Kamehameha the Great established a residence here after he conquered Maui in a bloody battle in Iao Valley. Some of the first missionaries from Boston came ashore at Lahaina in 1823. And Kamehameha III lived here when he granted religious freedom and drew up Hawaii's first laws and constitution.

In the middle 1800s, whalers came by the thousands to winter in this little port, anchoring their ships offshore. Humpback whales migrating to their Hawaiian breeding grounds from the Aleutians still make whale watching a popular winter pastime. Tour boats leave from Lahaina and Maalaea harbors for a close-up look at these leviathans, some of which swim right up to the boats. The best months to see whales are January through April, though you may spot some stragglers as late as June.

Lahaina is still partly the town it has been for a century and a half—streets are narrow, sidewalks few, trees old and spreading, family gardens a tropical hodgepodge. Most houses are simple cottages. Some shopping still takes place in false-front wooden buildings.

But Lahaina no longer exists as it did more than 20 years ago, when its primary purpose was to sell staples to west Maui's cane and pineapple workers. New shopping complexes, restaurants, and bars (some in recycled buildings) are constantly being added to the scene. Condominiums seem to spring up overnight. Today, Lahaina town is a popular and often crowded visitor destination.

Restoration activity. Lahaina is a national historic landmark, and its center is under Maui County Historic District protection.

Most of the additions and changes are in keeping with the town's restoration program, a joint effort of state and local government and the Lahaina Restoration Foundation. Weathered buildings (particularly on Front Street) are being refurbished, harmonious new building encouraged, and restoration and rebuilding underway for a few

(Continued on page 102)

SCRIMSHAW — WHALERS' ART

The meticulous art of scrimshaw—the carving or engraving of ivory, bone, and whales' teeth—goes back hundreds of years. Scrimshaw shops in Lahaina offer a wide variety of old and new pieces, ranging from a few dollars to collector's item prices.

Among the finest scrimshanders were the sailors who manned the whaling ships; many a whale's tooth took shape under the skilled hands of these seafarers who found scrimshaw to be a good way to pass the often lonesome weeks and months at sea. But since the Endangered Species Act of 1973 prohibited importation of whale products into the United States, scrimshanders have turned to other media, especially fossil ivory.

STROLLING THROUGH LAHAINA'S VIVID PAST ...

Fortunate is the history buff who visits Lahaina, because here—in one compact area—the flavor of the past can be sampled in reasonable time and with minimum wear on the shoes. A publication containing expanded information about the historical attractions mentioned on these pages can be obtained from Baldwin Home or other museums.

(1) Masters' Reading Room, built in 1834 by missionaries and ships' officers, is an appropriate home for the Lahaina Restoration Foundation. The lower floor was used by the mission; above was a reading room.

(2) Baldwin Home Museum includes Dr. Baldwin's dispensary-study and restored Baldwin Home, the New England style residence of medical missionary Dwight Baldwin and his family from 1836 to 1868. Built in 1834–35 of plastered coral and hand-hewn 'ohi'a beams, the home contains original furnishings and other period pieces. Dr. Baldwin's medical kit and theological books, and some early physician's implements are displayed in the dispensary. Museum is open daily; there's an admission fee.

(3) Site of Richards house, earliest coral stone house in the islands. William Richards was the first Protestant missionary to Lahaina. He traveled in the United States and Europe as envoy of Kamehameha III.

(4) Site of taro patch, visible as late as the 1950s, where Kamehameha III once worked to show his subjects the dignity of labor. Now the library lawn.

(5) Hauloa Stone is believed to have been used by early Hawaiians as a healing place.

(6) The "Brick Palace," thought to be the first Western style building in the islands, was built at the command of Kamehameha I.

(7) Carthaginian, a museum afloat, is a 93-foot replica of a 19th century brig. A project of the Lahaina Restoration Foundation, the ship contains a "World of the Whale" exhibit; there's an admission fee.

(8) Pioneer Inn was west Maui's only visitor accommodation until the late 1950s. The original building was constructed in 1901; the amusing house rules of that time are posted in the rooms. A wing added in 1964 reflects the same architectural style.

(9) Banyan Tree, planted in 1873 to commemorate the 50th anniversary of the arrival of Lahaina's first Protestant missionaries, is the largest banyan in the islands. It covers an entire square (about two-thirds of an acre) behind the Courthouse. At sundown, mynah birds strike up a chorus you won't soon forget.

(10) Courthouse was built in 1859 with stone from the demolished Hale Piula (15).

(11) Old Fort, next to the Courthouse, is a reconstruction of the ruins of a fort built here in the early 1830s and used chiefly to confine unruly seamen. The original fort was torn down in the 1850s to supply stones for the construction of Hale Paahao (21).

(12) Site of a canal (filled in 1913) dug to provide access for whaling ships. Before its construction, whalers had to drag boats across the beach to load fresh water.

(13) Site of old Government Market, where natives traded with sailors during the whaling days, is said to have earned its nickname: Rotten Row.

(14) Holy Innocents' Episcopal Church was built in 1927; Episcopal services at Lahaina actually date back to 1862, when the first services were held in Hale Aloha. The church has a unique painting of the Madonna and Child for which a Lahaina mother and infant posed.

(15) Site of Hale Piula, an old courthouse until damaged beyond repair by a gale in 1858. Its stones were used to build the present courthouse (10).

(16) Maluuluolele Park was once the site of a pond with an island where several Maui chiefs were buried.

(17) Wainee Church was the first stone church in the islands, circa 1830. Windstorms and fires have destroyed it several times since. The current church, dedicated in 1953, was renamed Waiola, "Water of Life."

(18) Wainee Cemetery, planted with fragrant plumerias and ancient palms, has gravestones with inscriptions dating back to 1823. Keopuolani, queen of Kamehameha the Great, is buried here.

(19) Hongwanji Mission has been a meeting place for Buddhists since 1910, when they erected a small temple. The present building dates from 1927.

(20) Site of house of David Malo, renowned Hawaiian scholar and philosopher who fought hard to preserve old Hawaii against growing outside control. A graduate of Lahainaluna Seminary, his gravesite is at the top of nearby Mt. Ball.

(21) Hale Paahao, the old prison, has walls of coral block taken from the old waterfront fort (11).

(22) Episcopal Cemetery contains the grave of Walter Murray Gibson, flamboyant and extravagant adviser to King Kalakaua in the 1880s.

THE DAYS OF KINGS, MISSIONARIES & WHALERS

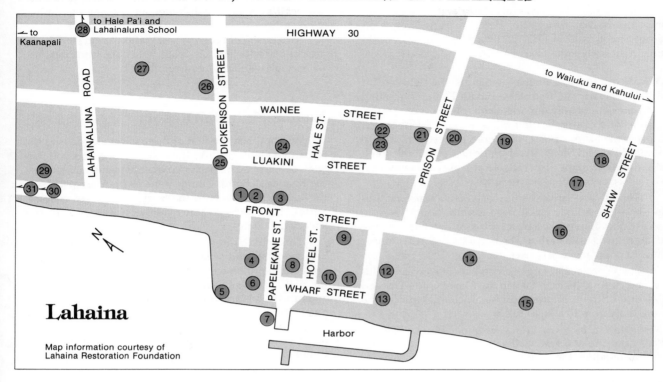

Lahaina

Map information courtesy of
Lahaina Restoration Foundation

㉓ Hale Aloha, built in 1858 and used as a church and school for many years, fell into ruins but was restored in 1974.

㉔ Shingon Buddhist Temple has the simple, wooden architectural style typical of houses of worship built during the plantation era when Japanese laborers were brought to Hawaii.

㉕ Luakini Street was the route of the funeral procession of Princess Nahienaena, who died tragically at age 21 in 1837.

㉖ Maria Lanakila Church was built in 1928. It replaced an 1858 frame structure established after the celebration of Maui's first Catholic Mass on Lahaina beach in 1841.

㉗ Seamen's Cemetery has only one inscribed marble slab and the fragment of another remaining. Buried here are a cousin and a shipmate of author Herman Melville.

㉘ Hale Pa'i and Lahainaluna School are across Highway 30 and 1½ miles/3 km up the hill. (Just before you begin the climb, you pass the old Pioneer Mill Company, which dates from 1860.) Hale Pa'i, a print shop at Lahainaluna Seminary founded by Protestant missionaries in 1831, produced Hawaiian textbooks and Hawaii's first newspaper. The school, the oldest educational institution west of the Rockies, now serves as the public high school for the Lahaina area. Hale Pa'i was restored in 1980–82 by the Lahaina Restoration Foundation. An exhibit features a replica of the early press and facsimiles of early printing. The museum is open to visitors daily except Sunday.

㉙ Wo Hing Temple is affiliated with the Chee Kung Tong, a Chinese fraternal society with branches all over the world. Recently restored, the temple has a small museum. The Chinese were among the earliest immigrants to Hawaii and became a powerful force in the commerce of Lahaina and throughout the islands.

㉚ Seamen's Hospital was precisely that, during the whaling era from 1840 to 1865. But it also has served as a girl's school, vicarage, and residence—and once as a hideaway for Kamehameha III. It was completely reconstructed in 1972.

㉛ Jodo Mission contains the Japanese Cultural Park, commemorating the first immigrants. Here you'll find a giant bronze Buddha imported from Japan, a temple, pagodas, and a bell tower.

...West Maui: Lahaina/Kaanapali

structures from each period of Lahaina's 19th-century history—from early monarchy days through the beginnings of plantations and the influx of workers from the Orient. The famed old sea wall (a favorite place for watching sunsets) was restored in 1980. Wo Hing Temple on Front Street, built in 1912, underwent extensive renovation in the early 1980s (see page 101).

A walking town. Lahaina town is just the right size for walking. Nearly flat, it stretches out for 2 miles/3 km along the water but is only 4 blocks deep. Shops, restaurants, and activity centers jostle for space along Front Street. Most of the historic points of interest lie between Lahainaluna Road and Shaw Street on or just off Front Street. Walking-tour maps are available at Baldwin Home Museum (see page 100) or at area hotels.

Though you can cover most of Lahaina's historic sites in about 1½ hours, you'll need several hours more to investigate shops, take a boat cruise, or watch the fishing boats return to the harbor. The bar at the colorful Pioneer Inn is a popular site at sunset.

For a spectacular large-screen look at Hawaii's natural and cultural history, take in the film at Omni Theater, 824 Front Street. Shows (admission charge) are on the hour daily from 10 A.M. to 10 P.M.

If you're in town Friday evening, don't miss Art Walk, starting at 6 P.M. Galleries are open and strolling musicians add to the festivities.

Lahaina to Kaanapali

The drive from Lahaina to Kaanapali on Highway 30 is short—less than 3 miles/5 km. The widened highway encourages cyclists. Just north of Lahaina, you can see the remains of a royal coconut grove, planted in 1827 by the wife of Maui's governor, Hoapila. Young palms are now taking the place of the older ones as they succumb to wind and age.

Two excellent beach parks, Wahikuli and Hanakaoo, are popular with local residents. Both offer sandy beaches, picnic tables, and changing rooms.

Kaanapali Beach Resort

As you approach the first of three entrance roads to the resort, you look out over the manicured greens and fairways of one of Kaanapali's two championship golf courses, the Kaanapali South Course. One clubhouse, just inside the turnoff, serves both the South and North courses. Parts of both courses climb to higher elevations and offer spectacular views.

This multifarious resort includes more than 600 developed acres and seven deluxe beachfront hotels. Several condominium complexes face the ocean; others flank the golf fairways. Kaanapali is a popular tennis center, and most hotels and condominiums have courts. Numerous restaurants, cocktail lounges, snack bars, swimming pools, and shops dot the grounds. Nightly entertainment, including an astronomy show at the Hyatt Regency, centers around the hotels.

Free trolleys provide shuttle service around the resort, to and from the Sugar Cane Train's Kaanapali Station (see below), and to Whalers Village. The latter, a multilevel, 8-acre complex of buildings and open plazas, houses a whaling museum along with shops and eating places.

"THE SUGAR CANE TRAIN"

One of the most unusual attractions in the islands is the 1890-style, open-sided train of the Lahaina Kaanapali & Pacific Railroad, which chugs along a 6-mile/10-km route, taking you back in time to the turn of the century when narrow-gauge trains were common on Hawaii's major islands.

The train runs on 36-inch, narrow-gauge, German-made tracks that were used by the Kahului Railroad before it stopped operating in 1966. It puffs its way through fields of sugarcane, crosses a 400-foot-long trestle, runs alongside the 4th hole of Kaanapali's south golf course (watch the golfers gawk!), and follows part of the roadbed of the cane haul line that traveled to and from Lahaina's Pioneer Mill between 1882 and 1952. As the train rolls along, passengers are entertained by a singing conductor.

Cars with wooden seats are modeled after coaches that King Kalakaua had built to his order in England around 1888. The steam engine, "Anaka," incorporates parts of five early Hawaiian locomotives, including brass-trimmed domes and headlight and a mahogany cab. It and the backup engine, "Myrtle," were rebuilt to 1890–1910 vintage from derelict Porter locomotives sitting on a track in Carbon, Ohio.

There are six scheduled departures daily from the Victorian style stations at Lahaina and Kaanapali and the boarding platform at Puukolii. Earliest is 8:55 A.M. from Puukolii; the last train, at 4:40 P.M., is one-way only from Lahaina to Puukolii. Tickets can be purchased at train stations or at activities centers. Jitneys transport passengers to and from Lahaina town or Kaanapali Resort.

NORTHWEST MAUI: NAPILI / KAPALUA

Less than a 10-minute drive north from Kaanapali, two vacation destinations attract an increasing number of visitors each year: Napili Bay and Kapalua. These adjacent regions have their own special characteristics, yet the two areas share at least one important asset—a spectacular view across brilliant blue ocean to the neighboring islands of Molokai and Lanai.

For those who enjoy auto exploring, the rugged north coast is right "next door."

Kaanapali to Napili Bay

North of Kaanapali, Highway 30 takes an inland route above the apartments, condominiums, and cottages lining both sides of the lower road, which travels through Honokawai to Kahana before joining the highway. A little more than a mile farther you come to Napili. Several condominiums and informal resorts with kitchen facilities preside over a lovely curve of sandy beach. Northern-

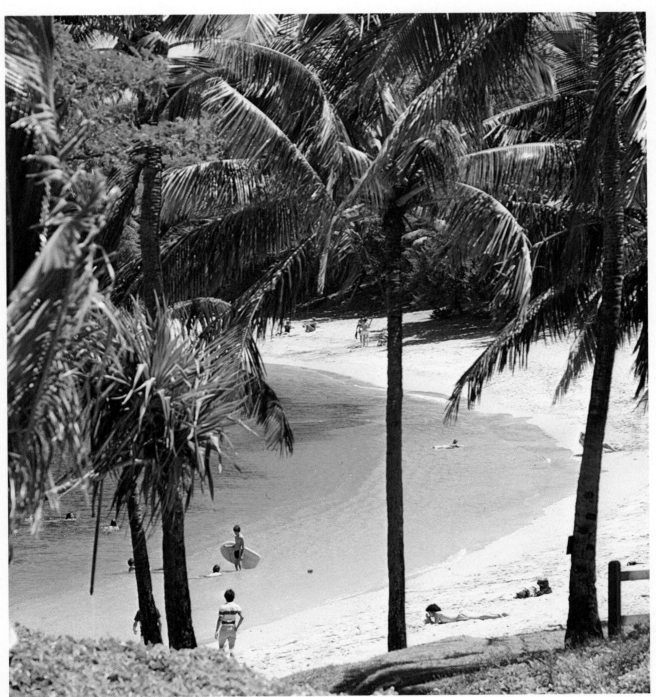

Kapalua Beach (formerly Fleming Beach), fronting Kapalua Bay Hotel, combines scenic beauty and safe swimming.

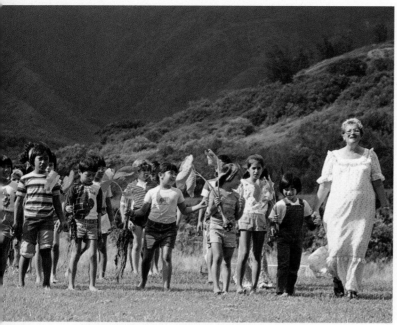

Kapuna program, *where senior citizens work with youngsters to keep old traditions alive, is popular with all ages—as witness this group with heart-shaped leaves picked from taro fields.*

most of these is Napili Kai Beach Club, composed of seven separate two-story wings scattered over 10 acres; here, on Napili Beach, Seahouse is a popular choice for dining and night life.

Kapalua Resort

Just to the north of Napili lies Kapalua Resort, one of the island's primary vacation destinations for golfers. Accommodations include deluxe Kapalua Bay Hotel, the latest Hawaiian entry by Ritz-Carlton, and several condominium complexes. A fine beach, interesting shops, and a variety of good restaurants are only some of the offerings.

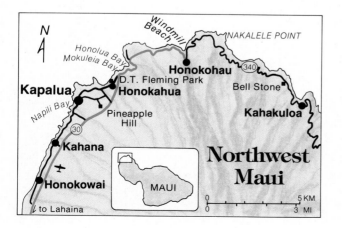

Kapalua's 750 landscaped acres include three 18-hole golf courses. Bay Course is the site of an international championship golf tournament; its terrain spreads from the lower mountain slopes down to the water's edge. Village Course combines a challenging hillside layout with dramatic views from just about anywhere. Plantation Course tests golfers' skills on its hills and gorges.

Tennis courts are located in a secluded garden area. Kapalua offers plentiful water sports—windsurfing, scuba diving, snorkeling, boating, and swimming. Flightseeing and horseback riding are only a few miles away.

Kapalua to Honokahua

Beyond Kapalua Bay are several excellent beaches favored—and sometimes nicknamed—by local people: Oneloa (Beach Camp) Beach; D. T. Fleming Park (Ball Park or Stable Point), fronting 600 feet of white sand *makai* of Honokahua village (swimming and surfing for experts only); Mokuleia Bay (Slaughterhouse); and Honolua Bay. Because of their wealth of underwater life, Mokuleia Bay and most of Honolua Bay have been designated by the state as a marine life conservation district.

Around the West Maui Mountains

The narrow, twisting, up-and-down road around the north end of the West Maui Mountains follows the course of an old royal horse trail and bears the extravagant title "Kahekili Highway." This isn't a good wet-weather drive; pavement ends just 5 miles/8 km east of Honokolau Bridge and begins again about 2 miles/3 km farther. Check car rental insurance coverage before making the trip.

Between a lighthouse at the island's north point and Honokohau, you cross weathered sandstone bluffs of various hues. There's a blowhole on the jagged coast. Windmill Beach, usually windy and rough, is splendid for diving on glassy days.

Honokohau is a jungle of fruit trees. Drive down into the valley a little way to see taro cultivated beside the stream and orchids on the slope. Just before you dip down into Kahakuloa village, try to get a ring from a roadside boulder known as the Bell Stone; you're supposed to listen on one side while someone bangs a rock against the other. (Results are dubious, but the stone is well worn from many trial bangs.)

Kahakuloa village stands at the mouth of a green valley in the middle of cattle country; a bold headland guards the southern approach. Amid the cluster of iron-roofed, wooden shacks fringed by a patchwork of taro, you'll find two picturesque churches—one Catholic and one Protestant. Villagers still pound poi, raise pigs, fish, beat the washing on rocks in the stream—but, at night, watch television.

Beyond Kahakuloa, the road winds along cliffs above fern gulches that stretch to the sea.

KIHEI & WAILEA

Until the early 1970s, Maui's southwest coast—from Maalaea Bay through Kihei and on south to Makena—was a quiet rural area where the only break in the lazy routine was a visit to Azeka's store, the post office, or Kihei's original and still charming resort, the low-rise Maui Lu. But, with its exceptional weather and multiplicity of excellent beaches, this region was destined to become the major tourist destination that it is today. It seems—to local residents who remember a kiawe-tree-covered area where seldom was heard the sound of a jackhammer—to have happened almost overnight.

This part of Maui is dry and usually sunny, receiving less than 10 inches of rainfall annually. Had it not been for this scarcity of water, tourism would have come to the region much earlier. When plans were laid for the Wailea resort area just south of Kihei, a major project was undertaken to import water from the rainy West Maui Mountains. By the early 1970s, condominiums and apartment hotels were under construction all along the coast; this development has continued, not only near the water but inland to the lower slopes of Haleakala.

Kahului to Kihei and Wailea

Highway 350 from Kahului Airport crosses central Maui from ocean to ocean; the drive takes about 25 minutes, depending on traffic conditions. Along the way you pass through miles of cane fields, with views of Maui's two mountain masses on either side—Haleakala to the left, the West Maui Mountains to the right. Kihei is most easily reached by following the highway all the way to Kihei Road, which runs the gamut of condominiums south along the ocean to the Wailea Resort turnoff. For a more direct route to Wailea, turn left from Highway 350 shortly before it reaches the ocean, onto the newer and faster Highway 31. You can also take this route to Kihei: several turnoffs lead down to Kihei Road. Or, if you are staying at the extreme southern end of Kihei, turn *makai* (toward the ocean) when you reach Wailea and then buttonhook back northward on Kihei Road.

Kihei—One Beach After Another

For sunny weather, sandy beaches, and good ocean swimming, Kihei (and south through Wailea and Makena) cannot be topped anywhere else on the island—or, for that matter, anywhere in Hawaii. Beach parks along this coast are popular with visitors and local residents alike. Reserve Kalama Park's pavilions in advance; they're usually crowded with festive groups on weekends and holidays. Kamaole Beach Park, just to the south, actually includes three separate beaches, with picnic tables, showers, and changing rooms.

A popular family vacation destination, Kihei has condominiums (more than three dozen) for just about any budget. Spaced throughout the region are several excellent restaurants. The popular Kihei Prime Rib features evening piano entertainment; its upstairs location gives

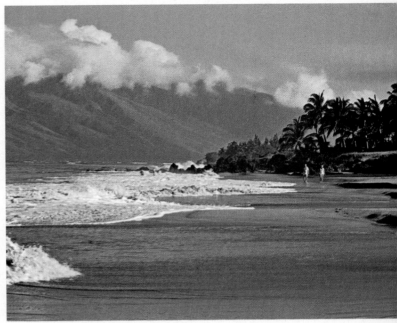

Early birds *enjoy stroll on a magical morning at Kamaole Beach Park #1. West Maui Mountains lie in distance.*

Gourmet favorites *such as 'ula 'ula and* ulua *come to end of the line at Maalaea's busy wharf.*

LOVABLE GIANTS—THE HUMPBACK WHALES

Breaching whale, seen close-up, is an awesome sight

With the arrival of winter each year, two groups of visitors make their presence known in Maui: the prime tourist season begins, and the humpback whales, having summered in Alaska and the Bering Sea, return to Maui's waters to breed, calve, and tend their young. First sightings usually occur in early December; by late May, all but a few stragglers will have departed.

The humpbacks are, to put it mildly, a sight to see. Once you've viewed them—particularly at close range from the deck of a whalewatcher cruise boat—you will begin to understand why the people of the islands have an ongoing love affair with these huge but gentle mammals.

Fewer than a thousand humpbacks remain in the North Pacific—about 600 of them visit Hawaii annually—but these are a small fraction of their numbers before they became prey to commercial hunters. Back in the mid-1800s, when as many as 450 whaling ships anchored in Lahaina each winter, perhaps 15,000 humpbacks inhabited the North Pacific. Though protected by international convention since 1966, the humpback population continues to decline. Both the Pacific Whale Foundation, headquartered in Maui, and the University of Hawaii are devoted to research, conservation, and education programs focused on whales (also dolphins and porpoises).

Humpbacks are 10 to 15 feet long at birth, weighing from 1 to 3 tons. During the first few weeks they gain about 200 pounds a day, due largely to the high percentage of fat in the mother's milk. When full sized, they average 45 feet in length, often weighing over 40 tons. Their long flukes (tails) have markings underneath which differ with each humpback; researchers who track their comings and goings can identify each individual from these "fingerprints."

Scientists have revealed that some male humpbacks "sing," or at least produce noises ranging from shrieks to low growling sounds that travel for miles in the water. Research continues as to what this might signify.

What to Watch for

Whalewatchers soon learn the meanings of four key terms: "breaching," "spy hopping," "fluking," and "fluke-slapping."

A whale "breaches" when it comes bursting out of the water head-first—maybe because it's disturbed about something or perhaps just having fun. If you see part of the whale's head out of the water for more than a couple of seconds, it's "spy hopping"—having a look-see above the surface. "Fluking" means that the whale is diving; the tail emerges and quickly submerges again. If its tail slaps against the surface in the process (an awesome "thwack"), the whale is "fluke-slapping."

...Kihei & Wailea

diners a good vantage point for watching sunsets. Azeka Place Shopping Center, on S. Kihei Road, is always busy. Both residents and visitors shop, bank, and browse through stores.

Wailea Resort

One of Maui's three world-famed luxury resorts, this 1,450-acre complex includes hotels (Stouffer Wailea Beach, Maui Inter-Continental, Grand Wailea, Four Seasons, and Kea Lani), upscale condominium villages, private homes, five beaches, a shopping center, and restaurants. Wailea Activities Center offers swimming, snorkeling, sailing, windsurfing, scuba diving, fishing, and whale watching. Three of Wailea Tennis Center's 14 courts are grass—hence the nickname "Wimbledon West."

Two clubhouses and three distinctively different 18-hole courses challenge resort golfers. The courses' straight-growing trees attest to the region's exceptional year-round golf weather. Compared to the wide fairways of the Blue Course, the tighter Gold Course is more demanding. A new Robert Trent Jones, Jr. links, the Emerald Course replaces the former Orange Course.

Makena

South of Wailea, the road continues to Makena. In the days when Ulupalakua Ranch was planted with sugarcane, the area contained Maui's second-ranking port. Makena now has the luxurious Maui Prince Hotel, an oceanside complex of low-rise condominiums, and two 18-hole golf courses.

Five beaches accessible by regular car are, north to south: Poolenalena, Maluaka, Oneuli, Puuolai, and Oneloa. All are swimmable, but safest are Poolenalena, Maluaka, and Puuolai. (Kahoolawe, an uninhabited island that was long used by the U.S. Navy as a military bombing target and recently returned to the Hawaiian people, looms large offshore. Fronting it is tiny Molokini, whose exceptional snorkeling waters can be visited by boat.)

In a 4-wheel-drive vehicle, you can continue on a rocky, rutty road down the coast to La Perouse Bay, named for the French explorer who anchored here in 1786 and then sailed away to mysteriously disappear at sea.

Ahihi-Kinau Natural Area Reserve encompasses the south end of Ahihi Bay and Cape Kinau. This ecologically important area has been set aside by the state to protect and preserve its unique natural resources. The lava flows forming Cape Kinau resulted from Maui's last volcanic activity, estimated to have occurred in 1790. Unusual species of marine life thrive in the reserve's tidal pools and offshore waters. Ninety species of larval fishes have been collected around the cape—more than four times the average number of species found elsewhere in Hawaii—and at least 23 species of stony corals have been found in the southern end of the bay. The ruins of Moanakala, a small fishing village also located in the reserve, is a focus for anthropological research.

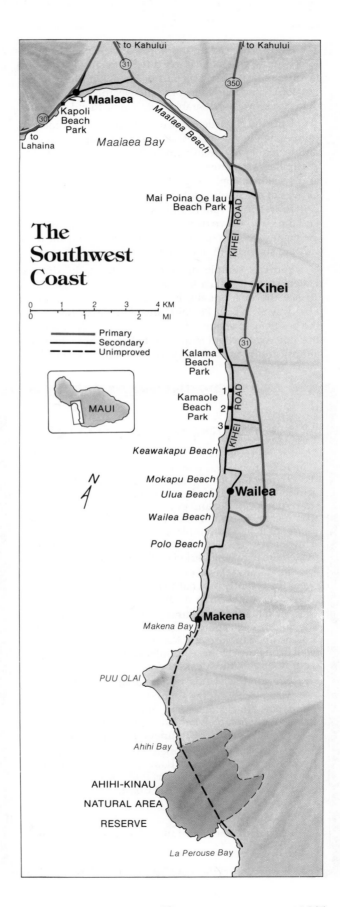

The Southwest Coast

MAUI

MAUI's QUIET UPCOUNTRY

When you head up the slopes of Haleakala from Kahului, you move into a different Hawaii. Though a favorite of islanders, this part of Maui is, unfortunately, overlooked by many visitors. The weather is cooler here than at sea level—a desirable trait to some island residents.

Upcountry gardens are usually ablaze with colorful, temperate-zone flowers. Cattle graze in lush pastureland, and farmers grow many kinds of vegetables—including cucumbers, tomatoes, most of the state's cabbage crop, and sweet Kula onions (perhaps the pride of the region). Groves of eucalyptus dot the green hillsides, soft clouds drift in and out of valleys and swirl over the higher slopes, and the views down over the isthmus and out to the coast are magnificent. In spring, jacaranda trees along the roadside are strung with purple blossoms.

You can sample upcountry Maui on the drive to Haleakala National Park along highways 37, 377, and 378. To see the heart of the big Kula district, continue on Highway 37 to Kula Hospital and Ulupalakua Ranch. But the best way to explore the upcountry is to drive some of the side roads. Maui maps don't always show them, but almost any road will carry you through a refreshingly rural countryside where the pace is slow, the people friendly, and the scenery restful. The road from Keokea to Kula Hospital has some exceptionally beautiful plantings just before you reach the hospital buildings.

Many of Hawaii's best-known families have year-round or part-time homes upcountry, especially in the southern region generally referred to as Kula. Early settlers, mostly farmers and plantation workers, came from China, Japan, and the Portuguese islands of Madeira and the Azores.

Kula's treasure, the octagonal Church of the Holy Ghost, reflects this heritage: the original parishioners of this 1897 Catholic church were mostly Portuguese. Perched on the hillside above the highway near Waiakoa, the church and its delicate steeple can be seen from many directions. If it's open, go inside to admire the gilded wooden bas-reliefs, Portuguese inscriptions, and the large, Austrian-made altar shipped in sections around Cape Horn.

Another example of the area's multiethnic heritage is St. John's Episcopal Church in Keokea, once a thriving Chinese community. The church was founded by a Chinese

STATE'S BEST LUAUS

The luau (feast) was once only a family celebration. Food consisted of a pig, roasted in a pit dug into the ground, accompanied by a bland paste made of ground taro root (poi). Pig and poi are still on the menu at commercial luaus, but they're only part of an expanded buffet that visitors sample while enjoying an evening of Hawaiian music and dance. At some hotels, you can watch the pig being buried earlier in the day.

Luaus are relaxed entertainment, a good time to wear the recently purchased aloha shirt and muumuu. A sweater might come in handy when the sun sets.

Most luaus cost around $50 per person, half-price for children. Except for fruit punch, drinks are usually not included in the price. Reservations are required well in advance at these popular gatherings; check with your hotel activities desk for details.

Some of the islands' best luaus are listed below.

Maui. Drums of the Pacific Luau, Hyatt Regency, Kaanapali; Hotel Hana-Maui, Hana; Old Lahaina Luau (particularly notable), Lahaina; Royal Lahaina Luau, Kaanapali; Maui Inter-Continental Luau, Wailea.

Hawaii. Hotel King Kamehameha Luau, Kailua-Kona; Kona Village Resort Luau (particularly notable), Kona Coast; Mauna Kea Resort Luau, Kohala Coast; Royal Waikoloan Luau, Kohala Coast.

Kauai. Tahiti Nui Luau, Hanalei; Coconut Beach Hotel Luau, Kapaa.

Oahu. Paradise Cove Luau, Ewa; Royal Hawaiian Luau, Waikiki.

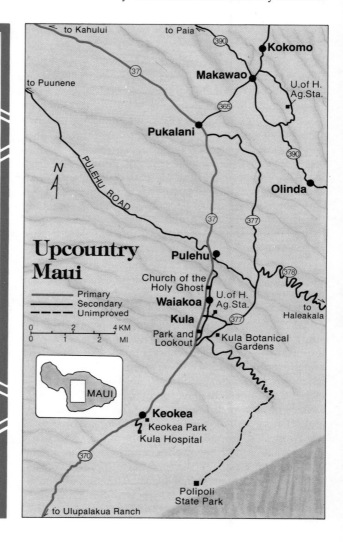

Upcountry Maui

——— Primary
——— Secondary
- - - Unimproved

0 2 4 KM
0 1 2 MI

MAUI

ULUPALAKUA —
PANIOLOS & HAWAIIAN CHAMPAGNE

Historic Ulupalakua Ranch, on Haleakala's southwest slope, encompasses 18,000 acres of the most scenic and pastoral country you are likely to see anywhere. Back in the 1850s and 1860s, James Makee (the erstwhile captain of a whaling ship) grew sugarcane here; he probably never dreamed that Ulupalakua would one day become one of the largest working cattle ranches on the island. And—though upcountry Maui turned out small quantities of wine for Hawaiian royalty even in the last century—Makee never could have envisioned Ulupalakua's producing Hawaii's first commercial grape wine with possibilities for eventual world-wide distribution.

A Lengthy but Scenic Drive

Ulupalakua (accent the first and last "u") is reached via Highway 37, east of Kahului. The drive takes a while; if you are coming from western Maui or Kihei/Wailea, plan on 1½ to 2 hours each way.

More than compensating for the length of the trip is the ever-changing scenery of oceanscapes, cane fields, the West Maui Mountains, Haleakala, colorful flower gardens, picturesque small farms and ranches, and—when you get to the Kula region—sweeping views of the southwest coast and the impressive (if forlorn) bulk of the uninhabited island of Kahoolawe.

Short minutes after you proceed southwest from Keokea, Ulupalakua's verdant grazing lands come into view up the slope of Haleakala to your left. This was once exclusively cattle land, but, in very recent years sheep (grown for meat, rather than wool) have been added to the scene. They, like the vineyards soon visible on your right, indicate that diversification has become not only advisable but essential to the area's cattle ranches.

Though the ranchlands continue up to about 6,500 feet, most of Ulupalakua's acreage extends down the southwest slope to sea level. As altitude decreases, rains become less frequent; grassy meadows and lush plantings gradually give way to scrubby growth, *kiawe* trees, and even cactus.

Paniolos—Old Maui on Horseback

If you keep an alert eye while driving through the cattle country, you may be treated to the sight of *paniolos* (Hawaiian cowboys) at work on the range. No place in upcountry Maui, or perhaps anywhere else, does the cowboy have a more distinguished tradition than at Ulupalakua.

More than 150 years ago, three Spanish-Mexican cowboys arrived in Hawaii, brought over from California by King Kamehameha III to control foraging cattle and begin raising them for beef. Islanders called them paniolos, the Hawaiian equivalent of *Españoles*. The Hawaiians themselves soon became paniolos, learning from the three "originals." Today, there are still a few paniolos working Ulupalakua whose fathers, grandfathers, and great-grandfathers rode the range many years before them.

Hawaii's "Napa Valley"?

The idea of a commercial vineyard at Ulupalakua was the concurrent dream of not one person but two: C. Pardee Erdman, owner of the ranch, and Emil Tedeschi, a young man who learned first hand about wine making while growing up in California's famed Napa Valley and was convinced that the climate and rich volcanic soil of upcountry Maui were exceptionally well suited to wine grapes. (To quote Tedeschi: "Napa Valley may be God's Country, but upcountry Maui is surely His vacation spot.")

In 1973, the two men went into partnership and began a venture that was to result, 10 years later, in 2,000 cases of Hawaii's first home-grown commercial wine. Four years of experimentation with 140 varieties of grapes were necessary in order to decide on the one best suited to the 2,000-foot elevation: Carnelian, a deep red hybrid of Cabernet Sauvignon, Grenache, and Carignane grapes.

The First Hawaiian Champagne

Having been advised that Carnelian could make not only red wine but a sparkling white, the partners opted for a champagne as their first commercial product (it has a faint blush of pink). On December 15, 1983, Tedeschi and Erdman hosted a formal celebration at the winery to celebrate Hawaii's entry into the world of grape wine.

Next, from the 1985 harvest, came two wines— Maui Blush and Maui Nouveau. Helping to ease the financial picture somewhat during the winery's struggling early years has been a popular and profitable pineapple wine, Maui Blanc.

In at least one respect, Tedeschi Winery is distinct from wineries on the mainland and elsewhere: It uses an old jail (1856) for a tasting room. Thick lava walls and shade from an ancient camphor tree keep it sufficiently cool for wine storage. (A trap door leads down to the dungeon, which is cooler yet.)

The tasting room is open from 9 A.M. to 5 P.M. daily; guided tours, offered from 9:30 A.M. to 2:30 P.M., allow a close-up look at the wine-making process.

...Maui's Quiet Upcountry

Lutheran minister who taught Chinese language and culture to the immigrants' children; the name of the church appears in Chinese characters over the doorway. If you bring a picnic, nearby Keokea Park is a pleasant place to stop.

Agricultural Experiment Stations

The University of Hawaii College of Tropical Agriculture operates two experiment stations on Haleakala's slopes: one of 20 acres in Kula and another, 34 acres, near Makawao. The Kula station is open to the public weekdays from 8 A.M. to 3 P.M. Its terraced plantings include new varieties of bedding plants, All-America award-winning roses, and a collection of ornamental proteas (see below). To get there, turn off Highway 37 on Copp Road, just south of Kula Elementary School, and follow the signs. The Makawao station specializes in macadamia nuts and avocados. Macadamia nut trees now grow on an increasing amount of the acreage formerly occupied by cane fields.

Kula Botanical Gardens

A visit to Kula Botanical Gardens (small admission fee) on Highway 377 will delight anyone who enjoys plants that grow in natural settings. Streams tumble down landscaped slopes on which flourish more than 700 types of plants, including orchids, ginger, protea, and koa and *kukui* trees. A bridge arches over a pond at the bottom of the property. From picnic tables and pergolas visitors can enjoy sweeping vistas.

THE EXOTIC PROTEA

Since the late 1970s, upcountry Maui, with its rich volcanic soil, has been the locale for one of Hawaii's burgeoning agricultural-floral pursuits—the growing of proteas. These astoundingly diverse South African natives belong to a plant family comprised of about 1,500 varieties—hence the name (say PRO-tee-uh), after the Greek god who was noted for his ability to change shape at will. (Macadamia nuts, another booming crop in Maui, are a protea relative.)

Protea blooms, with many colors to choose from, make superb cut flowers that hold their hue for weeks and retain their shape even after fading. Upcountry growers concentrate on varieties with large and exotic flowers (see the facing page for one example) which shippers then proceed to process and package.

Good places to see the flowers and learn how they are grown are Hawaii Protea Cooperative, Kula Lodge grounds; Kula Botanical Gardens, Highway 377; Kula Experimental Station, off Highway 37; Maui Enchanting Gardens, Highway 377; Maui Sunburst Farm, Copp Road; and Sunrise Protea Farm, Highway 377.

Auto Exploring

For the back-country explorer, an unimproved road climbs 10½ miles/17 km from Highway 377 to Polipoli State Park, a recreation area at the edge of a mixed conifer and hardwood forest. A car with 4-wheel drive is best for this trip. You can hike 1,000 feet to the top of Polipoli cinder cone, a Haleakala ridge vantage point from which you can see west Maui and the islands of Kahoolawe and Hawaii. The forest, with hiking trails, contains approximately 35,000 redwoods planted in 1927, some now 4 feet in diameter and 80 feet tall. A low-cost cabin in the recreation area can be reserved through the State Parks office in Wailuku.

Near the end of Highway 37, on a shoulder above the road, you'll find a Hawaiian sacred boulder to which offerings are sometimes still made. According to legend, the boulder is a man turned into lava by Pele, the volcano goddess, whom he had angered.

Highway 37 officially ends at parklike Ulupalakua Ranch (see page 109). If you keep going past Ulupalakua, you'll be on Highway 31 going south and then eastward along the coast as far as Hana. (This route is described on page 119.)

For a pleasant, little-traveled route from Kula back down to the Wailuku-Kahului area, turn west from Highway 37 onto Pulehu Road (about 3 miles/5 km south of Pukalani); it comes out near Puunene Mill. At the upper end of the road, lantana, morning glory, and California poppies bloom alongside grotesquely shaped cactus. Down near the coast, you drive through fields of waving cane.

Makawao. To see another part of Haleakala's slopes, take Highway 365 from Pukalani junction on Highway 37 to Makawao, the spiritual center of Maui cow country. This village once bustled with field hands and upcountry *paniolos* (Hawaiian cowboys), and experienced a boom when nearby Kokomo served as a Marine base during World War II. Although the town is quieter today, it is much more than just boarded-up doorways and dogs snoozing in the sunshine.

You can still find a hitching post for your horse and a watering hole for food and drink—Casanova's, Makawao Steak House, or Polli's. A "must" if you are visiting Maui in early July is Makawao's very popular 4th of July rodeo. Few rodeos anywhere can match it.

Galleries now jostle venerable western garb outlets along the main street, and boutiques compete for space with popular shops such as Komoda Store & Bakery and Kitada's Kau Kau Korner. Makawao's main street, Baldwin Avenue, meanders from the center of town to the former Baldwin estate, now home to Hui Noeau Visual Arts Center. A prestigious art show is held here every March and April.

From Makawao, Highway 39 leads uphill to Olinda, past Pookela Church, built of coral by missionaries in 1850, and Seabury Hall, an exclusive academy. Baldwin Avenue leads downhill to Paia.

Hard-riding paniolos, *born to the saddle and proud of their heritage, are an exhilarating part of the upcountry scene.*

Exotic protea flowers, *available in an astonishing variety of species, colors, and forms, are a Kula specialty (see feature on facing page).*

The quiet, eerie world *inside Haleakala Crater is a once-in-a-lifetime experience, even for seasoned hikers.*

HALEAKALA – HOUSE OF THE SUN

When you reach the overlook atop Haleakala, Maui's 10,023-foot volcano, you will have traveled the only paved road in the world that climbs to that height from sea level in just 40 miles/64 km. The views from the summit are spectacular. Off to the southeast, the tops of Hawaii's Mauna Loa and Mauna Kea float in a sea of clouds. As you turn clockwise, other islands and the rest of Maui come into view—unless clouds below blanket them. The air is bracing at this altitude, probably about 30 degrees cooler than in the valley. In winter you may encounter snow, and temperatures sometimes drop below freezing.

Haleakala National Park includes the summit and astonishing crater of this dormant volcano, which last erupted about 1790. The crater, low down on the southwest flank, is a vast depression carved out of Haleakala's dome by centuries of erosion. Later volcanic activity partially filled the crater with colorful cones and windswept banks of cinders. It measures 7½ miles/12 km long, 2½ miles/4 km wide, 21 miles/34 km around, 3,000 feet deep and covers 19 square miles/49 square km.

According to Hawaiian legend, from the crater rim the demigod Maui, son of Hina, snared the sun. He made it promise to go more slowly across the sky, giving crops more time to grow, fishermen more time to fish, and his mother's tapa cloth more time to dry. Now the sun is careful to travel slowly, and the great mountain is known as Haleakala—"The House of the Sun."

The total area of Haleakala National Park, 28,665 acres, includes an 8-mile/13-km-long strip that extends from the eastern edge of the crater down through Kipahulu Valley to the sea. The lower region of this addition, near the mouth of 'Ohe'o stream, is accessible, but the ecologically fragile virgin forest above 3,100 feet, now a biological preserve, is closed to entry.

The Drive to the Top

Before you start the 1½-hour drive from Kahului to the summit, phone 572-7749 for a taped report on current travel information and weather conditions. The message is updated during the day as conditions change. The crater's coloring shows up best in the afternoon, but clouds often roll in after 10 A.M.

Persons with high blood pressure or a heart condition are advised against driving alone, since the rarefied air can cause dizziness.

You climb first through cane fields and then through pineapple spreads into the Kula upland. From the turnoff onto Highway 378, a serpentine route leads up through pastures—and perhaps through a layer of clouds—into rocky wasteland.

Hosmer Grove. Just past the park entry sign, a paved side road leads in about ½ mile/1 km to Hosmer Grove, a small campground and picnic area ringed with North American pine, cedar, juniper, and spruce trees, deodar from India, cryptomeria from Japan, and eucalyptus from Australia. Trees are labeled along a short, level nature trail, and a sign at the start of the trail identifies birds commonly seen here. Open daily from 7:30 A.M. to 4 P.M., park headquarters lie at 7,030 feet, a mile past the entrance. Here you can pick up a park map-guide and other material and can get help in planning crater trips. An enclosure near the headquarters building permits a closeup look at Hawaii's state bird, the *nene*.

A SUNRISE TO REMEMBER

Few if any places in the world can match the sunrise view from atop Haleakala. Although it requires getting up at a wide-yawning hour (3 A.M. departure for the 2 to 3-hour drive from primary resort areas), the trip is an adventure—almost a pilgrimage—not soon to be forgotten. Recently arrived visitors from the mainland may not mind the early-hour departure too much, considering that Maui time is two or more hours earlier than the time back home.

You'll know that the long, winding drive through the dark was worth it when you look eastward to see the Big Island start to take shape as the murkiness of night gradually gives way to the first faint signs of daylight. When the huge, round, golden star of the show makes its dramatic appearance through the clouds, you will know, far more clearly than those who have missed the experience, what The House of the Sun is all about.

If you decide, before you leave home for Hawaii, that this is a trip you don't want to miss, bring along some winter clothing. The warmth of the resort areas is one thing; the cold, windy, sometimes freezing temperatures of Haleakala's 10,023-foot summit is something else. If you didn't pack warm clothes or can't borrow some, it's best to forgo this trip until another time.

Prefer Sunsets?

If early rising just isn't for you, climbing Haleakala later in the day to view the sunset is a good alternative. The view toward West Maui and Lanai, and the colors of sea and sky, are truly spectacular.

Whether you go for sunrise or sunset, phone 572-7749 for a weather report. Be sure your car has a full tank—no gas (or food) is available in the park.

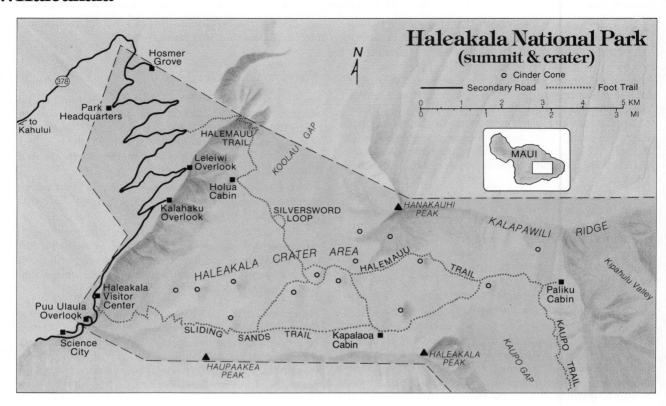

Some good view points. You can stretch your legs at several points along the 10¼ miles/16½ km between park headquarters and the top. At 8,000 feet, walk a mile on Halemauu Trail to the crater rim, where you can look across Koolau Gap, down Keanae Valley, and ahead to the trail zigzagging down the crater wall. There's a similar view at 8,800 feet from Leleiwi Overlook, just a 350-yard walk from the road. Here, in late afternoon, you may see the "Spectre of the Brocken"—your shadow against the clouds, encircled by a rainbow.

Just above, a road goes to Kalahaku Overlook, where you'll find some of Haleakala's famous silverswords and exhibits relating to the crater's cones and lava flows. The silversword, a relative of the sunflower, grows from 4 to 20 years as a rounded mass of stiletto-shaped leaves before sending up a flower stalk as tall as 9 feet with 100 or more purplish blossoms. Blooms develop from May through October. The plant flowers only once and then dies—but not before it sends out seeds to start new silverswords. Except for a few plants on the Big Island, this species of silversword is unique to its isolated habitat on Maui. Another variety grows in very wet areas in the West Maui Mountains.

When You Reach the Summit

Two visitor shelters sit atop the mountain: the Haleakala Visitor Center, on the rim at 9,745 feet, and Puu Ulaula Visitor Center, ½ mile/1 km farther up on Red Hill, the actual summit.

Exhibits at Haleakala Visitor Center explain the crater's features and formation. From here you look down on slopes of cinder blown by the easterly trade winds against the rocks of the original rim. Koolau Gap on the north and Kaupo Gap on the south cut the rim. Beyond Koolau, Hanakauhi's peak often protrudes from a blanket of clouds. On the opposite rim, Haleakala peak stands out like a fortress above Kaupo Gap. Symmetrical cones of varied hues look like small mounds of sand in the crater, but each is several hundred feet high. The largest, Puu o Maui, rises 615 feet from the crater floor. In remarkable contrast to the naked summit slopes are the meadow and stand of trees at the crater's east end, 7½ miles/12 km away, where the annual rainfall is 250 inches.

From Haleakala Visitor Center, a trail climbs 380 yards to White Hill, past ruins of stone wind barriers built by the Hawaiians for sleeping enclosures. The hill is formed of andesite, lighter in color than most Hawaiian lava. Walk a short distance down Sliding Sands Trail to get the feel of the crater; but remember, at this altitude it's an exhausting climb back up.

From Puu Ulaula Visitor Center at the summit, you have a 360-degree panorama of the crater and, on a clear day, of west Maui and the islands of Hawaii, Lanai, Molokai, and Oahu. You can continue for a mile beyond the park, along dead-end Skyline Drive through "Science City," with its domes and antennae for communications and space study. Although the facilities are not open to the public, you'll be rewarded with a precipitous view down to the Lualailua Hills and the south coast desert.

INTO THE CRATER'S DEPTHS

To truly claim you saw Haleakala crater, you should go down inside. The Park Service maintains 30 miles/ 48 km of well-marked trails and three rustic cabins (see below).

Two main trails, Halemauu and Sliding Sands, lead down into and across the crater. They meet near Paliku Cabin at the east end. Sliding Sands Trail takes you about 6 miles/9½ km down along the south face to Kapalaoa Cabin and then northeast 4 miles/6½ km to Paliku Cabin. On Halemauu Trail, you descend the west wall to Holua Cabin, a distance of 4 miles/6½ km, and then go 6 miles/9½ km farther along the center of the sloping crater floor. Short trails connect the two routes.

In half a day, you can make a round trip on Halemauu Trail as far as Holua Cabin. For a long day's hike (12 miles/19 km) or horseback ride, go down Sliding Sands Trail (avoid this steep trail as a way out), cross the floor on Ka Moa O Pele Trail, and climb out on Halemauu Trail—but unless you're willing to hike extra miles up the road, drive two cars to the park and leave one at the start of each trail. For a good overnight trip with no car problem, take Halemauu Trail all the way to Kapalaoa Cabin one day and return the next. You'll cover about 8 miles/13 km each way.

Crater-explorers should carry water for trail use (cabins have a limited water supply), a light raincoat, sun hat, suntan lotion, chapstick, and a light jacket or sweater. Be sure you have a good pair of hiking shoes, well broken in. And—perhaps most important of all— make sure you are in good physical condition for hiking.

Down in the weird environment of the crater, you'll see sandalwood trees; lichen, or Hawaiian Snow, the first plant to appear after a lava flow in higher altitudes; mountain *pili*, distinct from the lowland variety once used for grass houses; and volcanic dikes, remnants of an ancient divide that separated the heads of Keanae and Kaupo valleys.

North of Kapalaoa Cabin is Bubble Cave, formed when molten lava was forced up by gases; the lava stayed in that position until it cooled and later was opened when part of the top collapsed.

At rainy Paliku, large native trees (*ohia lehua, kolea, olapa*), tall grass, and ferns create a haven in the barren waste. Here you occasionally will see the *nene* (Hawaii's state bird).

On Halemauu Trail you pass Bottomless Pit, an old spatter vent, which looks like a 10-foot-wide well. The bottom is 65 feet down—so keep away from the crumbly edges. Nearby are Pele's Paint Pot, a colorful pass between cinder cones, and, on a cross trail, Pele's Pig Pen, a half-buried spatter vent. Near Holua Cabin you'll find the Silversword Loop Trail.

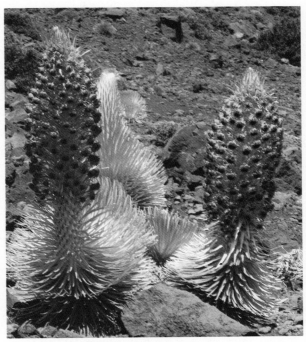

Silversword *plant blooms just once, then dies. The Silversword Loop, southeast of Holua Cabin, leads to a large concentration of them.*

Kapalaoa, Paliku, and Holua cabins. Each cabin accommodates 12 persons. Cabins have bunks, firewood cookstoves, and eating and cooking utensils. Cabin users must bring their own sleeping bags and light source. Reservations for cabins must be made by mail at least 90 days in advance and are limited to three nights per month with only two consecutive nights in any one cabin. Write Haleakala National Park, Box 369, Makawao, HI 96768, giving your social security number, the exact days, the number in your party, and which cabins you wish to use.

Campsites. Holua and Paliku also have camping sites. A permit is required (obtainable at park headquarters); length-of-stay limits are the same as for the cabins. No open fires are allowed, and campers should have a warm sleeping bag and tent with rain fly for cold or wet weather. Camping groups are limited to 15 people.

Guided horseback rides. Trail rides vary from a 2-hour trip to all-day excursions. For information, see page 121.

HANA – A VERY SPECIAL EXPERIENCE

The Maui visitor who leaves without dropping in on "heavenly Hana" misses an opportunity to see old Hawaii at its best. More—much more—than the little settlement usually known as Hana town, the "real" Hana ranges far up Haleakala's lush eastern slopes and stretches for miles along the ocean, roughly from Keanae to Kaupo (the inexactness of its extremities only adds to the Hana mystique).

You can drive the Hana Highway from Kahului to Hana town in about 2½ hours, but you really should allow more time to enjoy the magnificent scenery, perhaps stop for a picnic, swim in a freshwater pool, or just relax awhile in one of the pleasant wayside parks you'll find along the route.

Your trip begins on a fast, broad highway through cane fields. Just before you reach Lower Paia, you'll find H. A. Baldwin Park, a popular camping, swimming, and surfing spot. Next to it, Rin Zai Zen Buddhist Mission is notable for its graveyard with Okinawan-style family mausoleums resembling miniature houses. The old plantation town of Lower Paia has the look of the Old West, with many restored store fronts, restaurants, and shops. Right in town is handsome Manto Kuji Soto Buddhist Temple. The graveyard, above a sandy cove, has markers carved with Japanese characters.

Paia is the last stop for gas until you reach Hana. It's also a popular place to pick up box lunches for the trip; try Picnics, at 30 Baldwin Avenue.

A couple of miles east of town lies Hookipa Beach Park, a dangerous place to swim but the favorite haunt of surfers and windsurfers. An annual windsurfing competition is held here in October.

Once you hit the mile 19 marker, the road begins its tortuous route along ferny, pandanus-laden cliffs that drop abruptly into the pounding surf. The road twists in and out of gulches, many hung with sparkling waterfalls. Along the roadside is a jungle of breadfruit, koa, *kukui*, *'ohi'a*, and paperbark trees interspersed with groves of bamboo, tangled *hau* and guava, giant *a'pe* leaves, wild ginger, and even some rubber trees.

The road follows sections of open ditch—part of the system that takes water from these wet slopes to central Maui's farming areas. In this part of the island, people still live off the land and sea and respect the legends breathed by every cliff and hollow. The few villages are merely a sprinkling of houses and a general store; occasionally you'll spot old schools and churches. Just downhill from the highway at Huelo, shortly before you come to Kailua settlement, is Kualauapueo Church, built of stone in 1853.

Since the narrow road bridges streams and waterfalls in almost every gulch, you'll often be tempted to stop and look at roadside plantings or admire a distant view. (In any case, if traffic is stacked up behind you, it's a good idea to find a safe place and pull over until it passes.) It's not always easy, though, to find a safe place to pull off the winding road. But three wayside parks within a few miles of one another are especially inviting:

Kaumahina State Park. About 25 miles/36 km from Kahului, a shady park sits atop a cliff overlooking Honomanu Gulch and the Keanae Peninsula just beyond. Far below you can see Honomanu Bay's black sand beach, where natives fish and swim. Picnic tables and pavilions are spread over the neatly landscaped slopes.

Keanae Valley Lookout. A great two-way view awaits you at the lookout—down over Wailua to the sea, which breaks against Keanae Peninsula in the distance, and up through Keanae Valley to Koolau Gap.

Puaakaa State Park. Between the Wailua and Nahiku turnoffs lies a small park with picnic tables, trails, and a series of fern-banked waterfalls where you can enjoy a refreshing dip. Native plants are marked.

Spur Roads to Keanae, Wailua, Nahiku

From several high points along the road, you look down on small, quiet villages. The little clusters of houses, church steeples, banana groves, and taro patches resemble South Seas scenes.

Keanae. Take the side road down onto Keanae Peninsula, past the pebbly cove where villagers launch their skiffs. You may see someone pounding taro in the yards of the old wooden houses. Keanae's refurbished coral stone church is more than 100 years old. The surf pummels Keanae's lava shore, causing the jagged rocks to glisten from their constant washing. On a clear day, Haleakala looms up to the south.

Keanae Arboretum, above the peninsula, is planted with native Hawaiian and other plants, including 60 vari-

---

KAHOOLAWE

Off Maui's southwest corner lies the barren island of Kahoolawe, the only one of the state's eight major islands that is uninhabited. Kahoolawe has had a varied history, first as a fishing colony, later as a penal colony, and then as grazing land. In 1941, the U.S. Navy took over the 45-square-mile/115-square-km island and used it as a site for bombing exercises.

For nearly 50 years, residents of Maui and Lanai watched the nighttime aerial assaults with growing dismay. Hawaiian natives, who regarded the island as sacred, and environmentalists, who sought to preserve its archeological ruins, were finally rewarded when President George Bush ordered bombing stopped in 1990. The island was returned to the Hawaiian people in 1994, and will be used for religious rites.

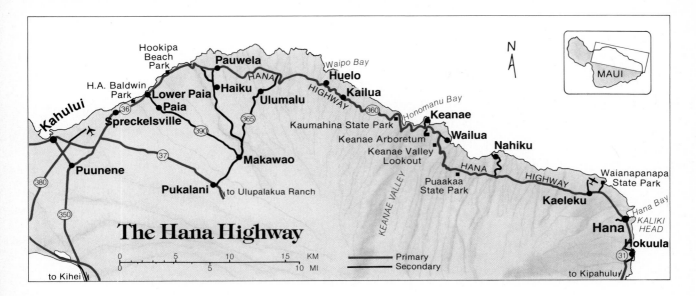

The Hana Highway

eties of wetland taro growing on reconstructed old taro patches.

Wailua. The spur road down to Wailua village passes churches and houses fronted with rows of ti and crotons and ends above a narrow cove at the mouth of the stream. Here villagers put out in fishing boats and children body-surf with homemade boards in the late afternoon while their elders relax on the porches and read—or just sit.

Quaint St. Gabriel's Church, with its painted trim of red hearts, is known as the Miracle Church. It is said that in 1860, when its builders set out to dive for coral and sand, they found these building materials heaped on shore by the waves. Some of the church's graveyard markers have photographs, and most are decorated—usually with artificial flowers in jars of water.

Take the road inland past Wailua's other row of houses for a close look at the taro and bananas grown for Maui and Honolulu markets. The geometrically terraced plots, set in a gently rising valley guarded by mountain walls, are as neat as a memorial park. Irrigation water trickles downhill from one patch to another in the old Hawaiian manner.

Nahiku. A 3-mile/5-km spur road takes you down through Nahiku village, now mostly covered by forest. You pass a few scattered houses, a school, and two churches, ending at the landing used at the turn of the century to unload equipment for building irrigation tunnels through the mountains. Trees here have been left from Nahiku's rubber plantation of more than 75 years ago. You can try out two good swimming holes: one reached by a path from the turn-around at the landing, the other about 400 feet from the wooden bridge and on the right after you pass the churches.

The road from Nahiku to Hana crosses much grazing land. Hana Airport is reached by a turnoff just before you get to the sign directing you to Waianapanapa State Park.

Waianapanapa State Park

Three miles from Hana town, a side road leads to Waia-napanapa State Park. Here, a footpath through lush tropical plantings takes you to Waianapanapa and Waiomao caves, two lava tubes near the sea that are filled with water and said to be connected. Waianapanapa Cave has a much-told legend: a Hawaiian princess, escaping from a jealous husband, hid in the underground cavern but, after being discovered by the husband, was slain. The slaying occurred in April, and Hawaiians tell you that the water still runs red with her blood each spring.

Certainly Waianapanapa Cave is an eerie place to swim, but some daring souls take a flashlight and brave the cold water. It's possible to swim underwater, past a point where the roof arches down, into another chamber; there a ledge is said to be the spot where the princess hid.

Out on a point, you'll see a natural rock arch and blowhole; on the grassy ledge where the sea gurgles beneath your feet, three old burial grounds are still in use. Below, Honokalani black sand beach fringes Pailoa Bay. Here you can scout for beach glass or swim when the bay is calm.

The trail to the south of the black sand beach follows the jagged lava coastline to Hana for about 3 miles/5 km. Now used primarily by fishers, the trail, called the King's Highway, was part of the original ancient highway built around east Maui by Chief Piilani before his death about 1527. Smooth steppingstones set into the rough lava and cinders have been washed away in places by high surf. Walking time to Hana town is about 1½ to 2 hours.

The park has inexpensive, furnished cabins available by reservation (see page 121).

Hana Town

Quiet Hana town is inhabited mostly by part Hawaiians, though more and more former mainlanders now make

Keanae Peninsula's *taro fields and quiet way of life represent the Hawaii of bygone years. The area can be explored on a short side trip from Hana Highway.*

their home here. The taro patches, banana clumps, and bits of stone terraces in the nearby gulches provide evidence of the Polynesians who once had a large settlement here. Subsequent sugar, pineapple, and rubber tree plantations were not very successful and finally sold. Since 1944, the fields have been gradually converted to grazing land for several thousand white-faced Hereford beef cattle.

Helani Gardens, a 72-acre commercial nursery, offers five acres of tropical greenery, fishponds, bridges, and a riverside picnic pavilion. Open daily, there is a small admission charge.

Lunch at the quiet and charming Hotel Hana-Maui is a pleasant experience and offers the day-trip visitor a welcome break after the winding drive from Kahului. The hotel, located just up from Hana Bay, has lovely tropical plantings in extensive gardens. Don't plan to stay overnight unless you have advance reservations.

Drive the mile to the top of Lyons Hill (Puu o Kahaula). On this cinder cone above town, a stone cross on a torch-lit platform serves as a memorial to Paul Fagan, who founded the ranch and hotel. There's a nice view down over the rolling hills to Hana Bay.

One of Hana's few modern touches is a compact shopping center. Sadly, the venerable Hasegawa General Store, the subject of a once-popular song, burned down in 1990, but will be rebuilt. Meanwhile, some of their "almost everything" contents are available in the renovated theater building on the main street. Hale Waiwai O Hana, the museum at Hana Cultural Center, is a treasure trove of old photographs and artifacts. The museum (small fee) is open daily except Sunday. Also in Hana are a fascinating Buddhist temple, the century-old Wananalua Church (Sunday services in both Hawaiian and English), and an impressive Catholic church.

Kauiki Head, a fortresslike cliff, guards Hana Bay. Here the armies of Kamehameha and the king of Maui tangled with slingshots. You can walk down the south side of Kauiki Head to an old cemetery and a red cinder beach, popularly called Red Sands Beach.

At the foot of Keawa Street, on the bay, is a place known locally as Punahoa. Here, many little springs of very cold fresh water gush out of the sand when the tide is low. You can feel them in the water even at high tide if your foot happens to land on one.

From Hana pier, you can walk along the base of the cliff to a plaque that marks the birthplace of Kamehameha's favorite wife, Kaahumanu, in a cave above.

Hana Ranch Restaurant and a snack shop on the bay are the only places besides the hotel to eat in Hana.

Hana to Kipahulu

Beyond Hana, Highway 31 continues for 10 miles/16 km to Kipahulu, in Haleakala National Park. Near Hana, a side road loops down to Hamoa Beach (facilities are for hotel guests only). Currents can be treacherous. At the Hana end of the loop, you pass Pele's Hill (Ka Iwi O Pele), where the fire goddess is said to have left her bones when she assumed a new body to go to the Big Island.

Where the road turns into Wailua Gulch, two impressive waterfalls topple from Haleakala's slopes. The concrete cross standing above the road is a memorial to Helio, a Hawaiian Catholic who converted hundreds to his faith during the 1840s. South of the falls, gnarled *kukui* trees on the mountainside are the remains of a grove. A few more turns bring you to the "Virgin by the Roadside," a shrine containing an Italian marble statue. Every day the statue is draped with leis, and once a year representatives from all of Hana's Catholic churches make a pilgrimage.

At 'Ohe'o Gulch (often called—erroneously—Seven Pools) you're in the national park. Look upstream and downstream from the bridge to see the pools; 24 of them topple into one another and finally flow into the sea. A path descends the south bank to the most accessible swimming and picnicking spots. On the north bank, about 600 yards above the highway is a restored taro farm, funded by the National Park Service and maintained by the Hana Cultural Center. Ranger-led walks and hikes are conducted all year.

The grave of famed aviator Charles A. Lindbergh can be reached by turning left, between two posts, about 350 yards before you would come to the gates of Kipahulu Ranch headquarters. Drive (slowly) along a bumpy gravel road for ¼ mile to Palapala Hoomau Church, where a clifftop graveyard looks down to a magnificent view of the sea.

Driving the Southern Coast

The scenic but sometimes rugged drive beyond Kipahulu should only be attempted in a 4-wheel-drive vehicle. And, even then, it can be a harrowing experience—narrow track, potholes, and lack of guard rails. Most rental car contracts ban travel on the road because of washouts.

Kipahulu to Kaupo. A one-lane gravel road links these two towns; you won't see pavement again for about 8 miles/13 km. The road hugs the edge of rocky cliffs above the water and dips straight into gulches. If you meet a car, one of you may have to back up to find a safe shoulder.

This country is drier than the Hana area, with open pastures divided by lichen-covered stone walls and abundant *hau* and koa trees. The road edges so close to Lelekea Bay that a heavy sea splashes spray right into your car. You'll see a few outrigger canoes on the rocky beach. A switchback trail visible on the hillside just south is the remains of the old King's Highway.

Kaupo's recently restored Huialoha Church (1859) and tidy graveyard perch on a grassy peninsula, an inviting place to picnic or camp. Nearby, ruins of a mission school and a heiau on the hill above the road invite exploration. A larger temple, Loaloa (circa 1730), lies at the start of Kaupo Gap Trail, behind the school off the spur road to Kaupo Ranch headquarters.

Whether or not you need to buy something, a stop at Kaupo Store is rewarding. Notice the hitching rail for horses. The store doubles as a post office—one in which all mail goes into one box and people hunt for their own.

Kaupo to Ulupalakua Ranch. More exciting views of the coastline and distant Hawaii island will greet you as you dip down to the sea at old Nuu Landing, where you'll find village ruins and a salt pond.

The road from here to Ulupalakua is paved and slightly wider. Soon after passing Nuu Landing, you cross a dry river bed, gutted by centuries of flash floods. Walking up to a pool at the head of the gulch, you'll discover caves and petroglyphs.

The gradual climb toward Kanaio carries you through the bizarre landscape of a Hawaiian dryland forest, more pastures, fields of yellow poppies, old lava flows, and cinder cones. About 5 miles/8 km farther stands the old Kahikinui ranch house. Nearby, below the road, you'll see the crumbling stone foundation of Santa Ynez Church, worshipping place of some Hawaiian Catholics whose arrest in the 1830s contributed to the subsequent granting of religious freedom.

The blue sea sparkles below as you drive along at 1,500 feet. Offshore you'll see tiny Molokini Island, to some Hawaiians a still-revered home of ancestral spirits, and Kahoolawe, the former military target island. Along the road are entries to a few grueling jeep trails; two link up with a footpath along the ocean that takes you west to La Perouse Bay.

Between Kanaio and Ulupalakua you look down on the surprisingly fresh-looking lava from Haleakala's last eruption, some 200 years ago. Puu Olai cinder cone, a Makena landmark, juts into the sea.

Maui's geography and close proximity to neighboring islands make it a land of recreational opportunity: from the undulating coastline to the desolate Haleakala moonscape, the Valley Isle's variety offers the spice of outdoor life. Several miles from its shores lie Molokai, Lanai, Kahoolawe, and exposed Molokini Crater, greatly expanding flightseeing and boating destinations.

For further details on any activity listed below, consult your travel agent, hotel activities desk, or the Maui Visitors Bureau, Box 1738, Kahului, HI 96732; 871-8691. The local area code is 808.

Flightseeing. A great way to gain an overview of the state's second largest island and the world's largest dormant volcano, crater-only and circle-island flights are available through the companies listed below. Most helicopter and fixed-wing plane flights are based at the Kahului Airport. Check with your hotel activities desk.

Helicopters. AlexAir, Blue Hawaiian, Cardinal, Hawaii, Kenai, Papillon, Sunset.

Planes. Kihele Maui Tours, Pacific Air, Paragon.

Golf. Maui and golf are almost synonymous. Three major golf tournaments are televised to mainland audiences every year. Most golf courses flank the western shore, so the Pacific figures prominently as a water hazard, if not a scenic distraction, on many holes. All courses listed are open to the public and are 18 holes, unless otherwise noted. Yardages are from regular tees.

Public courses. Pukalani Golf Club, Pukalani, 572-1314, par 72, 6,494 yards; Sandalwood Golf Course, Wailuku, 242-7090, par 72, 5,918 yards; Silversword, Kihei, 874-0777, par 71, 6,400 yards; Waiehu Golf Course, Wailuku, 244-5934, par 72, 6,330 yards.

Resort courses. Kapalua Golf Club, Kapalua: Bay Course, 669-8044, par 72, 6,151 yards, Village Course, 669-4871, par 72, 5,981 yards, Plantation Course, 669-8877, par 73, 6,547 yards; Kaanapali Golf Courses, Kaanapali, 661-3691: North Course, par 72, 6,305 yards, South Course, par 72, 6,250 yards; Wailea Golf Club, Wailea, 879-2966: Blue Course, par 72, 6,152 yards, Gold Course, par 72, 6,304 yards, Emerald Course, par 72, 6,825 yards; Makena Golf Club, Makena, 879-3344, par 72, 6,210 yards (another course coming soon); Waikapu Valley Country Club, Wailuku (private club, open to Four Seasons and Grand Hyatt guests only), par 72, 6,197 yards; Maui Country Club, Paia (private course, open to the public on Monday), 877-7893, 9 holes, par 37, 3,274 yards.

Tennis. More than three dozen hotels and condominiums have tennis courts. Guests usually play free; many courts are available to visitors. Check with your hotel activities desk. Major centers offer top facilities, lessons, and pro shops.

Courts. Wailea Tennis Club, 11 hard courts and 3 grass courts (3 lighted); Royal Lahaina Tennis Ranch, 11 courts (6 lighted); Kapalua Tennis Gardens, 10 courts (4 lighted);

Makena Tennis Club, Maui Prince Hotel, 6 courts; Hyatt Regency Maui, 6 courts; Maui Marriott Resort, 5 courts (3 lighted); Sheraton Maui, 3 courts (all lighted).

Swimming. Swimming is safe at the beaches listed below, but always check posted warnings and stay alert for strong tides or high winter surf.

Kapalua to Lahaina area: Kapalua Beach, Napili Bay, Keonenui Beach, Kahana Beach, Honokowai Beach Park, Kaanapali Beach, Hanakaoo Beach, Wahikuli State Wayside Park, Puamana Beach Park, Launiupoko State Wayside Park (includes a man-made ocean pool), Kulanaokalai Beach, Awalua Beach.

Kihei to Makena: Mai Poina Oe Iau Beach Park, Kalepolepo Beach, Kamaole beach parks, Keawakapu Beach Park, Mokapu Beach Park, Ulua Beach Park, Poolenalena Beach, Maluaka Beach, Oneuli Beach, Puuolai Beach, Makena Beach.

Central Maui: Waihee Beach Park (Wailuku).

East Maui: Hamoa Beach (Hana).

Surfing. Winter brings big waves to Maui's north shore; summer finds swells to the south. Activity centers in resort areas have surfing instruction and board rentals; check with your hotel or condominium front desk for information. The beaches below are some of the best for board surfing; bodysurfers also favor Mokuleia Beach, Kulanaokalai Beach, Kamaole beach parks, Keawakapu Beach, Wailea Beach, Polo Beach, and Hamoa Beach.

Northwest: Honolua Bay, D. T. Fleming Beach Park, Napili Bay, Hanakaoo Beach, Lahaina Beach, Puamana Beach Park, Launiupoko State Wayside Park, Awalua Beach, Olowalu Beach, Ukumehame Beach Park.

Southwest: Maalaea Beach, Kalama Beach Park, Mokapu Beach Park.

Central: Hookipa Beach Park, Hamakua Poko Papa, Lower Paia Park, H. A. Baldwin Park, Kahului Harbor.

Windsurfing. Maui attracts windsurfing champions from around the world as well as aficionados who want to challenge the big winds and waves at Hookipa Beach Park near Paia. Kahului's Kanaha Beach Park also provides good board sailing.

Many companies offer instruction and equipment for those who want to board sail. Among them are Hunt Maui in Paia; Maui Windsurf Co., Maui Windsurfari, Maui Magic Windsurfing Schools, and Hawaiian Island Windsurfing in Kahului; and Kaanapali Windsurfing School in Kaanapali.

Snorkeling and diving. Molokini Crater, just offshore, is very popular with snorkelers and divers. Go early with Blue Water Rafting, 879-7238, Kihei, or Trilogy Excursions, 661-4743, Maalaea Harbor. Other good snorkeling spots are Honolua Bay, Napili Bay, Black Rock at Kaanapali, and Puu Olai at Makena. In Lahaina, Dive Maui and Lahaina Divers are among companies offering equipment for certified divers.

Diving spots. Kaehu Beach, Waihee Beach Park, Honolua and Makuleia bays (protected by Marine Life Conservation District status—good diving, but removal of marine organisms is prohibited), Oneloa Beach, Kapalua Beach, Keonenui Beach, Honokowai Beach Park, Hanakaoo Beach, Wahikuli State Wayside Park, Lahaina Beach, Papalaua State Wayside Park, McGregor Point, Ulua Beach, Wailea Beach, Polo Beach, Ahihi-Kinau Natural Area Reserve, Hana Beach Park, Molokini Island.

Boating activities and cruises. Maui's heyday as an international port of call ended more than a century ago, but the Valley Isle still boasts a lot of aquatic adventure. Many combinations of water craft destinations and activities are available, as diverse as windsurfing clinics and inter-island outings on giant trimarans. Larger vessels offer trips ranging from 2 hours to a full day, and include fishing, swimming, skin and scuba diving, and meals. Sunset or dinner cruises, whale watching "in season" (during winter), excursions to neighbor islands, and charters are other options.

The numbers of companies and choices are too vast to cover thoroughly here; specific information can be obtained from hotel activity centers, the Yellow Pages (see "Boating Instruction" and "Boats-Charter"), and local travel publications, particularly near the major harbors of Lahaina, Kaanapali, Maalaea, and Kihei.

Fishing. Contact the Department of Land and Natural Resources (see address in next column) for spearfishing regulations and freshwater licensing and limits; there are no saltwater fishing licenses needed, or limits. For chartered fishing boats, check the Yellow Pages under "Fishing Parties." Based principally at Lahaina and Maalaea, these boats usually make ½-day to full-day trips.

Fishing locations. Channel waters between Maui, Kahoolawe, Lanai, and Molokai are good for trolling or bottom-fishing. Spots along much of Maui's shores provide fine shorefishing; among the most promising sites are Kahului Harbor, Paukukalo Beach, Waiehu Beach Park, Waihee Beach Park, the Kulanaokalai-Launiupoko area, Nuu Bay, Seven Pools Park, Waianapanapa State Park, and Hookipa Beach Park.

For spearing octopuses or small fish, try the waters off Lahaina, Makena, the Waiehu-Waihee area, Spreckelsville, and around Hana. Pier fishing is possible in Kahului, Hana, and Maalaea bays. *Hahalalu* (young bigeye scad) can be caught in late summer from harbor piers and breakwaters.

Cycling. The summit of dormant Haleakala is a popular place to start a run. Several companies offer guided rides from the chilly caldera down to the balmy seaside. Prices include specially equipped cycles, helmets and other gear, a meal along the way, and transportation to and from your hotel. Cruiser Bob's, 667-7717, the pioneer, offers sunrise, sunset, and afternoon rides. He's now joined by Maui Mountain Cruisers, 572-0195, Maui Downhill

Bicycle Safaris, 871-2155, and Chris' Bike Adventures, 877-8000.

Several companies rent bikes for those who want to explore the island on their own, including A & B Moped Rentals and Fun Bike Rentals in Lahaina and The Island Biker in Kahului.

Most of Maui's roads are narrow and traffic is heavy. Cycling is good around resort areas; the coastline north and south of Lahaina is best. Beyond Kapalua you'll happen upon secluded beaches and lovely panoramas of mountains and ocean.

A 2½-mile/4-km bikeway parallels the highway from the Lahainaluna Road intersection to Lahaina Civic Center (across the highway from Wahikuli State Wayside Park). Around Lahaina, this may be your safest option.

Horseback riding. The stables listed below offer rides ranging from Haleakala's slopes and crater to the Hana coast to the West Maui Mountains. Trips are geared to beginners and intermediates. Most stables won't accept children under 12 (a few have a minimum age of 18).

Stables. Adventures on Horseback, Makawao, 242-7445, 5-hour ride near Maui's north coast around Kaiku; Hana Ranch Stables, Hana, 248-8211, 1 or 2-hour rides on the Hana coast; Makena Stables, Makena, 879-0244, ½-day rides across lava fields and onto the Ulupalakua Ranch lands; Pony Express Tours, Kula, 667-2200, introductory rides near stable and ½-day and day rides in Haleakala National Park; Rainbow Ranch, Lahaina, 669-4991, trails through a pineapple plantation and into the foothills of the West Maui Mountains; Thompson Ranch Riding Stables, Kula, 878-1910, short rides around a cattle ranch on Haleakala's southwest flank, longer expeditions into the crater.

Hiking, camping, mountain tours. For maps, guides, and other information, contact Hawaiian Geographic Society, P.O. Box 1698, Honolulu, HI 96806; Hawaii Trail and Mountain Club, Box 2238, Honolulu, HI 96814; Hawaii Sierra Club, Box 11070, Honolulu, HI 96828; Department of Land and Natural Resources, Division of Forestry and Wildlife, 54 South High Street, Wailuku, HI 96793.

Camping information. For campsite specifics and permits, including the Polipoli Spring State Recreation Area and Waianapanapa State Park, contact the State Parks Division, Box 1049, Wailuku, Maui, HI 96793. For information on Haleakala National Park, write to Box 537, Makawao, Maui, HI 96768. A private camp with six cabins on a beach south of Lahaina is operated by Camp PECUSA (Protestant Episcopalian Camps, USA). For details, write to Holy Innocents Church, Box 606, Lahaina, Maui, HI 96761.

Mountain touring. Hike Maui, 879-5270, has day hikes focusing on Maui's history, geology, flora, and fauna. An astronomer leads Astronomy Tours Hawaii trips to Haleakala's summit to view the sunset and see the stars. Reserve at 667-9080. A meal is included in the price of both tours.

MOLOKAI

• TOURISM IS ASTIR IN OLD HAWAII'S SLEEPY OUTPOST •

Though sleepy little Molokai (population about 6,500) has long been a popular weekend destination for residents of Honolulu (only 26 miles/42 km away), not until recent years have other travelers been going out of their way to visit this lovely place, proudly referred to by its people as the "Friendly Isle."

Hawaii's fifth largest island, Molokai (pronounced moh-loh-kah-ee) is shoe-shaped, long (37 miles/59 km), and narrow (10 miles/16 km). It was formed by two major volcanic domes. The western end of the island, first to emerge, is now a rolling tableland that rises to only 1,381 feet. The jagged mountains of the northeast, topped by 4,970-foot Kamakou, were formed later by the East Molokai volcano. Kalaupapa, the little tongue of land that juts out from the north coast almost like an afterthought, was created by Kauhako volcano.

Slow-paced Tourism

Molokai's first large, master-planned resort area opened on the island's west shore in 1977. Despite its lovely setting and an 18-hole golf course that stacks up with Hawaii's best, Kaluakoi Resort has been slow to develop. Long-range plans call for another hotel, additional condominiums, and two more golf courses.

Molokai has more full-blooded Hawaiians than any island except Niihau. They're proud of their culture and slow to change their rural lifestyle. But with pineapple operations dwindling, Molokai's future appears to be tied to an approach that balances ranching and diversified agriculture with a gradual growth in tourism. The island's first macadamia nut farm and a new coffee plantation may be signs of that change.

Getting the Most from Your Visit

Unlike the large tourist meccas, Molokai won't "come to you"—you'll have to meet it on its own terms. You can bustle about or just do nothing; the mood and attitude are most decidedly "no push."

Spectacular scenery and fascinating historic sites are everywhere and within short driving distances. The south shore east of Kaunakakai, only a few hours driving on good roads from the airport or your hotel base, offers an excellent introduction to the feel of the island, as do western Molokai and the hill country northwest of Kaunakakai. The trip to Kalaupapa, possible by air, on foot, or by mule (see page 124), is an experience not to be missed.

The *pali*—the northern coast from Kalaupapa eastward to the Halawa Valley—has no roads, but you can charter a helicopter (from Honolulu or Maui), a small plane, or a boat to see this spectacular region of cliffs, waterfalls, and valleys.

Despite all its beauty and charm—and Molokai takes a back seat to none of the other islands in these and other natural attributes—Molokai is nonetheless not for everybody. If you thrive on a whirl of activities, and prefer restaurant-hopping and night life to sitting around quietly in the evenings, one of the bigger islands might be more to your liking.

But if you appreciate a quiet place, find fascination in history and old legends, don't mind roughing it a bit on occasion, and (most of all) can understand and identify with people who still value their generations-old way of life above all else—then, Molokai offers an experience you will never forget.

Kalaupapa peninsula

THE ESSENTIALS

Molokai is connected to Maui and Oahu by Air Molokai and Aloha IslandAir. Maui-based Paragon Air offers sightseeing tours from both Kahului and west Maui. The Lahaina-Molokai ferry, Maui Princess, departs Lahaina at 7 A.M. and returns from Kaunakakai at 4 P.M.

Getting Around

You can capture the flavor of Molokai in a day if you're content just to visit the celebrated places—Halawa Valley and the lookouts over Kalaupapa. But to explore and "get away from it all," the best reason for going to Molokai, you'll want more time.

You won't need to rent a 4-wheel-drive car to get around the island's few highways, though jeep tours are offered by Molokai Off-Road Tours. From Hoolehua Airport, driving time to Kaluakoi Resort is 25 minutes; it's 15 minutes to the town of Kaunakakoi. Gray Line runs an airline shuttle service. Taxis and limousines offer other choices.

Car rental. Avis, Budget, and Dollar car rental companies have offices at the airport. Reservations are recommended.

Special tours. Roberts Hawaii and Friendly Island Tours offer half and full-day van trips. Damien Tours operates ground tours of Kalaupapa (see below). Molokai Wagon Ride's offbeat tour includes a beach picnic.

Where to Stay

Lodging on Molokai is limited to one casual resort and two small hotels: Kaluakoi Hotel and Golf Club on the west shore and Hotel Molokai and Pau Hana Inn at Kaunakakai. Five condominiums round out the options: Kaluakoi Villas, Ke Nani Kai, and Paniolo Hale at Kaluakoi Resort; and Molokai Shores and Wavecrest at Kaunakakai.

See page 129 for a guide to Molokai's recreational facilities.

KALAUPAPA: WHERE FATHER DAMIEN BROUGHT HOPE

For almost a century, Kalaupapa, the tiny peninsula that juts out from the north coast's fortresslike cliffs, was the place of banishment and isolation for sufferers of leprosy. The once-dread disease has now been brought almost completely under control, and no new patients are admitted. Those who remain have arrested cases. Though free to leave, they prefer to live out their lives here in the place they consider their home.

The peninsula is also Kalaupapa National Historical Park and the park service staff is working with the state and with residents to preserve and restore historic buildings and interpret sites to bring to life the stories of the settlement's heroes. Father Damien, the colony's first white resident, devoted himself to relieving the victims' suffering from 1873 until he died in 1889 after contracting the disease. Though his body was sent to his native Belgium in 1936, a monument to this martyr (who has been proposed for sainthood) stands in the graveyard of St. Philomena, the church he built (see photograph, page 16).

The settlement welcomes visitors, and there is no health hazard if you follow the rules. You must have a permit from the State Department of Health to visit; but your airline or tour operator will get it for you. Minimum age for visitors is 15.

No roads lead to Kalaupapa. The only ways in or out are by air or on foot down the 3-mile/5-km zigzag trail along an abrupt and confining mountain wall. On the peninsula you must join Damien Tours (567-6171). Kalaupapa has no food service or accommodations. Hikers bring lunches; packaged tours include lunch.

Paragon Air (800/428-1231) includes Kalaupapa sightseeing on aerial tours from Maui. Flights leave from both Kahului and west Maui airports. The Maui Princess ferry (800/833-5800) out of Lahaina also offers tours. Air Molokai (877-0026) flies to Kalaupapa from Molokai's main airport and from Honolulu.

Though hiking is the only way to get down the trails at the moment, the popular mule ride from the top of the cliff (suspended in 1994) may be resumed at a later date. With sheer lava cliffs falling off at the edge of your path, this ride was not for the faint-hearted, but it was safe even for inexperienced riders—and a unique way to see some of Molokai's most majestic scenery.

Kalaupapa. Kalaupapa has several churches (St. Francis and Kanaana Hou are particularly charming), a community hall, general store, bar (beer and wine only), and wharf where barges come in twice each year to deliver vehicles and some other provisions. Three-fourths of the patients live in trim cottages, have gardens and television, and do their own cooking.

Kalawao. The easternmost district, Kalawao, lies 2½ miles/4 km across the peninsula. The colony was started here, but the settlement gradually moved to the Kalaupapa side, which is drier and less windy.

Kalawao has two historic churches: Protestant Siloama, set before a backdrop of mist-shrouded peaks; and St. Philomena, Father Damien's church.

Lawrence McCully Judd Park is a magnificent spot where you can picnic on a grassy bluff and watch the surf pound the green cliffs of the Pali Coast.

MOLOKAI

0   4   8   12 KM
0   4   8 MILES

Primary
Secondary
Unimproved
Foot Trail

Kaunakakai and the South Shore

Small Kaunakakai, 8 miles/13 km from the airport, is a lively place. At least once a week, people come from all over the island to shop and swap small talk. The bread at venerable Kanemitsu Bakery is famous all over the state. The Mid-Nite Inn got its name from a bygone era when it served saimin to travelers waiting for a midnight-departing interisland steamer; now it closes at 9 P.M. Saturday, the most popular market day, usually winds to a close with dancing and partying at the few night spots.

Gift stores, crafts shops, and grocers line three-block-long Ala Malama Street. To rent snorkeling gear and get information on the best fishing and diving sites, stop by Molokai Fish and Dive.

Barges load and unload cargo at Kaunakakai's wharf, where deep-sea fishing boats often offer sailing, fishing, diving, or whale-watching expeditions. Nearby, only the foundation of the home built for Kamehameha V remains.

Kaunakakai to Halawa. It's less than 30 miles/48 km from Kaunakakai to Halawa, but you should figure on at least 3 hours to allow time for sightseeing. Highway 450 (Kamehameha Highway) is easy driving as far as Pukoo; after that, the road becomes rough, narrow, and winding—but the views provide ample compensation. You gaze across the narrow channels to Lanai and Maui, while inland rise steep green mountain slopes, topped by 4,970-foot Kamakou.

Along this coast lies the only remaining concentration of offshore fishponds, built hundreds of years ago on all the major islands to stock and fatten fish for the tables of Hawaii's kings and chiefs (see page 128).

Onealii Park, just east of Kaunakakai, makes a pleasant picnic spot. It has a pavilion, rest rooms, drinking water, and a wading pool. Adjacent is a park for Kawela Plantation, a 6,000-acre agricultural/residential subdivision extending from the ocean to 4,000 feet elevation.

Kawela, a couple of miles beyond Onealii Park, was the site of a famous battle in the mid-1700s. Here the Molokai chiefs with their allies from Hawaii defeated attacking warriors from Oahu.

Forty-acre Kakahaia Pond, about 5 miles/8 km east of Kaunakakai, is a federal wildlife reserve and a refuge for the endangered Hawaiian coot and Hawaiian stilt.

Tiny Kamalo, a heavily populated area many years ago, has a small boat harbor and a wharf built sometime between 1850 and 1875. A sugar mill once stood just west of the present stream bed.

Stop at Kamalo's tiny St. Joseph's Church, a classic frame chapel with tall steeple and fine old glass windows. Built in 1876 and restored in 1971, it's the second of two churches founded on this side of the island by the famous Belgian priest, Father Damien (see page 124), who devoted his life to helping leprosy victims at Kalaupapa.

A mile beyond St. Joseph's Church, a monument marks the spot where, in 1927, Ernest Smith and Emory Bronte safely crash-landed their plane, ending the first civilian trans-Pacific flight after 25 hours and 2 minutes. The fliers, who took off from California, had hoped to reach Honolulu but ran out of gas.

Farther on, a Hawaii Visitors Bureau marker points to two *heiau* (temples) up on the ridge; though important ones, they are scarcely discernible.

Next comes long-abandoned Ah Ping's store; the only Chinese graveyard on the island (there are other gravesites) is located behind it.

Kaluaaha Church, a short distance past Ah Ping's, was built by the first missionaries and is Molokai's earliest church still standing. Its 3-foot-thick walls of plastered stone went up in 1844; the buttresses, iron roof, and faded red steeple (now fallen in) came later. The church is in disrepair now and the congregation meets elsewhere. Be very careful if you go inside—the roof is gradually collapsing.

(Continued on page 127)

Creamy waves *of Halawa Bay lap gently at Molokai's eastern shore, where Halawa Valley meets the sea.*

"High-rise" *on a low-rise island, giraffe is one of many African animals roaming in Molokai Ranch Wildlife Park.*

Father Damien's Our Lady of Sorrows Church, built two years before St. Joseph's Church and also recently restored, is just down the road in a palm grove. Anyone can attend the services, conducted only on special occasions. In a nearby pavilion stands a statue of the good father carved by a local artist.

Be content just to read about most marked places of historic interest from here on—often they're on private land and hard or impossible to see. Observe instead how the people live today. At scattered houses, you'll see nets drying and laundry flapping in the breeze. Families usually spend weekends out swimming, fishing, cooking, and camping.

Iliiliopae Heiau, 5 miles/7 km past Kamalo in Mapulehu Valley, is one of Hawaii's largest and most awesome temples. The heiau, about ½ mile inland from the road, is on private land, but you can reach it via the signed Wailau Trail. Treat the area with respect; it was the former site of human sacrifices. If you visit, wear good-gripping shoes and be prepared for some tricky walking as you ascend and descend the three platforms. The top platform is as large as a football field.

Between Pukoo and Waialua, you pass the site of a royal taro patch and the stack of a sugar mill that burned down about a hundred years ago.

Soon you are climbing through Puu O Hoku Ranch. Off the eastern tip of Molokai lies the islet of Mokuhooniki, used for bombing practice in World War II. There is a fine view of western Maui, with Haleakala looming shadowlike behind. Beyond the ranch buildings, between the road and sea, you'll spot a dense stand of trees: a sacred *kukui* grove that is the burial place of Lanikaula, a famous Molokai prophet for whom the grove is named.

Halawa Valley. Finally, the rough road zigzags down the ridge into Halawa Valley, guarded to the north by mighty Lamaloa Head. Here, in reach of an ordinary car, you'll find Hawaii's version of the South Seas of stories and paintings. Broad, deep, and green carpeted, the valley is backed by cliffs; two high falls plummet to a stream that meanders out to the sea.

Hundreds of people once lived in Halawa, considered one of the earliest settlements in the islands (about 500 A.D.). Even a few decades ago, taro farmers and fishermen were active. Though a few houses still stand, the jungle has gradually encroached on the geometric taro layout.

At the foot of the ridge, the road forks. One leg (paved) runs down to the shore, where you can swim in the bay if it's calm or at the mouth of the stream. The other road (dirt) heads into the valley a little way, past some old houses almost hidden in the lush foliage, a wooden church (still in use), and ruins of a mid-19th century stone church. The wooden church resembles a dollhouse.

Halawa's *pièce de résistance* is Moaula Falls, a pleasant hour's hike—but take along mosquito lotion and be wary of going too soon after a rain. The lower part of the main trail up the far side of the valley is overgrown now. To reach it, you have to ford the wide part of the stream, since a locked gate on the ranch jeep trail bars access to the bridge.

For an easier route, walk up the road to the last house and then follow a trail of sorts alongside a water pipe. You'll cross a couple of irrigation ditches and a narrow part of the stream where rocks serve as steppingstones. Don't lose sight of the pipe. When you come to a water tank, pick up the main trail; the pipeline continues alongside. As you walk through the tangle of *hau, kukui*, mangoes, Surinam cherries, *liliko'i*, and ginger, you'll spot the old stone terraces of many abandoned taro patches.

The falls drop from a towering cliff with such force that the surface of the pool below is a mass of bubbles. According to legend, you should swim only if the *mo'o* (lizard) is happy. To find out his mood, toss in a ti leaf—if it floats, all is well. Even if the leaf sinks, the mountain-cold water is too good to miss.

Upper Molokai

Heading west from Kaunakakai on Highway 460, you pass Kiowea Park. A coconut grove here was planted for King Kamehameha V in the 1860s. Across the highway and well worth a look is charming "church row."

Soon the road climbs 11 miles/17½ km from Kaunakakai on highways 460 and 470 to the crest of the island, high above Kalaupapa. At Kualapuu, Highway 480 branches toward Hoolehua Homesteads (homes are spread over many miles) and the airport and offers a view over the gigantic Kualapuu Reservoir. Water from wet, uninhabited Waikolu Valley is carried through the mountain to the reservoir through a 5-mile/8-km tunnel.

Kualapuu remains a pretty little plantation town despite the decline of pineapple growing in recent years. About 2 miles/3 km northwest of town at Hoolehua is a landmark, Puukapeelua or "Hill of the Caterpillar God"; its name springs from a legend in which a Molokai girl's lover turned out to be a giant caterpillar. When the people tried to burn the caterpillar, it released millions of tiny caterpillars that swarmed over the island.

Kamehameha the Great camped for a year at Kauluwai to get his troops conditioned and provisioned before attacking Oahu, which is visible from this high ground on clear days.

At Kalae, the steam-operated R. W. Meyer Sugar Mill, built in 1878, has been restored. On tours (10 A.M. to noon daily except Sunday; admission charge) you can see mementos of the German immigrant founder, whose home is next door.

Palaau Park. The road ends on a 1,600-foot cliff where a steep foot trail zigzags down to Kalaupapa, the only access by land to the settlement. The topside view of the cliffs stretching to the east is as awesome as the sight of the little peninsula laid upon the sea like a carpet, but a better vantage point is the lookout in Palaau Park. The park road, near the end of Highway 470, travels through a beautiful wilderness of koa, paperbark, ironwood, and cypress trees. After passing a small arboretum, which has 40 species of trees labeled, it ends at a campground.

Here you have a choice of two short trails. A footpath, arched with ironwoods that create a cathedral quality, leads to the Kalaupapa overlook. You can make out the wharf, churches, lighthouse, landing field, crater, and other features of the peninsula. The history of Kalaupapa is inscribed on a plaque at the viewing point.

The other walk follows a truck trail carpeted with ironwood needles for about 200 yards, and then turns right into a narrow footpath that climbs about 50 yards to a 6-foot-high phallic rock.

Waikolu Lookout and Kamakou Preserve. This remote area in central Molokai provides spectacular scenery and an opportunity to see some of Molokai as it existed a century ago. However, you must drive a gravel-and-dirt road (a turnoff from Highway 460) to reach it; drive this road only in dry periods and when the sky is clear over the mountains.

The drive takes you through a forest, planted since 1900 as watershed, that is resplendent with pines, cedar, eucalyptus, 'ohi'a, ferns, and clumps of ginger. After 9½ miles/15 km, you come to the Sandalwood Boat, a large depression in the ground the size and shape of a ship's hold, dug more than a century ago to measure the amount of sandalwood a ship could carry. Hawaiian chiefs bartered the wood for trinkets, whiskey, and finery from white traders who, in turn, sold it at great profit, especially in China where it was highly prized.

At Waikolu Valley Lookout, you step to the edge for a magnificent view of a deep, narrow gorge laced with high waterfalls.

Just beyond is a sign-in box at the entrance to the 2,774-acre Kamakou Preserve established to protect a precious high elevation rain forest with 250 kinds of Hawaiian plants and rare native forest birds. (See hiking information, page 129.)

West Molokai

Highway 460 heads west from the airport through Molokai Ranch lands. It's 8 miles/13 km to the end of the road at Maunaloa, a former pineapple plantation town. Hilly, picturesque, and graced with many Norfolk Island pines, Maunaloa attracts visitors with its market, colorful cafe and bar, and handful of shops, patronized not only by residents but also by vacationers staying at nearby condominiums. Local arts and crafts can be found at Plantation Gallery. Big Wind Kite Factory offers free lessons for its unusual high-flyers.

Kaluakoi Resort. From the turnoff it's 5 miles/8 km to Kaluakoi Hotel on Kepuhi Beach. From here you can see Oahu across the channel. On moonless nights, the lights of Honolulu gleam on the horizon.

The 6,700-acre Kaluakoi Resort sprawls along the beachfront. Currently, tourist facilities are limited to the casually elegant, cottage-style hotel, three condominium complexes, a 10-acre beach park, and an 18-hole oceanside golf course. Plans for a second hotel have been awaiting approval for several years.

Molokai Ranch Wildlife Park. The 350-acre Molokai Ranch Wildlife park offers guided photographic safaris around a natural game preserve. Though the park's primary purpose is to sell rare and endangered specimens to zoos worldwide, visitors can view over 1,000 African and Indian animals. On van tours, visitors get close-up looks at eland, oryx, Indian black buck, Barbary sheep, zebra, giraffe, and other species. At one stop, you can pet giraffes and other docile creatures. Two daily safaris and a separate beach adventure depart from nearby Kalaukoi Hotel. Make reservations at the hotel or call 552-2767.

The Pali Coast

The coastline from Kalaupapa to Halawa is one of the most spectacular in Hawaii. From its towering green cliffs, waterfalls plunge hundreds of feet into the ocean or disappear halfway down as winds blow them into a mist. The cliffs are honeycombed with caves. One at sea level is navigable to some 200 feet inside the island. Several beautiful valleys break the 2,000-foot pali.

Only from a boat or plane can you see it all. Airplane flightseeing tours take you by, as do regular interisland flights traveling the north route between Oahu and Maui. For a closer and longer look, you can hire a boat at Kaunakakai or charter a small plane.

FISHPONDS IN THE OCEAN

At least as long ago as the 15th century, ponds were built along shallow coasts and shores on all the major islands. A tasty assortment of fish was stocked and fattened in them to satisfy the appetites of Hawaii's kings and chiefs. Most ponds are now in ruins, but a few on Molokai are still in commercial use; you can see most of these as you drive eastward from Kaunakakai on Highway 450. Ponds were enclosed by thick walls of coral or basalt. Each had one or more breaks covered by grates with openings wide enough to let young fish in but too narrow to permit fattened fish to leave. The water had to be shallow—no more than 3 feet deep—so sunshine could penetrate it and promote growth of microscopic food on the bottom. Alii Pond, just east of One Alii Beach Park, has a 2,700-foot-long wall, recently restored. Two others of note are Niaupala (33½ acres) at Kaluaaha, and Kupeke (30 acres), just east of Pukoo.

MOLOKAI RECREATION GUIDE

 A glimpse of Molokai's uncomplicated yesteryears more than compensates for a lack of commercial recreation. For additional information on Friendly Isle attractions, contact Molokai Visitors Association, Box 960 Kaunakakai, HI 96748; (800) 800-6367. The local area code is 808.

Golf. The new Molokai Highlands course gives golfers a second 18-hole option. All courses are open to the public. Yardages are from the regular tees.

Courses. Kaluakoi Golf Club, Kepuhi Beach, 552-0144, par 72, 6,599 yards; Molokai Highlands Golf Club, Hoolehua, 553-3302, par 72, 7,200 yards; Ironwood Hills Golf Course, Kalae, 567-6000, 9 holes, par 36, 2,790 yards.

Tennis. Several courts are open to the public: Kaunakakai Community Center, Kaunakakai, 2 public courts; Kaluakoi Hotel & Golf Club, Kepuhi Beach, 4 resort courts; Ke Nani Kai, Maunaloa, 2 resort courts; Wavecrest, Kaunakakai, 2 resort courts.

Swimming. The waters along Molokai's accessible southeast shore are mostly too shallow or silty for swimming, but they are ideal for windsurfing. Frequent rough water limits swimming at the west end's beautiful beaches —long expanses of white sand interrupted by lava outcroppings—and also along western Molokai's north shore; the best beach here is Moomomi, at the end of Highway 480. Even on calm days swimmers should be alert to possible dangerous currents.

Farther east on the pali shore, you find safe water at the entrances to Pelekunu, Wailau, and Halawa valleys in calm water conditions (there is road access at Halawa). Streams running through these valleys to the bays are also nice for a dip. Coves with sandy beaches characterize the shoreline near Waialua, southwest of Halawa, though none are exceptional swimming beaches.

Surfing. Halawa Bay is one of Molokai's best beaches for both board and body surfing. Good surfing is also found at Rock Point, between Honouli Maloo and Honouli Wai on the southeast shore and at Kepuhi Beach on the west end.

Beachcombing, reef walking, skin/scuba diving. Mudflats constitute the majority of Molokai's southern shoreline, limiting shallow-water activities. The island's west end and Halawa Bay on the east end, though, are good for diving. Moanui Beach near Halawa Valley offers good reef walking on a fringing reef that borders much of Molokai's southern shore.

Boating and fishing. Though many boating companies, especially from Maui, consider the Friendly Isle a notable spot to drop anchor, only a few make Molokai their home port. Several fully equipped sportfishing cruisers and sailing yachts at Kaunakakai Harbor, among them Whistling Swan Charters and Molokai Charters, offer sightseeing, snorkeling, and fishing. *Alyce C.* and *Bali Hai* fish the noted waters of Penguin Banks. Hokupaa Ocean Adventures, (800) 553-3876, cruises from Halawa Valley in summer.

Cycling. If you brought a bike, Molokai has good cycling routes. One 2-wheel option follows the 28-mile/45-km coastal route (Highway 450) eastward from Kaunakakai as far as Puu O Hoku Ranch. Another safe run for cyclers is westward from Kaunakakai to Kaluakoi Resort on Highway 460.

Horseback riding. Molokai Wagon Ride, 567-6773, has 1½-hour guided rides from the cliffs overlooking Kalaupapa in east Molokai. For a less conventional ride, consider a Rare Adventures muleback excursion down a cliffside trail to Kalaupapa and back (see page 124); call 567-6088 or check with your hotel activities desk for reservations.

Kayaking. Pacific Outdoor Adventures, P.O. Box 61609, Honolulu, HI 96839, (800) 52-KAYAK, combines 5-day kayak trips along Molokai's windward coast with overnight camping.

Hiking. Rare Adventures, 567-6088, offers a fairly arduous hiking trip into Kalaupapa. The 7-hour excursion also includes a guided tour and lunch. Going down is not difficult, but remember you have to climb back up the rugged cliffs.

Nature Conservancy runs monthly member tours into the remote rain forest of Kamakou Preserve in central Molokai. For information, write or call them at 116 Smith Street, Honolulu, HI 96817; 537-4508.

A few precautions if you plan to hike on your own: Both the Wailau Trail, which crosses the island, and the track into Halawa Valley are not well signed and can be difficult in spots; also, residents in isolated areas do not welcome intruders. Before setting off on your trek, be sure to lock your car.

Camping. The forested mountain area overlooking Kalaupapa Peninsula includes camping facilities in Palaau State Park, as does Onealii Beach on the coast just east of Kaunakakai. Another fine spot for mountain camping is a meadow with a stream a few hundred yards east of Waikolu Valley Lookout (get permission to camp from the Division of Forestry, Kaunakakai).

The north shores of Halawa and Wailau valleys offer camping, too. The beach on the south side of Halawa is a county park with pavilion, rest rooms, and grills. To camp, you need a permit from the county office in Kaunakakai. At times (usually in the summer), Wailau Valley is accessible by boat.

Palaau and Onealii parks are especially inviting picnic spots. Lawrence McCully Judd Park on Kalaupapa Peninsula and Kiowea Beach Park near Kaunakakai also afford pleasant picnicking.

LANAI

• PINE TREES, WIDE-OPEN SPACES, AND SOME OF THE STATE'S FINEST BEACHES •

Long known for delicious pineapples rather than for tourism, Lanai has only recently begun to develop facilities for visitors. The island has long produced lots of pineapple, grown on more than 12,000 acres. It also retained 78,000 additional acres of open space. But two new luxury hotels and golf courses, one outside Lanai City and one at Hulopoe Beach, testify to the island's changing status from a pineapple plantation to an exclusive hideaway only half an hour by air from Honolulu.

Excellent swimming, snorkeling, and fishing along miles of coastline made to order for beachcombers await Lanai visitors. You can drive, hike, or ride a horse to lookouts above deeply eroded gulches or search for—and find—remnants of old Hawaii. Most of Lanai's 2,400 residents live in Lanai City; many formerly employed by the pineapple industry are now working in tourism.

Sixth in the island group in size—just 17 miles/27 km long and 13 miles/21 km wide—Lanai is actually an extinct volcano with a single crater, Palawai. Some say "Lanai" means a swelling or hump. If you look at the island from Maui, you will see that the name fits the contour of the land: a smooth, curved ridge rises from the southern base to an altitude of more than 3,000 feet and then slopes down again to the northern tip. Deep gulches cut into the ridge on the east side above a half-mile-wide coastal plain. On the west side, the ridge drops down to a plateau at 1,500 to 2,000-foot elevation, ending in cliffs above the sea. Vegetation on the plateau is scrubby, but gulches and hillsides on the windward side boast luxuriant growth. Rainfall in high areas averages 42 inches a year; in lower areas, 12 inches.

Ghostly Beginnings

One of Lanai's legends claims that the island was inhabited only by ghosts or evil spirits for a thousand years after the Polynesians had settled the other islands. Then Kaululaau, nephew of Maui's king, was banished to Lanai as punishment for one of his mischievous acts. Though he was not expected to survive, Kaululaau won out by driving all the ghosts from the island, making it safe for humans.

Protestant missionaries arrived on Lanai in 1835. Twenty years later, a Mormon colony was started in Palawai Basin. The colony later dissolved in a dispute between the church and the leader, Walter Murray Gibson, who refused to turn over his land acquisitions. His extensive holdings eventually passed on to sugar interests and then cattle ranchers; by 1910, most of the island had been bought up by a single ranching company.

"Fruit Basket" with a Future

Ranching gave way to farming after the land was purchased in 1922 by Dole Company (today part of Castle & Cooke). For many years the island produced 90 percent of the country's pineapples. But cheaper labor costs elsewhere have resulted in a sharp decrease in pineapple production; soon, the company will scale down its operations to about 100 acres, which will be just enough to supply local needs.

The company has plans to diversify into cattle ranching, tourism, and other agricultural crops, such as organic vegetables for stores, hotels, and restaurants.

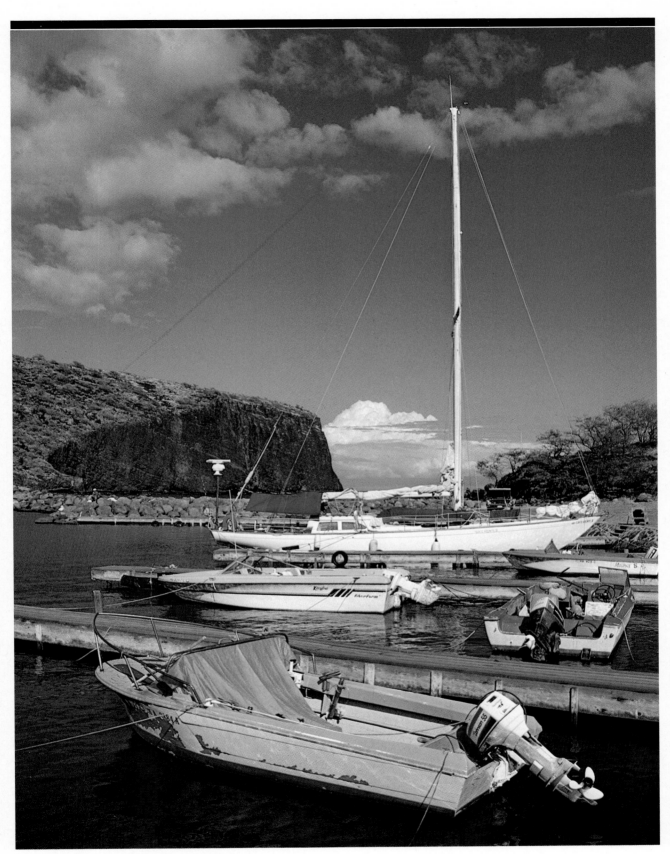

Tiny Manele harbor, a drop-off point for day-trippers

THE ESSENTIALS

Hawaiian Airlines and Aloha IslandAir offer daily air service to Lanai's airport from Oahu and Maui. Air Molokai has daily flights to Lanai from Kahului, Maui. Expeditions runs round-trip ferry service from Lahaina, Maui, to Manele Bay; call 661-3756 for details. Several Maui companies offer full-day snorkeling and exploring trips to Lanai from Maui.

Getting Around

Lanai's airport is a 10-minute drive from Lanai City. Complimentary shuttles pick up hotel guests. Taxis are also available. Four-wheel-drive vehicles (which you need to explore the island) can be rented from your hotel or from Dollar Rent-A-Car (565-7227); advance reservations are a must. Oshiro Drive & U-Drive, Lanai City Service, and The Lodge at Koele offer off-road tours, the latter for guests only.

The only paved roads radiate out from Lanai City. Ask for directions before exploring the island on your own; attractions can be hard to find.

Where to Stay

The Lodge at Koele and Manele Bay Hotel, both managed by Rockresorts, offer premier settings and all the amenities you'd expect from new luxury resorts. The 102-room Lodge, tucked into pines upcountry, has the look and feel of a country estate. The 250-room Manele Bay Hotel tops a bluff overlooking Hulopoe Beach. Your other choice is the comfortable 10-room Hotel Lanai, a recently refurbished white-frame building in Lanai City with a popular bar and restaurant.

See page 137 for a guide to Lanai's recreational facilities.

PINEAPPLE —
TO LANAI BY WAY OF HARVARD

No one is certain just how or when the pineapple first came to Hawaii. It was not brought by the early Polynesians. The first mention of it appears in the diary of Don Francisco de Paula y Marin, a counselor to King Kamehameha I, who wrote on January 21, 1813, "This day I planted pineapples and an orange tree." Commercial production began on Oahu in 1882 when Captain John Kidwell, an English horticulturist, brought from Florida a shipment of the Smooth Cayenne variety grown almost exclusively in Hawaii today.

The pineapple is a true fruit, but it grows on a low plant, not on a tree where many visitors expect to find it. New plants are started by planting the crown, taken from the top of the fruit. After the fields are prepared, machines lay long rows of plastic mulch strips, simultaneously fumigating the soil beneath. The strips conserve moisture, increase soil temperature, and discourage weeds. New plants (around 20,000 per acre) are inserted in holes poked through the strips at regular intervals.

It takes from 18 to 22 months from the planting to the harvesting of a pineapple. In the first crop, each plant bears one 4 to 5-pound fruit; a ratoon (second or third) crop may have one or two smaller pineapples.

Harvesting is done by hand because pineapples must be picked when they are fully ripened. Workers move through the field, picking the ripe fruits and placing them on long-armed harvest machine conveyors. Sometimes crews work around the clock. The pineapples move by conveyor belt into bins on waiting trucks.

Most pineapple goes to canneries, but a growing proportion of fresh fruit is airlifted directly to mainland market areas.

James D. Dole—Pineapple Pioneer

Lanai underwent many years of decline during the late 19th and early 20th centuries. Attempts to make the island agriculturally productive didn't succeed; within a few years after experiments with sugarcane failed in 1901, the island's population—once well over a thousand—dwindled to less than two hundred.

All this changed when, in 1922, James D. Dole's Hawaiian Pineapple Company acquired control of the island and began growing pineapple. Kaumalapau, on Lanai's southwestern shore, was developed into the harbor necessary for shipping pineapples to the company's cannery in Honolulu.

Dole came to Hawaii in 1899 after graduating from Harvard. (Sanford B. Dole, president of the Republic of Hawaii at that time, was his first cousin once removed.) He soon began experimenting with pineapple plantings on 60 acres of homestead land at Wahiawa, in central Oahu. From these humble beginnings the pineapple industry expanded dramatically until, 25 years later, it became vital to the economy of all of Hawaii's islands.

Recently, Castle & Cooke decided to phase out Lanai's pineapple business in favor of more profitable endeavors. Now, resorts and golf courses sprawl across land where golden fruit once grew.

LANAI

Lanai City

No place else in the islands is quite like Lanai City. Situated at 1,600 feet, just below the mountains, its climate resembles a California mountain town in summer—comfortably cool days, crisp nights. Immediately noticeable as you enter town is the stately presence of hundreds of towering Norfolk Island and Cook Island pine trees, planted by the pineapple company.

The village is very much a plantation town, a holdover from another era. The three main roads have no stoplights and only a few stop signs. Locals gather every morning for coffee at the counter in S&T Properties, and locally baked pastries are still sold at the glass counter of Blue Ginger Cafe. But changes are coming. Designer bottled water is available at both Richard's and Pine Isle groceries, and Island Collections gallery features paintings, quilts, and other handicrafts made by local artists.

Lanai City, the island's one and only residential area, houses virtually the entire citizenry, the great majority of whom are Filipino. The modest homes cover a number of blocks outside the business section with their metal roofs and seemingly endless variety of colors and add-ons. Home gardens feature giant mango trees and a variety of tropical plants, but many azaleas, camellias, lilies, and other colorful temperate-zone flowers also thrive at this elevation.

Kaumalapau Harbor

Highway 440 from Lanai City to the harbor at Kaumalapau passes through acres of pineapple for 6 miles/9½ km, the fields broken only by red dirt roads that crisscross them. You may see irrigating and harvesting machines; the latter load fruit onto trucks at the rate of 10,000 pineapples per hour. But planting and picking are done by hand. During the harvesting peak in summer, you see scores of pickers, many with their heads all but covered by scarves, big hats, and goggles.

The road descends in curves to the harbor, which is backed by steep bluffs. The company-built harbor accommodates the barges that carry pineapples to the cannery in Honolulu; it always has a few fishing boats as well. At the 400-foot dock, cranes transfer the pineapples from trucks to barges.

North of Kaumalapau, the plateau ends in a bluff above the sea. To the south, jagged cliffs rise as high as 1,000 feet out of the water.

Hulopoe Beach and Manele Bay

Another pineapple-lined trip from Lanai City is the 8-mile/13-km drive to Manele Bay on a different section of Highway 440. Along the way you can detour to the Luahiwa petroglyphs, located near the base of the steep slopes around Palawai Basin, but you'll need a guide or

The luxurious Lodge at Koele,
*situated in Lanai's highlands, resembles
a private mountainside retreat.*

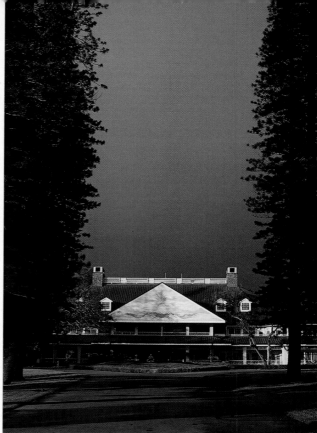

With its gentle waves, *lovely stretch
of white sand, and palm-shaded campground, Hulopoe Bay is Lanai's best—
and only swimmable—beach.*

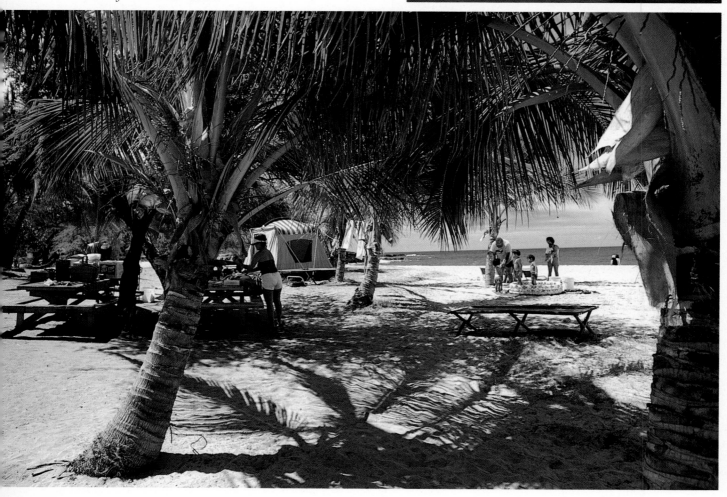

good directions to find them. You take a dirt road off the highway, then scramble up grassy banks to boulders that have one of Hawaii's most concentrated and best preserved collections of ancient rock carvings.

Manele Bay has a small boat harbor with a breakwater and berths for pleasure craft. Just beyond the breakwater, anchored in a cliff, is an old wooden chute; many years ago it was used to load cattle onto ships. Low lava stone walls and platforms on the hill above are remains of early native houses.

To the west is Hulopoe Bay, with a beautiful tree-fringed swimming beach (best on the island, but with an abrupt offshore dropoff) and an adjacent rock-rimmed pool for children. The park here contains the island's only improved picnic site, with tables, barbecues, showers, and restrooms. Bluffs along this coast were once submerged, and marine fossils have been found as high as 1,200 feet.

It's only a short walk or drive to the southeast end of the Hulopoe shore, and well worth the time for the view of Pu'u Pehe, an impressive sea stack known as "Sweetheart Rock." The story has been passed down through the years of a young Lanai warrior whose wife, captured from a Maui chieftain, died in a storm. After burying her atop the rock, the grief-stricken husband took his own life by flinging himself down into the churning sea.

Both Manele and Hulopoe are part of a marine life conservation district. Be sure to heed the restrictions posted throughout the region.

Kaunolu Village

Probably the most extensive and best preserved ruins in the islands are those of Kaunolu Village at the end of a rutty, rocky 3-mile/5-km jeep trail through grasslands south of the pineapple fields. Remains of 86 houses, 35 stone shelters, and various grave markings and garden sites are scattered across a point above the sea.

(Continued on next page)

WHAT'S IN A NAME?

No sooner do arriving passengers deplane in Hawaii than they become aware of the sight and sound of the islands' colorful place names. Unfortunately, most visitors depart knowing little more about the significance of these names than they knew upon arrival; they've missed an opportunity to share something special with the people of Hawaii.

Below you'll find a small sampler of meanings of some of Hawaii's better-known cities and towns, streets, and landmarks. Certain prominent names about which you might be curious aren't included because researchers and historians disagree on their translation—the words "Oahu," "Kauai," and "Hawaii" itself, for example. But you can read about these three and thousands of other Hawaiian names in the excellent book, *Place Names of Hawaii*, published by the University of Hawaii Press and available in many bookstores. Organized alphabetically for ready reference, it contains not only meanings but also pertinent background information on each place listed.

Ala Moana . . . . ocean street	Kaunakakai . . . . . . beach landing	Makawao . . . . forest beginning
Haena . . . . red hot	Kaupo . . . . landing of canoes at night	Makena . . . . .abundance
Haiku . . . . speak abruptly		Manele . . . . sedan chair
Haleakala . . . . . . house of the sun	Kealakekua . . . . .pathway of the god	Maui . . . . the demigod Maui
Halekulani . . . . . . house befitting royalty	Keanae . . . . the mullet	Mauna Kea . . . . . .white mountain
	Keauhou . . . . the new era	Mauna Loa . . . . . . .long mountain
Hanalei . . . . .crescent bay	Kihei . . . . cloak	Napili . . . .*pili* grass
Hanapepe . . . . .crushed bay (due to landslides)	Kokee . . . . to bend	Nawiliwili . . . . . . .the *wiliwili* trees (Hawaiian natives)
Honolulu . . . . .protected bay	Koko . . . . red earth	
Iao . . . . .cloud supreme	Kona . . . . leeward	Paia . . . . noisy
Ilikai . . . . surface of the sea	Koolau . . . . windward	Poipu . . . . crashing (as waves)
Kaahumanu . . . bird feather cloak	Kula . . . . plain	Punahou . . . . new spring
Kahala . . . . amberjack fish		Ulupalakua . . . . .ripening breadfruit
Kahului . . . . .the winning	Lahaina . . . . cruel sun	
Kalaupapa . . . . .the flat plain	Lanai . . . . . . day of conquest	Waianapanapa . . .glistening water
Kamehameha . . . . . the lonely one	Lihue . . . . cold chill	Waikiki . . . . spouting water
Kapalua . . . . two borders	Lunalilo . . . . very high (of royalty)	Wailea . . . . water of Lea (canoe makers' goddess)
Kapiolani . . . . arch of heaven (rainbow)	Makaha . . . . fierce	Wailua . . . . .two waters
Kailua . . . . .two seas	Makapuu . . . . bulging eye	Wailuku . . . . . water of destruction
		Waimea . . . . reddish water

Now a national historic landmark, Kaunolu was once an active fishing community and a favorite recreation spot of Kamehameha the Great after he conquered all the islands. His house, on the edge of the eastern bluff above a usually dry stream bed, overlooked the bay, the village, and Halulu Heiau on the west bank.

Today you can see remains of this *heiau* (temple) and, spread along the east bank, parts of rock platforms where grass houses once stood enclosed by sections of stone walls. Many boulders have petroglyphs, a few with bird-like figures peculiar to Lanai.

From Kahekili's Jump, a break in a cliff above the sea, fleeing warriors are said to have leaped into the 12 feet of water 62 feet below. Their survival depended on clearing the ledge of rock that protrudes 15 feet into the sea at the base of the drop.

From Kaunolu you can walk about 2 miles/3 km along cliff tops to Pali Kaholo, at 1,083 feet the highest point in Lanai's coastline. You can also go from Kaunolu to Manele along the shore, but this difficult and rocky walk takes most of a day.

Garden of the Gods

You'll find the Garden of the Gods about 7 miles/11 km along a dirt road out of Lanai City; ask for good directions. The road passes first through pineapple fields and then through an area of lantana, *poha*, Norfolk Island pine, ironwood, and eucalyptus.

The garden is a varicolored canyon of windswept sand with fantastic lava formations standing all around, weird survivors of the decomposition and coloring wrought upon the less durable substances by wind, rain, and sun.

Dirt roads and jeep trails traverse the arid, uncultivated plateau that is northwestern Lanai. One road goes all the way to the white sands of Polihua Beach. Here surf casting is rewarding, but the strong current makes swimming dangerous and the windblown sand is often intolerable.

The Munro Trail

Lanai has beautiful forests, deep in gulches and high on mountain ridges. Munro Trail (also called Lanaihale Road), a dirt road best driven in a 4-wheel-drive vehicle, takes you to Lanaihale at the top of the island. On a clear day, you can see all of the major islands except Kauai from this 3,370-foot elevation.

The 7-mile/11-km route extends from the southeast hills near Waiakeakua to Koele's rolling grasslands. Near the top of the ridge, it cuts through a heavy rain forest of tree ferns and other exotic tropicals, most of them planted years ago by Hawaii's late naturalist, George C. Munro. Stands of Norfolk Island pines, in particular, were planted to increase the island's ground water, tapped for irrigation. Weather studies show that the trees collect moisture from the hill-hugging clouds.

A trail leads off to a lookout over 2,000-foot Hauola Gulch, Lanai's deepest ravine. From the road, you can see man-made notches in Hookio Ridge at the head of Maunalei Gulch. Warriors used these for protection and as bases for attack in 1778 during a battle in which the king of Hawaii massacred many Lanai natives.

The road overlooks the pumping station down in Maunalei Gulch, the island's watershed, which has tumbling waterfalls, a *kukui* grove, and lush valley plants.

The Windward Coast

About 3 miles/5 km from Lanai City, the narrow, paved road (Highway 44) that runs northeast to the windward coast passes a particularly pretty picnic area: rolling green hills and grassy knolls, shaded by a few *lama* and *olopua* trees that were once part of an extensive forest. There's a fine view over the 7-mile/11-km-wide channel between Lanai and Molokai. Then the road cuts a corkscrew course down to the shore.

Shipwreck Beach. At pavement's end, you can drive or walk (at low tide only) northwest on a dirt road to an old lighthouse foundation and along part of Shipwreck Beach—a stretch of 4 miles/6 km or more where a few hulks of old ships lie rotting and rusting on the reef. The shore (part sand, part black lava, part tidal flats) is littered with timbers and other remnants of once-proud vessels. Beachcomber shacks near the lighthouse ruin are built mostly of lumber from outmoded steamers purposely abandoned in this shallow reef graveyard.

From road's end, walk about 100 yards west along a marked trail to Kukui Point, where a score of petroglyph-covered boulders feature the carved figures of strange "birdmen" like those at Kaunolu.

The road to Naha. From the end of Highway 44, a jeep road of dirt and hard-packed sand follows the coastline south for about 15 miles/24 km to Naha, an old village site. A parallel road of sand and silt hugs the shore for part of the way. Spots become flooded during high tide, but beachcombers can cross over to it on one of many connecting spurs. Clumps of *kiawe* trees here are so wind-bent they look like banks of tall wild grass. *Kiawes* along the somewhat protected inland route have old, gnarled trunks and branches that reach over the road in places to provide a lacy green canopy.

Keomuku, an abandoned village on the coast road, consists of a few old houses and a picturesque, weathered church (built in 1903), nestled in an oasis of palm trees. Just beyond, you can walk inland to see the remains of Kahea Heiau on the bluff above. At the foot of the bank is a boulder covered with weathered petroglyphs. Stones from the heiau were used for the Maunalei Sugar Company's plantation railroad bed.

The road ends at Naha. Off its narrow sand beach are good grounds for spearfishing, casting, and squidding. You can hike uphill for a mile or so along an old trail.

LANAI RECREATION GUIDE

Lanai, the smallest developed island in the Hawaiian chain, offers limited visitor entertainment beyond resort activities such as golf, tennis, and horseback riding. For more information, contact Destination Lanai, Box 700, Lanai City, HI 96763; 565-7600. The local area code is 808.

Golf. When the 18-hole Manele course joins Greg Norman's Koele layout in 1994, golfers will have splendid options. Yardages are from regular tees.

Public course. Cavendish Golf Course, Lanai City, 565-7044, 9 holes, par 36, 3,071 yards. *Resort course.* The Experience at Koele, 565-7231, 18 holes, par 72, 6,628 yards.

Swimming. You'll find Lanai's best swimming on the southern shore. Coconut-fringed white sand beaches highlight neighboring Hulopoe and Manele bays; both feature public facilities (picnic sites, barbecues, showers, restrooms), the only ones on the island. Hulopoe also has a rock-rimmed pool for children's swimming.

Beachcombing. Shipwreck Beach on the north shore consists of more than 4 miles/6 km of white and black sand and tidal flats. The lucky beachcomber's booty from this marine graveyard may include glass fishing net floats or the rare paper nautilus shell. On the southeast coast, the shore-hugging unpaved road to Naha provides access to sand and silt exploring grounds.

Skin and scuba diving. Hulopoe and Manele bays are both underwater conservation districts; though diving is excellent, removing any marine life from these areas is prohibited.

Fishing. On the northwestern cape, you might be tempted to swim at Polihua Beach's white-sand shore—don't, for the strong current is dangerous. Instead, try your luck at surfcasting here. The waters off Naha provide opportunities for spear fishing, casting, and squidding. Both shore and deep-sea fishing lure anglers to the water off the coast between Naha and Hulopoe. You can also shore fish at Kaumalapau Harbor.

Boating. Both resort hotels offer boat rentals and snorkeling and sailing tours.

Horseback riding. Guided 1 and 2-hour trail rides leave daily from the stables across from The Lodge at Koele. For reservations, call the hotel concierge.

Hiking, biking, and 4-wheel-drive touring. Resort hotels offer organized hiking, mountain bike rentals, and off-road tours on 4-wheel-drive vehicles. If you explore on your own, carry food and plenty of water. Hikers will need sturdy shoes. Poor maps and a lack of signs make navigating difficult.

The most popular hike and mountain bike route is strenuous Munro Trail, a 20-mile/30-km loop along the volcanic ridge behind Lanai City to the top of 3,370-foot Lanaihale. On clear days, it affords views of Molokai and Maui.

Another favorite destination is Kaunolu Bay on Lanai's rugged southern coastline. Here lie some of the state's best-preserved ruins of an ancient fishing village—house sites, stone shelters, gardens, and gravesites.

It's roughly 12 slow-going miles/18 km from Lanai City to the white sands of Polihua Beach. En route you pass through the native forest of Kanepuu, a Nature Conservancy preservation project, and the dramatically barren volcanic moonscape called Garden of the Gods. Dangerous currents at the beach make swimming unsafe.

PETROGLYPHS – FRAGILE MEMENTOS

Petroglyphs, ancient rock carvings found on all the islands and mentioned frequently in this book, offer a fascinating glimpse of the Hawaiians of earlier times—how they perceived their world and what they considered to be important.

Some of the finest (and best preserved) examples are in caves, where people could patiently scratch and chip at the rock walls while taking shelter from heavy rains and storms. Petroglyphs are also found along old trails, where travelers stopped to rest.

Earliest carved figures were composed of straight lines, looking a little like bent matches or "stickman" drawings. Later came triangular forms, distinctively Hawaiian; and, lastly, more fully shaped and rounded forms.

Tragically, vandals have defaced many of Hawaii's finest petroglyphs. Those who view them should remember that these historical carvings—though chiseled in rock—are both fragile and irreplaceable and should be treated accordingly.

HAWAII

• THE ORCHID ISLE
…FLOWER-FILLED PLAYLAND OF PELE •

Hawaii, youngest and southernmost island in the Hawaiian chain, is almost twice as large as all the other islands combined; hence its most common nickname, the "Big Island." Because it's also one place in the United States where you are likely to see volcanic action and is world-famous for its orchids, it has two other nicknames—the "Volcano Island" and the "Orchid Isle."

Dominated by Giants

In spite of its Big Island title and its area of 4,050 square miles/10,492 square km, Hawaii is a small piece of land indeed to contain two single mountains that are probably the tallest and bulkiest on earth. Mauna Kea and Mauna Loa rise 30,000 feet from the ocean floor. Mauna Kea, a dormant volcano, peaks at 13,796 feet above sea level; Mauna Loa reaches 13,677 feet.

Of the five volcanoes that formed the Big Island, only Mauna Loa and Kilauea (on Mauna Loa's southeast slope) are active. Although Mauna Loa has erupted only twice since 1950 (for a few hours on July 5, 1975 and, more recently, on March 25, 1984), Kilauea has spouted off dozens of times in the last decade. Volcanism has ceased in the north corner of the island, and the old Kohala Mountains (5,480 feet) have been eroded into cliffs and canyons where they face the northeast trades.

A Vast Land of Variety

Much of the Big Island is lava wasteland, but there is an amazing variety of terrain, climate, scenery, and things to do. In 40 miles/64 km you can travel from tropical beaches into fields of waving cane, up through rain forest or grassy pasture, and over lava slopes with snow banks and below-freezing temperatures. This southernmost piece of the United States has the nation's only coffee industry and is the state's biggest producer of sugar, papayas, avocados, macadamia nuts, anthuriums, vegetables, beef, and Christmas trees—but grows none of its pineapple.

More and more of the 121,000 Big Island residents are turning to the care and feeding of visitors. Most of the island's hotels, condominiums, and luxury resorts are concentrated on the sunny Kona and Kohala coasts.

Outdoor experiences on this island range from swimming to skiing. Because Hawaii is not as well endowed with beaches as the other islands, resorts provide their own, trucking in sand to lay over the lava base. Swimming pools often nudge the ocean's edge. If you like to hike, hunt, ride, or camp, Hawaii presents territory unsurpassed. A special sport is 4-wheel-drive exploring through rough and primitive country, much of it high and cool.

Peering Into the Past

Hawaii was the first to have Western ways implanted. It boasts Hawaii's most famous historic and legendary personalities: Kamehameha the Great, born in Kohala about 1753, ruled his kingdom from Kailua, where he died in 1819; Captain James Cook, who put the islands on the world map, was killed at Kealakekua Bay in 1779; the first company of missionaries landed at Kailua in 1820; and the state's most fascinating lady, the volcano goddess Pele, still lives on Hawaii in Halemaumau, Kilauea's firepit.

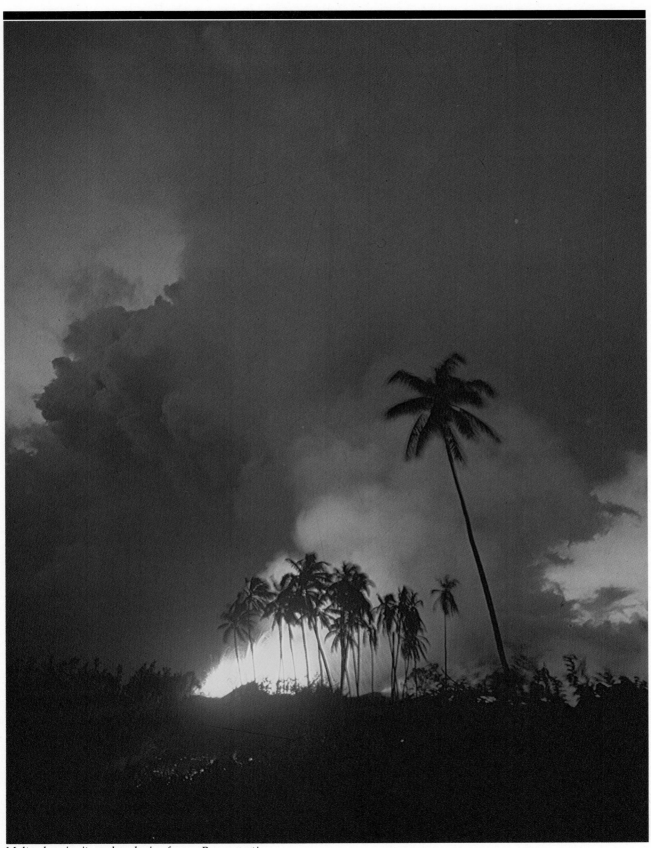

Molten lava ignites palms during former Puna eruption

THE ESSENTIALS

Hawaii, the Big Island, lies 200 miles/320 km southeast of Oahu. It's one of four islands that has direct air service from the west coast of the mainland. This makes it possible to arrive at Honolulu, visit other islands (either by regularly scheduled flights or on special tours), and leave for the mainland from Kona on United Airlines. Or you can reverse the trip, going into Hawaii and out through Honolulu.

Aloha Airlines and Hawaiian Airlines serve both Kona's Keahole Airport and Hilo International Airport; Mahalo Air flies between Honolulu and Keahole. Travelers to the north end of the island might consider Aloha IslandAir's daily service to Waimea's Kamuela Airport. Those whose schedules prohibit a more lengthy stay can visit Hawaii's major attractions on a daylong flightseeing tour from Honolulu or Maui.

Taxis serve Hilo and Keahole airports. A limousine company operates from Kailua-Kona. Some resorts offer airport pickup; check when you make your reservation.

Getting Around

Most all-island tours stop for a night or two on the Big Island and take sightseers to major attractions in minivans. Island-based companies also offer ground and aerial tours. The best way to explore is on your own; plan to spend at least 4 days.

A good paved road loops around the island (216 miles/346 km). From the Kona and Kohala coasts, the road heads east across the top of the island through Waimea and Honokaa to Hilo, south toward Hawaii Volcanoes National Park, and along the southern part of the island back to Keauhou and Kailua-Kona. The drive between Kailua-Kona and Hilo can easily take a day if you stop at Waimea, Honokaa, and the Waipio Valley. You'll need at least another day to tour Hilo's quaint stores and nearby gardens and to view Kilauea's volcanic activity.

Saddle Road across the north central part of the island provides access to rugged roads that climb Mauna Loa and Mauna Kea. It's an alternate route, albeit slower, between Kohala and Hilo, but off-limits to rental cars.

Cars, bicycles, mopeds, and 4-wheel-drive vehicles. All national and local car rental agencies have vehicles at the airports in Hilo and Keahole. Bicycles and mopeds can be rented in Kailua-Kona.

Bus service. The island's best transportation bargain is the bus that provides round-trip service Monday through Saturday between Hilo and the Kona Coast. It costs only a few dollars each way, with an additional charge for luggage that won't fit under the seat. For information, stop by the County of Hawaii Transit Agency, 25 Aupini Street, Hilo, or phone 935-8241.

Local buses connect downtown Hilo with outlying rural areas and provide access to Kona Coast towns. A free, double-decker London bus runs daily between Kailua-Kona and the Kona Surf Resort. Keauhou shuttles run between shopping centers and golf courses.

Where to Stay

To reduce driving time, consider establishing two bases of operation, one on the Hilo side of the island and another along the popular west coast. (For information on Big Island bed and breakfasts, turn to page 149.)

Among Hilo's bayside hotels are Hawaii Naniloa, Hilo Hawaiian, and Hilo Bay. Other choices around the city include Waiakea Villas and Dolphin Bay.

Historic Volcano House perches on the lip of Kilauea Crater in the national park. Kilauea Lodge and smaller Hale Kilauea guest house are nearby. Sea Mountain at Punaluu (golf course) lies southwest of the park. Military families can stay at Kilauea Military Camp, an in-park recreation center.

The largest hotels from Kailua-Kona south to Keauhou Bay include King Kamehameha (at Kailua Pier), Kona Bay, Royal Kona, Crown Lands of Keauhou, and Kona Surf. Area condominiums come in all sizes and price ranges.

North of Kailua-Kona, along the North Kona and South Kohala coasts, sprawl the island's most glamorous resorts, which encompass both upscale hotels and luxury condominiums. From south to north lie once-isolated Kona Village with its soon-to-be Four Seasons neighbor, Royal Waikoloan and Hilton Waikoloa Village, Mauna Lani Bay Hotel and Ritz-Carlton Mauna Lani, and the Mauna Kea Beach Hotel (closed for remodeling until 1996) and neighboring Hapuna Prince Beach Resort.

Elsewhere, look for accommodations at Kamuela Inn or Parker Ranch Lodge in cool Waimea or head south to the inexpensive Manago Hotel (good restaurant) in Captain Cook. For information on stays in national or state park cabins, see page 171.

Touring the Island

Local ground tour companies (Grayline and Roberts, Kailua-Kona; Jack's, Hilo) schedule trips to Hawaii's main attractions. Tours can be booked through hotel travel desks or directly with tour operators and travel agents. Big Island Air, Hawaii Airventures, Hawaii Island Hoppers, Hilo Bay Air, 'Io Aviation, Kainoa Aviation, Kenai Helicopters, Mauna Kea Helicopters, Papillon Helicopters, and Volcano Heli-Tours offer aerial tours.

The Shopping Experience

Boutiques in Hawaii's deluxe hotels carry original resort attire. Restaurants and attractive settings make Kings' Shops at Waikoloa Beach Resort and Hale Kea in Waimea popular shopping malls. For best local souvenirs, try Kailua-Kona, Keauhou Shopping Village, and downtown Hilo. Arts and crafts stops include Kamaaina Woods factory, Honokaa; Gallery of Great Things, Waimea; Kimura's Lauhala Shop, Holualoa; and Volcano Art Center (in the park's original Volcano House). Shop for chocolate at Kailua Candy Co.; macadamia nuts at factories in Hilo, Honokaa, and South Kona; coffee at plantations in South Kona; and anthuriums and orchids at Hilo nurseries.

Dining Options

Restaurants offer varied cuisine, from seafood (Kona restaurants) to Parker Ranch steak (Waimea). Japanese food is popular around Hilo and Honokaa. For imaginative island fare, choices include The Canoehouse at Mauna Lani, Hawaiian-oriented Coast Grille at Hapuna Prince, and Merriman's and Eidelweiss in Waimea. Kona Village is noted for its Friday night luau. Supermarkets stock Hilo Homemade Ice Cream, Kona coffee, and wine from Volcano Vineyards.

On pages 172–173, we've included a guide to the island's recreational facilities. For information and addresses of specific accommodations, excursions, and attractions, contact the Hawaii Visitors Bureau offices, Kona Plaza Shopping Arcade, 75-5719 W. Alii Drive, Kailua-Kona, HI 96740, or 250 Keawe Street, Hilo, HI 96720.

Backdropped by snow-topped Mauna Kea, Hilo sprawls along magnificent crescent-shaped bay.

HILO – THE BIG ISLAND'S "BIG CITY"

Hilo is a cane field town now grown up to be the fourth largest "city" in the state, though its population is only 42,000. It sprawls along the crescent-shaped edge of Hilo Bay; Mauna Loa and Mauna Kea are backdrops on clear days.

Though Hilo has hotels, restaurants, and intriguing shops housed in wood-frame buildings with metal roofs, tourists en route to Hawaii Volcanoes National Park tend to overlook the unpretentious town. Busy with the flower and macadamia nut industries, Hilo also serves as Hawaii county seat and as home to a campus of the University of Hawaii.

To savor the flavor of the friendly town, stroll through galleries and crafts shops downtown. A colorful farmers' market takes place on Wednesday and Saturday mornings at Mamo and Kamehameha streets.

Along the Waterfront

Hilo's waterfront is a greenbelt sculptured into a handsome park. Following a disastrous tsunami (seismic wave) that destroyed the bayfront in 1960—including homes and businesses that had been rebuilt after an even more destructive tsunami in 1946—the spunky little town was rebuilt again, this time on higher ground. The waterfront, now lined with paths and gardens, is exceptionally lush and green because Hilo receives almost 140 inches of rain a year (most of it at night and in the early morning).

Banyan Drive, a tree-shaded parkway, rounds Waiakea Peninsula past most of Hilo's hotels. Each banyan along the drive bears a plaque with the name of the celebrity who planted it.

Coconut Island, the palm-fringed islet in Hilo Bay, was once a Hawaiian sanctuary with birth and healing stones. Now it is a pleasant picnic spot reached by a bridge from Waiakea Peninsula.

Liliuokalani Gardens spreads over almost 30 acres of Waiakea Peninsula, with stone lanterns, pagodas, curved bridges, and plants and trees representative of both Japan and Hawaii.

Suisan Fish Market, 85 Lihiwai Street, bustles with activity around 8:00 A.M. Monday through Saturday. That's when the fish are auctioned off in two or three languages, including "pidgin"—an exotic island blend of Hawaiian, English, and Japanese. You can look and listen, but only licensed fish dealers can bid. At Sampan Harbor, the "sampans" unload their catch around 5:30 A.M. and 4 P.M.

Wailoa River State Park includes the area around the Wailoa River, Waiakea Pond, and the Waiolama Canal. The Wailoa River has the distinction of being the state's shortest river; it flows less than half a mile. The park's picnic area can be reached from the end of Piilani Street or by crossing footbridges near the Wailoa Visitor Center.

Wailoa Cultural and Visitors Center has changing exhibits on the Big Island's culture, history, and scenery and an information counter. The center is open Monday through Saturday 8 A.M. to 4:30 P.M.

Downtown Hilo

Stop by the Hawaii Visitors Bureau at 250 Keawe Street for a self-guided tour booklet that allows you to explore downtown Hilo on your own. Or join a historical walking tour; call 935-8850 for information.

Central Christian Church, corner of Haili and Kilauea streets, was originally known as the Portuguese Church. This wooden Victorian was built in 1892 by immigrants who became Protestants to have services in their native tongue rather than the Latin required in Catholic churches.

Haili Church, 404 Haili Street, was built by Protestant missionaries. This yellow frame, New England style church, recently renovated following a 1979 fire, has services in Hawaiian and English. The choir is justifiably famous.

St. Joseph's Catholic Church, corner of Haili and Kapiolani streets, is Hilo's largest church. Complete with cracked bell, it resembles an early Spanish mission.

Lyman Museum and Mission House, 276 Haili Street (Monday through Saturday 9 A.M. to 5 P.M., Sunday 1 to 4 P.M.), returns the visitor to 19th century Hilo. Hand-hewn timbers from local forests and stones mortared with coral were used in the construction of this 1839 home built by the Rev. and Mrs. David Belden Lyman, missionaries who arrived in the islands in 1832. The house is furnished with antiques and curios from the missionary period; each year a traditional New England Christmas is reenacted. The Lyman Museum next door opened in 1973. In the Island Heritage Gallery, exhibits focus on the belongings of the early Hawaiians and the various ethnic groups who immigrated to the Big Island. Man's Heritage Gallery contains artifacts fashioned of glass, wood, crystal, and jade. The Earth's Heritage Gallery displays large collections of both lava formations and minerals from around the world. The museum admission fee covers the entrance charge for both buildings.

The Naha and Pinao Stones are museum pieces in front of the Hawaii County Library on Waianuenue Avenue. In ancient days, the huge, rectangular Naha Stone stood before the temple of Pinao, near the present library site, while the Pinao Stone was the temple's entrance pillar. The Hawaiians used the Naha Stone to determine the legitimacy of claimants to the Naha royal bloodline. One who could move the stone would become king of the island; one who overturned it would conquer all the islands. It's said the prophecy was fulfilled when Kamehameha the Great overturned the stone while still a young boy—even though he was not of Naha blood.

East Hawaii Cultural Center, 141 Kalakaua Street, includes galleries, workshops, studios, and a gift shop. The 1932 building, listed on the National Register of Historic Places, once housed the county's police station and the district courthouse. Its architecture combines traditional Hawaiian style and art deco design.

In and around Hilo

Visit temples and churches, learn about the art of growing orchids and anthuriums, try a taste of macadamia nuts, or relax at one of the beaches along Highway 12 (see the next page).

Hilo Hongwanji Temple, 398 Kilauea Avenue, was built in 1925 for the oldest Japanese Buddhist mission in the state, founded in 1889.

United Community Church, on the corner of Kinoole and Mohouli streets, resembles an oriental temple. Built in 1937 as the Hilo Chinese Christian Church, it now has a "melting pot" membershp and English services.

Ke Kilohana O Ka Malamalama Church, 588 Manono Street, serves about 200 members of a small Protestant sect, Hoomana Naauao O Hawaii. The church has Hawaiian-English services, two choirs, and Hawaiian language classes.

Wailuku River State Park lies along the banks of the Wailuku River, which empties into Hilo Bay. The state's second longest river, the Wailuku flows 32 miles/51 km from its source high on the slopes of Mauna Kea.

Rainbow Falls. The rainbow that gives the falls its name is visible many mornings in the spray and mist. A short trail to a secluded picnic spot starts near the lookout.

Boiling Pots. This site is a mile farther inland at the end of a foot trail from the corner of Wailuku and Peepee Falls drives. The "pots" are a series of deep, round pools, 20 to 50 feet across, cut in the lava stream bed and linked by falls and rapids. Turbulent water flows beneath the lava and bubbles up as if boiling. The pools are inviting, but the currents can be treacherous—check conditions before entering the water.

Kaumana Caves are on Kaumana Drive about 5 miles/ 8 km from downtown. From the picnic ground, a stairway descends to a fern grotto between two large lava tubes. The two tubes and their many branching caverns were formed during Mauna Loa's 1881 flow, which lasted for 9 months. The cave leading toward Hilo can be explored (wear old clothes and take a flashlight); it's been followed for more than half a mile. The other is dangerous and should not be entered.

Gardens and nurseries flourish in Hilo's rainy climate. The Big Island is famous for its anthuriums and orchids, many of which are grown around Hilo. The Hawaii Visitors Bureau (180 Kinoole Street) can provide information on the gardens and nurseries open to the public; some of the larger ones are listed below. The greatest concentrations are along Highway 11 and around Pahoa. Many nurseries also offer plants for sale (make sure purchases are properly packaged and certified for export to the mainland) or they will arrange to ship plants back to you or to friends on your gift list.

Akatsuka Orchid Gardens, on Highway 11 at 22-mile marker between Hilo and Volcano (daily 8:30 A.M. to 5 P.M.), is a fully covered display garden of orchids and other island plants. Both flowers and plants are for sale.

Hilo Tropical Gardens, 1477 Kalanianaole Avenue (daily 9 A.M. to 5 P.M.), is a 2-acre garden of orchids, tropical flowers, shrubs, trees, and natural tidal pools. The gift shop has a fine selection of Hawaiian handicrafts.

Hilo Orchidarium, 524 Manono Street (9 A.M. to 5 P.M., closed Sunday; donation requested), is the headquarters for the annual orchid show. Orchids are the only plants displayed in its landscaped gardens.

Bloomers Hirose Nurseries, 2212 Kanoelehua Avenue (daily 7:30 A.M. to 5 P.M.), features a variety of tropical plants and flowers, along with a large gift shop.

Nani Mau Gardens, 421 Makalika Street off Highway 11 (daily 8 A.M. to 5 P.M.; free for children and seniors), displays more than 100 varieties of tropical fruit trees and more than 2,000 varieties of orchids, red ginger, and anthuriums in its 30-plus acres. Visitors can take a narrated tram tour, drive a golf cart, or stroll through the grounds, which include a Japanese garden, a waterfall, and a miniature lake. A restaurant (open daily for lunch) overlooks the grounds.

Rainbow Tropicals, on the corner of Mamaki and Kealakai streets off Highway 11 (daily 8:30 A.M. to 5 P.M.), is a leading floral exporter, with more than 20 of its 62 acres devoted exclusively to anthuriums. A walk through the well-cultivated orchards and gardens of the nursery takes visitors past a collection of rare palm trees.

Mauna Loa Macadamia Nut Mill, 4 miles/6½ km south of Hilo on Highway 11 (weekdays 8:30 A.M. to 5 P.M.), offers self-guided tours through its processing plant and state-of-the-art chocolate factory. You can also walk through the orchard and sample the company's products. Don't expect bargains at the gift store.

Hale Manu Crafts, off Highway 11 near the Panaewa Rainforest Zoo, specializes in weaving with *lauhala,* the leaf of the pandanus tree. Available for sale are hats, purses, mats, and baskets all woven of lauhala, along with other gift items.

Panaewa Rainforest Zoo, Stainback Highway (daily 9 A.M. to 4:30 P.M.), is Hilo's charming zoo. Situated in the Panaewa Rainforest south of Hilo, the zoo is designed around the theme of animals and plants found in the world's tropical rain forests.

Onekahakaha Beach Park, 3 miles/5 km from Hilo on Highway 12 (Kalanianaole Avenue), is Hilo's largest developed beach park. You'll find a strip of white sandy beach, a tidal pool perfect for children's wading, plus picnic pavilions and firepits.

James Kealoha Beach Park, a mile farther along Highway 12, also has picnic tables and a strip of sandy beach.

Leleiwi Beach Park, five miles/8 km from Hilo on Highway 12, offers sheltered coves, a lava-rock beach, and cooler swimming because of some freshwater inflows.

WHAT DO THEY CALL THAT FISH?

Whether you plan to catch them, look at them, or just eat them, chances are that you'll encounter fish of some kind during your Hawaiian vacation.

The names of many of the fish on the menu or in fish markets may be unfamiliar to you. To aid in identification, we've put together a listing.

'ahi . . . . .yellowfin tuna
aholehole . . . . mountain bass
aku . . . . .skipjack tuna
akule . . . . bigeye scad
'ama'ama . . . . mullet
a'u . . . . .marlin, swordfish
awa . . . . milkfish
'aweoweo . . . . red bigeye
hahalalu . . . . young bigeye scad
hihiwai . . . . .freshwater limpet
humuhumu . . . . triggerfish
kaku . . . . barracuda
kalikali . . . . .pink snapper
kamanu . . . . Hawaiian salmon
kawakawa . . . . little tuna
mahimahi . . . . dolphin fish

moi . . . . threadfin
'oama . . . . .young goat fish
'o'io . . . . .bonefish
ono . . . . wahoo
'o'opu . . . . goby
'opae . . . . freshwater shrimp
'opakapaka .pink snapper
'opelu . . . . mackerel scad
'opihi . . . . saltwater limpet
puhi . . . . eel
uhu . . . . parrot fish
uku . . . . gray snapper
'ula'ula . . . . .red snapper
ulua . . . . jack crevalle
u'u . . . . squirrel fish
weke . . . . goat fish

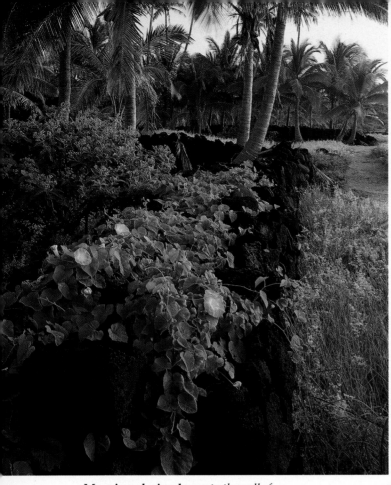

Morning glories decorate *the wall of the heiau at Kamoamoa on the coast of Hawaii Volcanoes National Park.*

Bright anthuriums *thrive in the shade of giant tree ferns near Pahoa. The long-lasting blooms are a favorite tourist buy.*

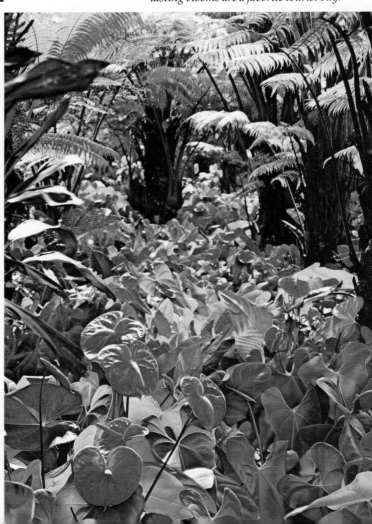

THE PUNA DISTRICT

The triangle-shaped Puna District reflects the Big Island's geological youth. Fresh lava flows and the pounding sea combine in an ever-changing landscape and seacoast—a living museum showing how the Hawaiian Islands were formed.

This diamond-shaped district also forms the easternmost tip of the Big Island—and of the state. A region of contrasts, the Puna District offers subdivisions and isolated settlements, tropical forests and areas laid bare by lava extending from the eastern shoulder of a very active volcano to the rugged coastline. An agricultural area, it's a major producer of papayas and anthuriums. Orchid nurseries and macadamia nut groves also flourish.

Puna's usual bucolic tranquility is occasionally interrupted by upheavals from Kilauea, one of two active volcanoes in the area. Lava has made its way to the sea in several places, adding hundreds of acres of land but covering towns, forests, and roads en route. In a surprisingly short period of time, Puna's mineral-rich soil and rainy climate enable new plant life to replace the desolation.

The Puna coast is lined with Hawaii's famous black sand beaches, formed when lava hits the ocean, explodes into bits, and is ground fine by the waves. But these beaches also change and eventually disappear as the sea, reclaiming some of its own territory, washes away the lava bits.

Freakish evidences of volcanic activity show up throughout the area. A few signs of Kapoho village still poke above the lava flows that buried it in 1960; its devastated lavascape served as a training ground for astronauts. In 1991, a fiery flow overran the town of Kalapana, the national park's Wahaula Visitor Center, and two of the island's most scenic black sand beach parks—Kaimu and Harry K. Brown.

Highways through Puna

Prior to recent eruptions, you could make a loop trip from Hilo to Hawaii Volcanoes National Park and back through the Puna District on Highway 11 from Hilo, Chain of Craters Road (see page 152) in the park, and Highway 130, which began at the park's eastern edge. However, lava flow from the 1991 eruption now covers much of the eastern end of Chain of Craters Road, severing this round-trip route.

Though you can no longer reach the park from Puna, the region is worth a detour. Gentrification is proceeding apace, but most of the area still has a rakish charm.

To reach the Puna District from Hilo, follow Highway 11 south to Highway 130 at Keaau. Highway 130 travels through the district toward the remains of Kalapana. A turn onto Highway 132 at Pahoa leads to Lava Tree State Park and on to Highway 137, a coastal route that once joined Highway 130 at Kalapana. The latter highway is now closed 4 miles before this intersection, but from the end you can view the 1991 destruction and even venture onto the lava for a closer look.

Highway 11 to Hawaii Volcanoes National Park

Highway 11 is also known as the Hawaii Belt Road or the Mamalahoa Highway. This is the circle-island route that provides access to nearly all of the Big Island. South of Hilo, Highway 11 skirts the western edge of the Puna District while climbing to the rim of Kilauea's caldera (see page 150). Along the way you'll pass fields of anthuriums and scattered towns.

Mountain View. Mountain View is the center of anthurium nurseries along Highway 11. In the town itself, St. Theresa's Church was built and decorated by Father Evarist, who was also the artist for the Star of the Sea Painted Church (see page 148). He finished in 1936; the paintings in the church show fine baroque detail. Opposite the church is a Japanese shrine. Try the stone cookies at the Mountain View Bakery before leaving town.

Gardens and nurseries. Many nurseries in the area are open to the public; look for a "Visitors Welcome" sign outside. Among the larger ones are Anthuriums of Hawaii and Hawaiian Flower Gardens in Mountain View, and Hawaiian Tropical Orchids near Volcano.

Along Highway 130

Keaau sits at the junction of highways 11 and 130. Highway 11 continues directly to the park; Highway 130 heads through the heart of the Puna District. South of Pahoa, the road cuts through tropical forests and an old lava flow before ending at barriers marking the most recent eruption and the end of the road. (This highway used to intersect Highway 137, which runs along the Puna coast, and met Chain of Craters Road at the park's eastern entrance.)

Keaau. This old plantation town is growing. Plantation quarters in the town have been restored and converted to shops for local artisans. Across the street, the Christmas Store has a variety of Hawaiian Christmas ornaments and other items. Also note the town's fine Hongwanji Buddhist Temple.

Pahoa. A town of false-front buildings and some wooden sidewalks, Pahoa is the home of the school that has several times been converted to eruption headquarters for volcanologists, evacuees, reporters, and spectators. Note the attractive Sacred Hearts Church.

Gardens and nurseries. Anthuriums abound in this area; you'll see these colorful flowers growing in lava-encrusted yards under orange and tangerine trees. Some of the major nurseries in the area include Hawaiian Greenhouses, Anthuriums of Pahoa, Taira's Big Isle Anthuriums, and Puna Flowers & Foliage. Check locally for gardens and nurseries open to the public.

Lava flows. As you're southward-bound on Highway 130, park at the marked turnout about 4 miles/6km out of Pahoa and have a look below at the impressive remains of the 1955 eruption. But watch out for obscured holes and cracks. You can climb a 20-foot cone and peer into its still steamy interior. Note the deep cracks in the old, now partly brush-covered roadway that was cut off by the eruption. From here, scientists actually watched an eruption start: a fissure opened, the road split, and small explosive fountains shot up through a bulge of lava. "Pele's Kitchen" contains old tree molds, yellowish from sulphur and other gases that steamed out of them after this eruption.

The highway crosses two 1955 lava flows that reached the sea. You can see the cones from which they came outlined against the sky.

Along Highway 137

Highway 137 follows the coast between Honolulu Landing on Hawaii's east shore to its present stopping point a few miles beyond the settlement of Opihikao. The road, which hugs the seashore, leads past old villages and some of the island's picturesque black sand beaches. The beaches along this section of Hawaii's coast are ideal for picnicking or exploring, but currents make swimming dangerous.

Houses closer together than others in the region identify two old villages—Opihikao and Pohoiki. As you approach Opihikao, watch for concrete tombs atop old lava. The settlement's wooden church, on a side road *mauka*, is more than 100 years old. Country lanes heading inland from the two villages pass small farms, houses,

and sources of 1955 lava, emerging onto the main roads below Pahoa.

Up the coast from Pohoiki lie some startling contrasts: a vast wasteland of recent origin and fields of orchids and papayas thriving in crushed old lava.

In 1960 Pele went on a month-long rampage in this region, destroying two villages, 1,500 acres of cane and other farm crops, a photogenic natural pool, inshore waters rich in mullet, and beach lots so desirable they're in use again. Lava fingers buried a dozen homes, but others have gone up to take advantage of the newly formed black sand beaches. Near the junction of highways 137 and 132, you'll pass a few things miraculously spared.

Along the entire route from the park back to Honolulu Landing, you'll find a mixture of old and new Hawaii, with both natural and manmade attractions.

Lost beaches. In addition to the destruction of Kalapana, the 1991 eruption covered two of Puna's best-known seaside parks. Harry K. Brown Beach Park, near Kalapana, contained legendary boulders (some large enough to be arranged as picnic furniture under umbrellas of palms and pandanus trees), a saltwater swimming pool built into gray sand dunes, and the Kekaloa Heiau, an ancient Hawaiian temple supposedly built by a wizard.

Kaimu Black Sand Beach, a few road curves east of Harry K. Brown, once boasted the island's most photogenic black sand beach. With its backdrop of coconut trees, Kaimu's curving strand repeatedly starred in advertisements describing Hawaii's charms.

Star of the Sea painted church. One of Puna's most beloved landmarks, this tiny treasure house of painting once stood on the Kalapana shore. It was saved from the 1991 lava flow and temporarily relocated.

Father Evarist Gielen, the Belgian artist who painted the pictures in the interior of the church, completed his work in 1929. The priest had studied briefly in Europe with Father John, the artist of the Kona Coast's painted church (see page 161). Other examples of his work can be seen in St. Theresa's Church in Mountain View.

In the church, two barrel-vaulted ceilings, one over the altar recess, appear to be supported by columns that are only painted on the wall. Six pictures with large designs and soft colors float on painted ceiling ribs; windows have painted canopies. The large nativity scene over the door is Florentine in tone. To the Hawaiians, accustomed to worshipping outdoors, the paintings represented a compromise between their old and new religions.

MacKenzie State Park. The park campground sits in a shady grove of ironwoods along the coast just past Opihikao. The shore fishing is good, and a portion of an ancient Hawaiian foot trail runs through part of the park. The currents are dangerous—don't swim here.

Isaac Hale Beach Park. On Pohoiki Bay, this was once Puna's shipping port. Now it's a launching place for small boats. There is good fishing and hiking, but no swimming.

Kapoho Cone. You can get a good look at this green-cloaked prominence from an old eruption. Drive up a grassy road to the cone's low rim, then walk down inside to jungle-shrouded "green lake" of perhaps 10 acres. Its green color is caused by the great quantity of algae.

Cape Kumukahi Lighthouse. The lucky lighthouse stands on the shore at the end of Highway 132, near where it crosses Highway 137. The river of lava from Pele's 1960 flow crushed the station's cottages and then stopped, split, and continued to the sea on either side of the lighthouse. Local residents claim Pele spared the fishermen's beacon and consider the spot a special place. The lighthouse tower, now automated, stands on the state's easternmost point.

Koae. Highway 137 continues north to Koae through a blanket of cinders that are alive now with orchid fields. A cream-colored church punctuates the blackness around this settlement. Koae was virtually abandoned when its houses buckled under a heavy cinder shower. Fishermen's trails lead to more black sand beaches.

Honolulu Landing. Passenger cars can travel as far as Honolulu Landing. Through a grove of ironwoods, you'll see 1840 cinder cones hard enough to drive on. The beach at Honolulu Landing washes away each winter—proof of the ocean's force in changing the coastline. Do not swim here—the currents are dangerous.

Cape Kumukahi to Pahoa

Highway 132 completes the triangle of roads through the Puna District, connecting the coast with Pahoa. Off the road, you'll see a few things miraculously spared during the 1960 lava flow. Left on the side of an old cinder cone are 16 gravestones, usually flower-decked. The molten river temporarily forked and went around them.

Kapoho. On Highway 132 you pass right over the buried village of Kapoho. To the north is the 420-foot black cone built up on the eruption site. Most of the Kapoho's 250 people moved to Pahoa and now grow their anthuriums there, but their new orchid fields lie above the old town site in a graben that has ideal growing conditions. The Kapoho region's newest crop is Norfolk Island pines.

Lava Tree State Park. Hidden in a tropical forest are the "petrified Hawaiians"—weird, lava-encrusted tree trunks. Two centuries ago this was a grove of large ohia trees; then came the 1790 eruption from Kilauea. A flow of hot lava poured through the forest and around the trees. The tops were burnt off by the heat. Moisture in the tree trunks chilled and hardened the lava, forming a shell around each tree. After the molten lava drained away, the lava trees were left. A deep fracture runs through the park and there are other dangerous cracks throughout it—these may be siphons that drained vast quantities of lava back into the earth.

BIG ISLAND BED AND BREAKFASTS

Private cottages in cool Waimea, rustic lodges near the action in Hawaii Volcanoes National Park, a wayside retreat in photogenic Waipio Valley, a plantation house near green and black sand beaches, or a rambling inn high above the Kona Coast—these are just a few of the choices available to you in bed-and-breakfasts inns on the Big Island. Accommodations range from separate buildings, or at least private entrances, to a spare bedroom in a private residence with a shared bath and a breakfast with the family.

Run by friendly, knowledgeable hosts, these resort alternatives offer less expensive accommodations than most island hotels and include a morning meal (or supplies for making your own). Innkeepers are usually very happy to act as travel agents, recommending restaurants, suggesting activities, and pointing out "must-see" attractions in the area. Some even take guest along on family outings or suggest itineraries for forays on your own.

Most bed and breakfasts can be booked in advance through local reservation agencies. Several are listed at right. For still other suggestions, contact the Hawaii Visitors Bureau offices in Hilo or Kailua-Kona (addresses on page 141).

Hawaii's Best Bed & Breakfasts
P.O. Box 563
Kamuela, HI 96743
(800) BNB-9912; (808) 885-4550

All Islands Bed & Breakfast
823 Kainui Drive
Kailua, HI 96734
(800) 542-0344; (808) 263-2342

Pacific Hawaii Bed & Breakfast
19 Kai Nani Place
Kailua, HI 96734
(808) 254-5030

My Island Bed & Breakfast
P.O. Box 100
Volcano, HI 96785
(808) 967-7110; (808) 967-7216

Hawaii Island Bed and Breakfast Association
P.O. Box 726
Volcano, HI 96785
(brochure only)

The best known and most popular of the Big Island's many attractions is Hawaii Volcanoes National Park. Each year a large number of visitors journey to this park in hopes of witnessing the fire goddess, Pele, in one of her tempestuous moods. She's unpredictable, though; Pele does perform often, but she may not be at her fiery best during your visit.

Even without flashy shows of molten lava rivers and mountains spewing fire, Hawaii Volcanoes National Park is a fascinating place to explore. Within its 344 square miles/894 square km are two live volcanoes, Mauna Loa and Kilauea; a bizarre volcanic landscape abounding with fantastic features; rain forest; and rare plants and birds. Established in 1916, the park encompasses the summit caldera and upper northeast flank of Mauna Loa, Kilauea's caldera and southern and eastern flanks, and a stretch of Puna's coast at Kalapana.

The park's main entrance lies 30 miles/48 km southwest of Hilo on Highway 11. A second entrance, through the park's Kalapana section along the Puna coast, was closed by lava flows in 1991 when a vent on Kilauea's east slope buried the village of Kalapana, overran the Wahaula Visitor Center, and severed Chain of Craters Road. When current activity ceases and the roads are reopened, you'll be able to make a 90-mile/144-km loop trip from Hilo or visit the Kalapana section separately.

The Kilauea Visitor Center (open daily 8 A.M. to 5 P.M.) at the park entrance is stocked with maps and information on volcanoes, plants, and wildlife. A film on the recent eruptions is shown hourly from 9 A.M. to 4 P.M. Seismographs at the observatory overlooking Kilauea Crater track volcanic activity; for recorded eruption reports, phone 967-7977 at any hour.

Getting to Know the Volcanoes

Mauna Loa's summit is 13,677 feet; Kilauea's is 4,090 feet. In contrast to the explosive behavior of many steepsided volcanoes in other parts of the world, these gently sloping volcanoes erupt relatively quietly with spectacular fire fountains and fluid lava flows that form lakes, rivers, and falls. Often, crowds of people can get close enough to have good views of the eruption. In fact, Kilauea is called the "drive-in volcano" because of its easy visitor accessibility.

Mauna Loa. At times erupting lava from this volcano has stayed within its summit caldera, Mokuaweoweo. Still other times, the lava has spilled over and down the slopes or issued from rifts in the mountainside far below. Mauna Loa's flows have covered half the island and even journeyed as far as the sea. During the volcano's March, 1984 eruption, lava emerged from a vent in the northeast rift near Red Hill and flowed to within a few miles of Hilo. That period of activity, lasting 22 days, was the longest on the northeast rift in 103 years. It was also the first time that Mauna Loa and Kilauea had erupted simultaneously in 116 years.

Kilauea. This volcano's huge crater—2½ miles/4 km long, 2 miles/3 km wide, 400 feet deep—contains Halemaumau, the crater within a crater that is said to be the firepit which Pele, the volcano goddess, now calls home. This main vent is less than a mile in diameter. Its depth changes with each refilling or collapse of its bottom. For more than a century, Halemaumau was a bubbling, sometimes overflowing lava lake. The almost continuous activity ended with steam explosions in 1924. Since this vent is connected with a reservoir of molten magma deep beneath the earth, lava lake activity continues sporadically, marked by the rise and fall of the crater floor.

Kilauea's outbreaks in the last two decades—so many it's hard to keep count—have also included fireworks in its satellite craters and flank eruptions some miles from the summit along both east and southwest rift zones. A five-year period of intermittent activity began in February, 1969, in and about several pit craters along the Chain of Craters Road. Lava traveled both by surface streams that covered the road and through underground lava tubes. Since 1969, flowing lava has repeatedly reached the sea to form a couple hundred acres of new land.

Fountains played along a stretch of Ka'u Desert near Mauna Iki in September, 1971, the first activity along Kilauea's southwest rift zone since 1920. Kilauea's joint eruption with Mauna Loa in March, 1984, was part of a series of eruptions along the eastern rift that began in January, 1983, and is still continuing. The 1983 lava flows covered homes outside the park's eastern boundary. In 1986, lava flows destroyed homes in Kapaahu and in Kalapana, an area lost completely in the 1991 eruption.

Crater Rim Drive

The 11-mile/18-km Crater Rim Drive takes you from Kilauea Visitor Center around and into the summit caldera, across both rift zones, and over bleak desert. En route you'll see two types of lava flows, *pahoehoe* and *aa*. The smooth-looking, ropey lava is *pahoehoe* and the blocky, jagged lava is *aa*. The chemical composition of both types of flow is the same. Usually a flow begins as pahoehoe and becomes aa somewhere down the slope.

Volcano House. Before you begin your trip along Crater Rim Drive, stop at the Volcano House, located across the street from the visitor center. Styled like a hunting lodge, the hotel has 37 rooms and a rim-side view of Kilauea Crater; Halemaumau smokes in the distance. The Volcano House makes a good base for park explorations; note the continuously burning fire in the lobby. Lunch is crowded; dinner is more relaxed.

The 3-mile/5-km, self-guiding Halemaumau Trail starts near Volcano House and crosses the scorched and scarred floor of Kilauea caldera to the rim of Halemaumau. This is the park's most popular hike. If you take it, start early before the sun bakes the crater floor. Arrange a ride back from Halemaumau Overlook, or walk out of the crater and back 3½ miles/5½ km on Byron Ledge Trail.

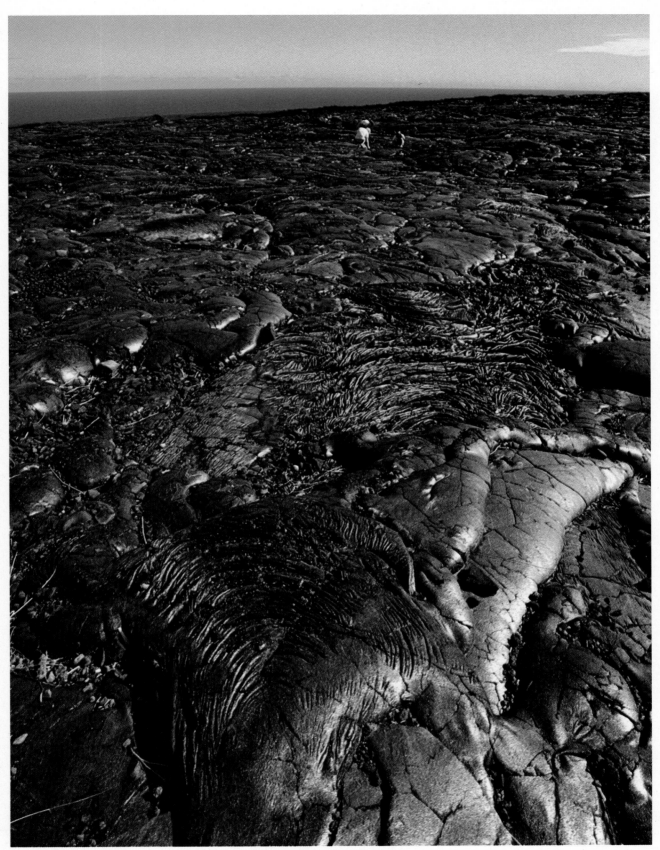

A sea of lava *dwarfs visitors in Hawaii Volcanoes National Park. This ropy lava is called* pahoehoe; *rough, cindery type is* aa.

...Hawaii Volcanoes National Park

Volcano Art Center. The current Volcano House was built in 1941. Part of the original 1877 structure was moved across the street adjacent to the visitor center and now houses the Volcano Art Center. This first-class gallery features local artists' work. Exhibits include paintings, photos, and sculptures—all inspired by the volcanoes.

Sulphur Banks. Heading west on Crater Rim Drive, you come first to the Sulphur Banks, where volcanic fumaroles emit gases and vapors that cool when they reach the surface, leaving colorful mineral deposits. Along Steaming Bluff, you can be engulfed by steam from hot water released through deep ground cracks.

Mauna Loa Strip Road. This side route takes you up the mountain to a shelter and overlook at 6,662 feet, the start of an 18-mile/29-km trail to Mokuaweoweo caldera. Along the road's lower reaches are tree molds as large as 5 feet across, formed when liquid lava cooled around tree trunks, crusting on the outside but burning out the inside.

The road passes Kipuka Puaulu (Bird Park), an oasis (*kipuka*) created when a Mauna Loa flow divided. It left intact 100 vegetated acres with unusual native plants, including some edible berries and a few plant varieties found nowhere else. Here are picnic grounds, an exhibit describing the plants and native birds, and a pamphlet to guide you on an easy, mile-long nature trail. From Bird Park, the Mauna Loa Strip Road continues up over 10 paved but narrow miles (16 km). You're rewarded with a panoramic view on clear days.

Thomas A. Jaggar Museum. Continuing counterclockwise on the Rim Drive, you come to Kilauea Overlook, a picnic spot on the edge of the vast, lava-streaked depression. Half a mile farther is the Thomas A. Jaggar Museum, housed in the former Hawaiian Volcano Observatory building. Exhibits, video monitors, and seismographs tell the story of Hawaiian volcanoes both past and present. Brightly colored murals by Herb Kane illustrate Hawaiian volcano legends, including the story of Pele, goddess of the volcano. Just beyond the museum's wall of windows is Kilauea Caldera.

Next door is the Hawaiian Volcano Observatory. Located on the high point of the caldera's west wall, this facility's research program is geared toward gaining a better understanding of volcanic behavior and improving methods of predicting volcanic activity. It is closed to the public.

Halemaumau Overlook. From the halfway point on the drive, walk the short trail to the overlook on the east edge of Halemaumau, right along its cracked and crumbly—but safe—brink. Depth and coloring of the firepit depend upon Pele's current mood; the temperamental lady just may send up sulphurous smoke to irritate your eyes and throat.

Devastation Trail. Park at Devastation Trail, a half-mile of boardwalk atop cinders that takes you through a skeleton forest wrought by the violence in Kilauea Iki (Little Kilauea) Crater in 1959. Note how the ohia trees are once more coming to life with new foliage. The walk ends at Kilauea Iki Overlook (also accessible from the rim drive).

Kilauea Iki. Straddling Kilauea Iki's rim is Puu Puai, the 400-foot cone of pumice and ash formed during the 1959 eruption when dazzling fountains of lava shot as high as 1,900 feet. It rears up 150 feet from the old, now-buried roadbed. The Kilauea Iki trail takes you across the floor of the chasm. As on the Devastation Trail, plant life is once more taking root. You'll see ohia and fern seedlings growing in the crater's cracks.

Thurston Lava Tube. This easternmost point on the drive is in the famous Fern Jungle, a moist tangle of giant tree ferns and several varieties of smaller ferns growing in the shade of weathered ohia trees. You can walk on a ¼-mile loop trail through forest to a 450-foot tunnel, 10 or more feet high. This ancient tunnel was created during an eruption when the outer crust of a lava flow hardened while the molten river within continued to travel. When the supply of lava stopped, the tube drained out and left a tunnel. Lava tubes or tunnels are common in Hawaii.

Chain of Craters Road

You'll need to backtrack from the Thurston Lava Tube in order to take the turnoff for the Chain of Craters Road. It's a 27-mile/43-km drive from Kilauea Caldera, at the 4,000-foot mark, to the coast.

You'll drive by three active fault escarpments, edges of the east rift zone, and approach the smoldering base of Mauna Ulu (growing mountain)—a 385-foot-high vol-

Kipuka Puaulu
Bird Park
Golf Club
Tree Molds
Sulphur Banks
Kilauea Visitor Center
Volcano
MAUNA LOA STRIP ROAD
to Kona
Steaming Bluff
Kilauea Overlook
Volcano House
to Hilo
Observatory
Thurston Lava Tube
HALEMAUMAU TRAIL
KILAUEA CALDERA
Byron Ledge
KILAUEA IKI CRATER
Halemaumau Crater
Devastation Trail
Fern Jungle
CRATER RIM DRIVE
Keanakakoi Crater
CRATER RIM TRAIL
Lua Manu Crater
Puhimau Crater
CHAIN OF CRATERS ROAD
Kokoolau Crater
Kilauea Caldera
0   1   2 KM
0   1 MI
HAWAII
——— Primary
— — Secondary
········· Foot Trail
to Kalapana

cano built up by the eruptions. From the vents of Mauna Ulu came the lava and cinders that blanketed the old road; from its depths, lava flowed through tubes to the ocean. The best view of Mauna Ulu is from the top of Puu Huluhulu, an older crater lightly forested with ohia trees.

The road is now closed 1½ miles east of Kamoamoa campground. A rough trail leads 2 miles over glassy lava to the Wahaula Heiau, an ancient temple surprisingly spared by the 1991 flows that destroyed the visitor center.

The Park's Kalapana Section

Near the coast, make a stop at the trailhead at Puu Loa. Walk the old Puna-Ka'u Trail for ½ mile east over pahoehoe fields to mounds etched with petroglyphs.

Chain of Craters Road winds westward along the Puna coast. As you drive through this section of the park, you'll follow a road atop 60-foot cliffs with views inland over the undulating pahoehoe lava. Kilauea's current activity centers above this area in the East Rift Zone just east of the park's boundary.

Kamoamoa. The coastal Kamoamoa campground and picnic area overlook an arch created when wave action eroded a 100-foot lava tube. On its south side, back of a canoe landing, are long, narrow enclosures that were canoe sheds. The rock walls you see in all directions formerly outlined village compounds. One long wall, from sea to pali, is of turn-of-the-century construction and now separates the campground from the partially repaired ruins of Moa Heiau.

Wahaula Heiau. Currently accessible by a rough 2-mile trail that starts beyond the Kamoamoa campground are the ruins of Wahaula Heiau, one of the islands' oldest heiau. The temple was built in approximately A.D. 1250 by the Tahitian priest Paao, who introduced the severe system of taboos and sacrifices practiced in Hawaii until 1819.

A coastal trail from the heiau leads to a lookout point where you can view clouds of steam created by lava flowing into the sea through lava tubes. Nature is creating a black sand beach along this stretch of coast.

The Road Westward from the Park

From Kilauea's summit, Highway 11 swoops down the volcano's southwest slope—the Ka'u Desert, barren and bleak except when winter and spring rains make it bloom with native yellow *mamani* and white *alahee* (a coffee relative with a carnation scent). Highway 11 then circles westward toward the Kona Coast.

Just inside the park boundary, less than a mile walk on the Mauna Iki (Footprints) Trail will lead you to a spot where, in 1790, warriors battling Kamehameha the Great for control of this island were asphyxiated by fumes and dust while fleeing boulders and mud balls belched from Halemaumau. (Hawaiians believed that Pele interceded to help Kamehameha.) Most of the footprints left in the hardening ash have eroded, but one set is protected under glass. The trail continues a mile to a dome that fired in 1920 at the head of the Great Crack, a huge fissure that extends to the sea. In this area, lava fountains broke out again in 1971.

CONDOMINIUMS: HOMES AWAY FROM HOME?

If you're traveling with small children and you want to avoid having to eat every meal in a restaurant, or if there are more than two of you and you're planning a visit longer than a week, staying in a condominium can save you money and provide space and comfort.

Are you a condominium candidate? Ranging in size, price, and style from exclusive, luxurious hideaways to inexpensive, compact lodgings in high rises, condos offer space and value for families and groups of friends. On the other hand, the cost can be prohibitive for a single traveler or even a couple.

Remember, however, that not all condominiums offer daily maid service. If your family likes fresh towels and clean beds every day, find out before you book if these amenities are included. Though buying breakfast and lunch supplies cuts costs and allows evening dining splurges, you'll have to find a market, do the shopping, prepare the food, and clean the kitchen.

Where are condominiums located? Currently, the Big Island has some 45 condominium complexes, most of them in resort areas along the Kona and Kohala coasts. Many are indistinguishable from their hotel neighbors. If the amenities include use of hotel facilities, as a condo guest you will have access to the island's finest golf courses and best beaches and restaurants.

The most deluxe units are sprinkled around resorts at Mauna Kea Beach, Mauna Lani Bay, and Waikoloa Beach. Kailua-Kona, heart of the fishing and boating scene, has a number of moderately priced properties. Aston Royal Sea Cliff Resort and Kona By The Sea are award-winning developments. Keauhou's scenic coastline and golf course settings make Colony Resort's Kanaloa at Kona a good choice.

How do you rent a condominium? To find a space that's suitable for your needs, contact your travel agent. Knowledgeable agents check condominium properties personally; they can also suggest tour companies that include condominiums and car rentals as part of vacation packages.

For additional information and listings of units, contact the Hawaii Visitors Bureau, 250 Keawe Street, Hilo, HI 96720; (808) 961-5797.

Drier in climate than other island areas, Ka'u is farm country, rich in macadamia nuts, sugarcane, and cattle-feeding grasses. The cane grows at higher elevations here than anywhere else in the country, some at 3,300 feet. You'll sample the district when you drive the 50-mile/80-km stretch of highway between Hawaii Volcanoes National Park and the Kona Coast. If you have time, you can explore side roads and visit the southernmost point in the United States.

From the Park to Punaluu

Between the boundaries of the park and Waiohinu, the road travels through mixed grasslands ribboned with windbreak trees that run up onto Mauna Loa's steeper flanks. The cane fields in the area take more than three (rather than the usual two) years to mature because of their elevation.

Pahala. To reach pretty little Pahala village, drive the cane haul road uphill several miles to luxuriant Wood

Fierce wooden replicas *of ancient gods guard Puuhonua O Honaunau National Historical Park.*

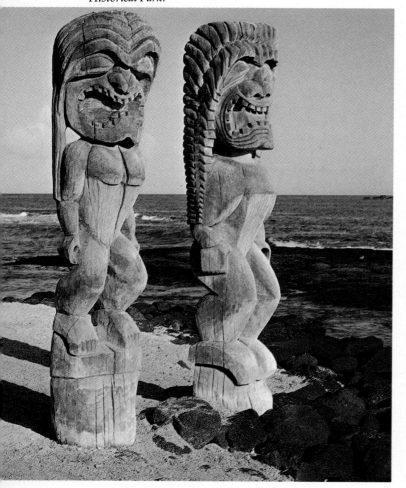

Valley. In 1868, the mightiest cataclysm in Hawaii's history smothered a village here with an avalanche of mud set loose by an earthquake. The quake also triggered simultaneous eruptions of Mauna Loa and Kilauea and lethal seismic waves that swamped Puna and Ka'u villages, depressing the southern coastline about 7 feet.

In town, you'll notice the colorful Wood Valley Temple. Winding southward back to the highway on a parallel strip of the old Belt Road, you'll pass weathered houses, eucalyptus and African tulip trees entwined with bougainvillea, and part of a large orchard of macadamia nut trees. Navel oranges, grapefruit, mangoes, guavas, and avocados also sprout in Ka'u pastures, along with scattered remnants of old sisal.

Punaluu. Drive south to the black sand beach at Punaluu. A visitor center and museum show exhibits from the area. The ruins of Kaneeleele Heiau lie about 500 feet east of the beach. A 404-acre resort complex here, Sea Mountain at Punaluu, includes condominiums, an 18-hole golf course, a restaurant, and a center for the Aspen Institute for Humanistic Studies.

A tiny church on the hill above Punaluu guards the settlement. In its graveyard is a shrine to Henry Opukahaia, a Punaluu boy who sailed to New York in 1809, became a Christian, and died in New England—but not before he had influenced missionaries to come to Hawaii to teach his people.

The road south from Punaluu continues in a loop back to the main highway. At Ninole Cove, fresh water bubbles up through lava at the ocean's edge. There's a pebbly beach with "stones that give birth" (stones with holes that contain baby stones said to multiply). On the hill above the golf course clubhouse, ruins of two ancient temples are accessible to walkers.

Punaluu to South Point Turnoff

Honuapo sits where the main highway meets the shore. A spur road opposite a former sugar mill (now used as a community center) leads into Whittington Beach Park and to a decaying old sugar-shipping wharf.

Naalehu, 3 miles/5km beyond, and Waiohinu, a little farther, are the last places at which to buy gasoline for South Point exploring or, if you are Kona-bound, for the next 50 miles/80 km. Naalehu has a shopping center, several small restaurants and grocery stores, and an old grandstand and community center in the main park.

Jungled Waiohinu village is distinguished by having the Mark Twain Monkeypod Tree, a new tree growing from the roots of one planted by Mark Twain in 1866 and felled by a storm in 1957. It also possesses the island's most elegantly trimmed frame church, Kauahaao, built in 1842 and set beside a tidy old cemetery. The Shirakawa Hotel resembles an oversized house with its parklike gardens of hibiscus and orchids. The hotel offers *furo* (and conventional baths). Locals from the Kona area make the trek for dinner in the hotel's dining room.

The Nation's Southernmost Tip

Ka Lae, or South Point, is the most southerly piece of ground in the United States. A ruggedly beautiful, wind-swept cape, it contains remnants of one of the oldest known Hawaii settlements (A.D. 750).

To explore this area, take the marked turnoff from Highway 11 about 3½ miles/6 km west of Waiohinu. Drive downhill for about 10 miles/16 km through pasture that is sometimes parched, sometimes verdant and abloom with lantana and native wildflowers. Along the way you'll see some of the large windmills designed to generate power for the area. Any people you see will likely be fishermen; the currents that meet off the treeless point create outstanding fishing.

Salt pans (lava boulders with depressions in which sea water was allowed to evaporate) are scattered on the grounds of an automated light tower where the pavement stops. Here, too, are the remains of Kalalea Heiau, a fishermen's shrine and part of a complex of ruins designated a national historic landmark. Fishers still bring offerings of food and drink to the *mana* (spirits) in the shrine.

On the point where the lava slope dribbles away, look for rings (more than 80 of them) chipped in leeward edges; the early Hawaiians secured their canoes by running bowlines through these rings. The moorage of today's anglers is just up the west side beneath a 50-foot cliff that has hoists and ladders welded to its face. Just inland, you'll spot a turbulent, rock-bound pool—a lava tube formed when a hot spot in the cooling flow collapsed into the ocean. A bit farther north, a spur road goes out to the edge of the shore, where along the rising bluff you'll get a fine view of black rock to Mauna Loa.

On the windward side of the cape, breakers pound dunes of yellowish ash and patches of green sand. Bishop Museum archeologists, excavating a habitation site dating from A.D. 1000 1 mile/1 km east of the canoe mooring holes, turned up a fish hook "factory." Just inland is Palahemo, the early settlers' well—a tidal waterhole on which fresh water floats. On its rim are petroglyphs.

Along a spur road of sorts that connects Kaulana Bay with the main road lies Makalei Cave, where ancients slept on stone platforms.

South Point to Kona

West of the South Point turnoff, Highway 11 crosses miles of old Mauna Loa lava flows. Because of rainfall differences, some more recent flows have forest cover; other, older ones remain barren and black. Though the land here is harsh, it does have a delightful oasis—Manuka State Park, a wayside picnic ground and arboretum of native and imported plants.

Milolii, at the south end of Kona, is a tiny Hawaiian-Filipino fishing community about 2,000 feet below the highway. It's reached by a winding, bumpy side road of

The Ka'u District

about 6 miles/10 km. Even though the village is strung out on lava rubble that supports only *kiawe* and palms, villagers grow anthuriums and ferns on hauled-in soil. Anglers return to the village in the afternoon with their catch, which they truck to Hilo's fish auctions.

Houses are of old lumber and corrugated iron. You'll see goats tied up outside and pigs nosing about for food. Most families have kerosene or gas stoves and refrigerators and generator-powered lights, television, and telephone. The store has canned and packaged goods and cold drinks—honk your horn out front to have it opened.

Services are conducted at the century-old Hauoli Kamanao Church (there's a Catholic church, too). Children go *mauka* to school; the older ones board during the week.

South of town, roads fit only for 4-wheel-drive vehicles lead to petroglyphs, lava tubes, caves, coconut groves, and Ahole Heiau.

A Kona Stopover

If you're driving from the national park, you won't have much time for exploring between Milolii and your next stopover (probably in the Keauhou Bay to Kailua resort area). So Puuhonua O Honaunau and other places of interest in the southern Kona region are covered in the following pages as excursions from there.

THE KONA COAST

You'll often hear and read references to "Kona" and "the Kona Coast." These vague designations refer to about 60 miles/96 km of Mauna Loa's and Hualalai's western slopes that are part of the two big districts of North Kona and South Kona. This sun-soaked region of Hawaii is marked by jagged fields of lava for much of its length. Offshore, tropical waters teeming with fish lure snorkelers and deep-sea anglers. Planes from the mainland as well as commuter flights land at Keahole Airport, the site of the Onizuka Space Center, named for the Hawaiian astronaut killed in the Challenger disaster.

At the heart of the Kona Coast lies its major resort town, Kailua-Kona. The town's real name is Kailua; since there are two other Kailuas in Hawaii (one on Oahu and one on Maui), the U.S. Postal Service designated it Kailua-Kona. Many locals just call it Kona. To make matters even more confusing, the Hawaii State Board on Geographic Names has now decided it should be called simply Kailua. Kailua-Kona by any of its names encompasses both the town and the area stretching south 5 miles/8 km to Keauhou.

Exploring Kailua-Kona

Kailua-Kona may be the Kona Coast's major resort town, but it still possesses the atmosphere of a small village. Easily explored on foot, the town offers a wonderful array of things to see and do.

The main part of town runs along Alii Drive between the Hotel King Kamehameha and the Royal Kona Resort. Strolling this banyan-shaded stretch of road bordering Kailua Bay, you'll discover open-air restaurants, snack bars, shop-filled arcades, tiny boutiques, and several historical treasures. At the north end of the strip, you can sit on the seawall and people-watch or view the bay. The Kona Coast is famed for its fantastic, golden sunsets.

The royal compound. King Kamehameha the Great spent his final ruling years in the Kailua-Kona area. You'll find his royal palace grounds north of the seawall on a tiny peninsula of land adjacent to the Hotel King Kamehameha. These few acres, known as Kamakahonu, were the center of governmental activities from 1813 until King Kamehameha's death in 1819. Here, also, King Kamehameha II held a feast marking the overthrow of the religious *kapu* system (see page 160).

The restored royal compound (a national historic landmark) includes Ahuena Heiau, an imposing lava rock platform complete with thatched buildings and fierce-looking wooden gods. Artifacts and illustrations depicting early Hawaiian life are on display in the Hotel King Kamehameha's lobby and adjoining shopping arcade.

The hotel offers traditional hula performances (free of charge), guided tours of its historic grounds, and ethnobotanical forays that highlight plants used by the early Hawaiians. Seaside luaus take place several times a week. Check with the hotel's front desk for tour information and luau reservations.

Kailua Pier. Across the cove from Kamakahonu is Kailua-Kona's busy wharf area, embarkation point for charter fishing trips, scuba and snorkeling excursions, and various boat cruises. Captain Beans' unusual double-hulled vessel with its bright red sails, a familiar sight in the bay and along the coast, provides daytime glass-bottom boat rides as well as evening dinner cruises. Two other vessels, the Atlantis submarine and the semisubmersible Nautilus II, provide underwater peeks at beautiful coral formations and at multitudes of colorful tropical fish. For information, stop by their offices near the Kailua pier.

Walk out on the pier in late afternoon to welcome back the charter fishing boats. You may even see a lucky angler proudly posing with a record catch. The waters off Kailua-Kona are world-renowned as excellent deep-sea fishing grounds for Pacific blue marlin, *ahi* (yellowfin tuna), *ono* (wahoo), *ulua* (jack crevalle), mahi mahi, and swordfish. Annual fishing tournaments boast cash prizes rivaling those of some golf and tennis tournaments.

For more information on fishing charters and boat excursions, see page 172.

Hulihee Palace. In the middle of town stands this gracious, two-storied building with verandas overlooking the bay. It was built in 1837–38 by Kuakini, brother of Kamehameha's favorite wife and governor of the island in 1820. In the 1880s the handsome building served as King David Kalakaua's summer palace. This fine home, now a museum, has been restored to the elegance of the Kalakaua period. Featured are 19th century furnishings made from native woods as well as fascinating Hawaiian artifacts.

The palace is open daily from 9 A.M. to 4 P.M., with the last guided tour at 3:30 P.M. There is an admission fee.

Mokuaikaua. Directly across Alii Drive from Hulihee Palace stands the oldest church in the islands, Mokuaikaua. Completed in 1837 by the first company of missionaries, the church has rock walls mortared with coral, and hand-hewn ohia wood beams more than 50 feet long joined by ohia pins. The white, New England style steeple is a Kailua-Kona landmark. You enter the grounds through a 1910 missionary memorial arch.

St. Michael's Church. Two spreading monkeypod trees frame this church on Alii Drive at the south end of town. St. Michael's was finished in 1848 at the site of the first Catholic mission established on the Neighbor Islands. It has a quaint, coral grotto shrine. Hale Halawai, Kailua-Kona's open-sided community hall, is in a coconut grove opposite the church.

Kailua Candy Company. Two of Hawaii's most famous products, Kona coffee and macadamia nuts, star in the homemade candies produced by this candy manufacturer. A Hawaiian warrior marker pinpoints the location of the factory/store located on Kaiwi Street, a short drive north of the town center. Guided back-of-the-house tours, conducted Monday through Friday between 9 A.M. and 3 P.M., include some tasting. Candies produced by the Kailua Candy Company include mouth-watering morsels like Kona coffee swirls, chocolate macadamia nut fudge, and chocolate "turtles." The store is open weekdays from 9 A.M. to 5 P.M., Saturday from 9 A.M. to 1 P.M.

South to Keauhou

South of the Royal Kona, Alii Drive winds along the coast for about 5 miles/8 km to its end at the moderately priced resort of Keauhou, now known as Crown Lands of Keauhou because of its connection with Hawaiian royalty. On this stretch of road, lined with beach houses, condominiums, and hotels, you still see tangles of gnarled *kiawe*, wave-splashed shoreline, and occasional brilliant accents of bougainvillea. You'll also pass White Sands Beach, sometimes called Disappearing Sands Beach because the waves and currents that challenge expert body surfers occasionally carry away the sand, exposing its lava base.

Alii Drive is a popular walking and biking route. Even when there is no sand, the shoreline is fascinating. You'll often find vendors along the roadside selling flowers, fruits, and vegetables.

Historic sights. The coastal area between Kahuluu Bay and the Kona Country Club, once a playground for Hawaiian royalty, is dotted with a number of historical sights, including a half-dozen heiau, ancient home sites, burial platforms, and petroglyphs.

You'll see several temples and petroglyphs on the grounds of the Keauhou Hotel at the Crown Lands of Keauhou resort. The spring-fed Po'o Hawaii Pond, a king's bathing pool, sits in a lush coconut grove. Adjacent to the pond is a reconstruction of King Kalakaua's beach house, a frame structure built more than a century ago. Rock pools and a gray beach strand line the shore.

St. Peter's Catholic Church. Also known as the "Little Blue Church," St. Peter's is scarcely larger than a playhouse. It was built on a lava beach on the site of a heiau to surmount superstition. The austere interior is marked with a plain wooden cross.

Just north of the church is Kuemanu Heiau, a well-preserved temple dedicated to surfing.

Kahaluu Beach Park. A tiny beach park spreads over the bay's south shore. An ancient stone breakwater, believed to be built by the *menehune* (legendary race of dwarfs), once protected the bay from treacherous currents. Storms and heavy surf have taken their toll, though, and the wall is crumbling, making the bay a less safe place to swim and snorkel.

Crownlands at Keauhou. Though it's now the location of the North Kona Coast's planned resort development, Keauhou Bay was previously an anchorage and canoe landing for Kona fishermen. A monument just south of the pier marks the birthplace of Kamehameha III.

The Kona Coast

...The Kona Coast

Looking across the undulating fairways of Keauhou's championship golf courses, it's difficult to believe that this area of hotels, condominiums, and shops was once nothing more than a sea of bleak, black lava.

Royal slide. High on a hill above Keauhou Bay lies part of the ancient royal *holua* (slide). The hand-laid rock course originally extended about a mile to the sea. Kings and chiefs covered the 50-foot-wide channel with *pili* grass and ti and banana leaves and rode down it on wooden sleds. Replicas of these sleds can be viewed at the Bishop Museum in Honolulu. From Alii Drive, the slide is accessible by foot from a spot opposite the Kona Country Club's entrance.

A Drive Through Coffee Country

Between 800 and 2,000 feet, Kona is coffee country—cool and green, with dependable afternoon cloud cover. Here grows the only coffee commercially produced in the United States.

The coffee belt extends from Honokohau in the north to Kealia in the south. It's bisected by Highway 11 and, above Kailua-Kona, by Highway 180 (which eventually joins 11 near Honalo). You can reach the area on Highway 11 from Kailua-Kona or, from Keauhou, by taking Kamehameha III Road uphill from Alii Drive. Highway 182 (Hualalai Road) out of Kailua-Kona also intersects with Highway 180 just south of Holualoa.

As you drive the narrow roads through coffee country, you'll see grove after grove of the bushy, glossy-leafed trees whose product has made this area famous worldwide. About March each year, the trees turn snowy with fragrant white blossoms. In fall, the berries from these blossoms turn bright red and are ready to harvest.

In spite of Kona coffee's popularity as a gourmet brew, the industry has been waning. Statistics show a fall in production and a decline in coffee acreage, partly due to the scarcity and high cost of labor. Many farmers now grow macadamia nuts for diversity. Production has begun to pick up slowly in the last few years, however, perhaps indicating a reversal.

Much of the coffee country's charm comes from its string of towns cluttered with old wooden buildings, country stores interspersed with modern ones, and little box houses perched precariously on the hillsides. Roads wind under spreading trees and past colorful garden plantings: white and yellow ginger in summer; gold Timor shower trees and wild sunflowers in November; red and white poinsettias in winter; jacaranda, coral shower, and silver oak trees in spring.

Upcountry arts. A renovated coffee mill in Holualoa on Highway 180 is the setting for the Little Gallery's arts and crafts collection. Here local painters, woodworkers, ceramists, and quilters display their work. Across the street is the town's tiny restored Congregational Church, the gallery's previous home.

Amateur theatrical performances take place a few miles south in Kainaliu's restored Aloha Theater. If you enjoy healthy cuisine, try the Aloha Cafe inside for moderately priced breakfasts, lunches, and dinners. Sit on the terrace for the best views.

19th century temples and churches. In Honalo, near the junction of highways 180 and 11, you can visit charming St. Paul's Catholic Church, built in 1864, and the serene Daifukuji Buddhist Temple. Rural Kealakekua, the business and banking center for the Kona area, is home to the Hongwanji Buddhist Temple and three fine mission churches: Central Kona Union Church, built in 1859 of rocks mortared with coral plaster; diminutive Lanakila, a wooden chapel that has stood since 1868; and Christ Church, the island's oldest Episcopal sanctuary.

Mrs. Fields Macadamia Nut Factory. While in Kealakekua, stop by the nut-processing factory operated by Mrs. Fields of cookie fame. Fifteen-minute tours (no charge) of the plant on Hale Kii Street explain the factory's operations; free samples are passed out at the end. The factory is open daily from 9 A.M. to 5 P.M.; nuts, candies, and cookies are sold in the store.

Kona Historical Society Museum. Kona's historical exhibits are housed in the old Greenwell Store in Kalukalu Ahupua'a, upcountry from the town of Captain Cook. Artifacts, photographs, and memorabilia revive Kona's colorful past. Built around 1867 of native stone and burned coral lime, the Greenwell Store was restored to its original condition in 1979. The museum is open Tuesday through Friday from 9 A.M. to 3 P.M. and Saturday morning.

Kona coffee mills. From Captain Cook, site of South Kona's civic buildings, Napoopoo Road winds down through coffee trees to the ocean. Stop by the Royal Kona Coffee Mill and Museum for a free cup of coffee, a fine photographic display of this area's coffee industry from infancy through modern times, and a look at equipment that has been grinding and roasting local beans for more than a century. If the mill is operating, you can watch the sorting, bagging, and drying operations. The museum is open daily from 8:30 A.M. to 4:30 P.M.

Smaller coffee roasters around Kealakekua offering free samples include Bong Brothers (restored mill), Captain Cook Coffee Company, Kona Coffee Company, and Kona Kai Farms.

Kealakekua Bay Area

Continuing along Napoopoo Road, you'll journey through groves of coffee, mango, and avocado trees before you reach beautiful Kealakekua Bay.

Napoopoo. On the shore of Kealakekua Bay is the village of Napoopoo, where typical houses are engulfed in foliage and set behind low stone walls. Townsfolk market

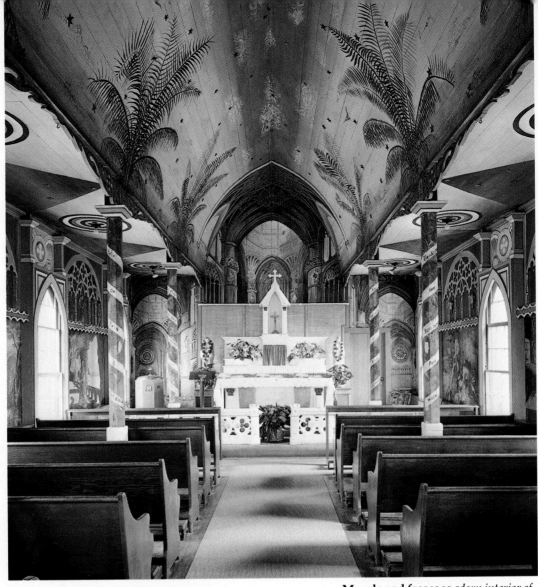

Murals and frescoes *adorn interior of St. Benedict's, one of the island's two "painted churches."*

Alii Drive, *the Kona Coast connection between Kailua and Keauhou, passes shops, hotels, and fine spots to watch the surf meet the lava shoreline.*

leis and bracelets of seeds and shells at the road turnaround by the bay.

At Napoopoo County Park the beach is pebbly, but you can swim in remarkably clear ocean waters laced with cool springs in a bend of the bay. This body of water is so rich in sea life that it has been made a marine preserve. Kealakekua Underwater State Park offers snorkelers and divers 100 feet of visibility with a myriad of tropical fish and spectacular coral growths.

Captain Cook Memorial. Tranquil Kealakekua Bay was once the scene of violence that resulted in the death of Captain James Cook, famous explorer and the island's European discoverer. He was killed in 1779 while trying to end a melee between his men and the natives. Only a month before, on his first landing, the Hawaiians had mistaken Cook for their god Lono and led him into Hikiau Heiau, where he was honored in a special ceremony.

In the same heiau on the shore of Kealakekua Bay, Cook read the islands' first Christian burial service over one of his men. At the foot of the stone path leading up to the sun-scorched temple platform, you'll see plaques commemorating both this ceremony and Henry Opukahaia, the Hawaiian boy who was instrumental in bringing the first missionaries to the islands.

From the heiau or Napoopoo's shore, look across the vast bay to the wooded spit of land on its north side. Midway along this spit stands a 27-foot white obelisk erected in 1874 near the spot where Captain Cook died. The monument is isolated by soaring bluffs riddled with ancient burial caves. Though a rough jeep road links the town of Captain Cook with the obelisk, the best way to see the monument up close is on one of the tour boats that cruise down from Kailua-Kona or Keauhou Bay (see page 172).

Ancient battleground. A narrow, 3-mile/5-km coastal road takes you from Napoopoo to Honaunau Bay and Puuhonua O Honaunau. En route you cross the barren Keei plain, a stretch of lava rock and wispy grass. This was the site of a battle in the early 1780s between Kamehameha's forces and those of Kiwalao, the rightful heir to the neighboring districts. Kiwalao was defeated and killed.

On the hill above Keei, notice the handsome stone church. It's old Kahikolu, completed in 1841 and then rebuilt in 1853. The church, with its interesting graveyard, has been restored. A road leads to it through the brush about ½ mile up Napoopoo Road, on the way to the Royal Kona Coffee Mill and Museum.

Puuhonua O Honaunau

In Hawaii's pre-Christian era, a *puuhonua*, or "place of refuge," was a haven for the lawbreaker and war-vanquished. Though there were similar refuges on the Big Island and other islands in the chain, the one on the shore of Honaunau Bay—associated with the Kamehameha dynasty—is historically the most important.

For perhaps 400 years, people scurried by trail from the south or swam Honaunau Bay from the north to reach this sacred place ahead of their pursuers. After they were purified, they were free to leave and return home, protected by the amnesty bestowed upon them by the priests.

Kapus. Hawaii's people were governed by *kapu* (sacred rules of life). These kapu included laws forbidding commoners to go near a chief, touch his possessions, walk in his footsteps, or even let their shadows fall on royal grounds. Women weren't allowed to eat with men. Fishing and hunting times were governed by kapu.

If a kapu was broken, it was feared that the gods would become angry and create a lava flow, tidal wave, or some other form of devastation in retaliation. The penalty for breaking a kapu was death; escape to a place of refuge was the only salvation.

A puuhonua also protected noncombatants during battles as well as defeated warriors.

History of Honaunau. Wooden figures facing out to sea guarded this place of refuge from waterborne assault; on the landward side, it was secured by a wall more than 1,000 feet long, about 12 feet high, and 17 feet thick—and hand laid without mortar. About 1650, Hale-o-Keawe Heiau was built to honor the reigning king of Kona. When Keawe died, his bones were placed in the temple. Between then and 1818, the bones of 22 other ruling chiefs were also interred in the temple. It was believed that the royal line of high chiefs had a special power or *mana* that remained with them even after they died; this power protected the puuhonua.

In 1829, the refuge temple was razed by the Hawaiians, who by that time had rejected the old religion and system of laws. This historic site was set aside in 1961 as a national historical park with the goal of restoring the area to its late-1700s appearance. Today you can see the wall, another temple platform built around 1550, and the reconstructed Hale-o-Keawe Heiau, rebuilt from sketches and descriptions made by early European visitors. Replicas of the wooden gods were carved from giant ohia logs and once again face menacingly seaward.

The shady coconut grove outside the wall was formerly the palace grounds for the ruling chief. Here you'll see some reconstructions of early thatched houses, the royal canoe landing, a few Hawaiian canoes built in the traditional manner, and the royal fishpond.

Park details. The park visitor center is open daily from 7:30 A.M. to 5:30 P.M. Plan to go early while the park is still cool and quiet; tour buses begin arriving around midmorning. A self-guiding booklet lets you wander through the grounds on your own. Tile murals and recorded messages at the entrance tell the story of ancient Hawaii. Rangers give talks in the amphitheater; demonstrations of canoe carving, thatching, weaving, and most other early Hawaiian crafts take place most days between 9 A.M. and 4 P.M. near the visitor center.

Along Highway 160

En route to Puuhonua O Honaunau on Highway 160, the curving connection between Kealakekua Bay and Highway 11, lie some of the area's most beautiful macadamia nut orchards and many thriving gardens containing a myriad of plant varieties. Most nut farms are small; some have stores. Fuku-Bonsai Center's miniature plants are found in mill stores here but are grown in upcountry Keauhou near the junction of highways 11 and 180.

Just off Highway 160 lies Kona's famous painted church, well worth a stop. Signs at the turnoff direct you to the site.

St. Benedict's painted church. A side road from Highway 160 leads to St. Benedict's, a charming church tucked amid lush, tropical foliage. In December, brilliant red poinsettias lend vivid color to the tiny white structure.

The exterior of the church has intricate carpenter's Gothic details—a frontal lattice and a belfry that resembles a storybook castle. A few of the adjacent fenced gravestones have iron-pipe crosses and markers with photographs. Some inscriptions are in Chinese, some in Hawaiian, and others in Portuguese.

But it's the church's interior that has won all the acclaim. The elaborate decoration was applied by Father John Berchmans Velghe, a Belgian priest who wanted to bring to his parishioners the splendor of medieval Europe. In 1902, he turned his gable-roofed church into a miniature cathedral—and folk-art masterpiece—by painting its walls, ceiling, and columns with copies of religious works. Because many of his congregants were unable to read or write, he used Hawaiian motifs to relate the story of Christianity. On the wall behind the altar, a trompe l'oeil painting of the light dome, apse, and transepts of Burgos Cathedral in Spain gives the illusion that the vaulted nave continues.

Father Velghe had studied briefly in Europe with Father Gielin, the artist of the Star of the Sea painted church in Puna (see page 148).

The South End of Kona

Southern Kona contains lava flows from Mauna Loa, new forests and orchards, and a few settlements.

Highway 11 passes below the 100,000-acre Honaunau Forest, where more than 800,000 Australian red cedar and tropical ash trees were planted for harvest at the end of the century. The road crosses all three 1950 Mauna Loa flows, which buried several buildings in their path to the sea. It spans Honomalino farmlands, occupied by a huge macadamia nut orchard and healthy plantings of bananas, avocados, citrus, and vegetables. In the scattered housing tracts, flower gardens provide colorful accents in the rough lava.

Hookena, a couple of miles down a narrow, twisting spur road, is almost a ghost town. You'll find a handful of cottages, a swimming beach, and park pavilion (no drinking water or lights). A few families are still in residence; others come on weekends to camp and fish. Notice the pilings of an old wharf where interisland steamers once loaded coffee, oranges, cattle, lumber, and passengers; it was abandoned in the early 1930s when the road from Hilo finally reached Kona. To the north lie remnants of the main street—a stone wall with gates, shade trees, posts that supported gas lamps, ruined houses, and a Congregational church, built in the mid 1850s, with a still-visible altar inscription in Hawaiian. The cliff above the beach is honeycombed with burial caves.

Milolii settlement, at the southern end of the Kona Coast, is described on page 155.

North Kona to Kohala

Two highways lead from Kailua-Kona through North Kona to the South Kohala district: Palani Road connects with the Hawaii Belt Road (190) that travels a high route for about 40 miles/64 km to Waimea; Queen Kaahumanu Highway (19) follows the coast just above the sea for about 35 miles/56 km to Kawaihae.

The coast road traverses bleak lava wasteland, passing the turnoff to Honokohau Harbor, which was blasted out of lava and dredged to create a small harbor. To see remnants of ancient Honokohau, continue north on the highway for 1¼ miles and turn seaward on a gravel road. The fish ponds and the surrounding village sites are being restored as part of Kaloko-Honokohau National Historical Park. The ponds (still in use) were built to raise King Kamehameha's favorite fish. Some historians believe his bones were hidden in or near the ponds, though the burial site has never been found.

Farther north at Keahole, strange circular house platforms and shelter and burial caves have been discovered. Still farther north on the coast is Kona Village Resort, a luxury hideaway featuring Polynesian atmosphere and plush, thatched bungalows. The resort's accommodations and lush gardens nestle between the fingers of a lava flow from now-dormant Hualalai's last sputterings in 1801.

The Hawaii Belt Road, the alternate route north from Kailua, starts out past hillside homes, goes through coffee farms, wilderness, and ranch land, and finally emerges onto the Waimea plateau. It passes through a seemingly endless landscape of dry grass and cactus that stretches from the sea to the domes of the great volcanoes. Cattle graze along the roadside. On a clear day, you can see Haleakala on Maui.

Around Puu Waawaa Ranch, swaths of black lava that once flowed from Hualalai and Mauna Loa cut through the grasslands. You'll see cupcake-shaped Puu Waawaa, the island's largest cinder cone, which furnishes pumice for the manufacture of a lightweight aggregate.

For information on the South Kohala coastal resorts, see page 163. You'll find details of North Kohala on page 164, and a history of cool Waimea and its neighbor, the Parker Ranch, on page 165.

Framed by palms, *a Kohala lifeguard sits atop tower, reaping the day's reward: a sky-painting sunset.*

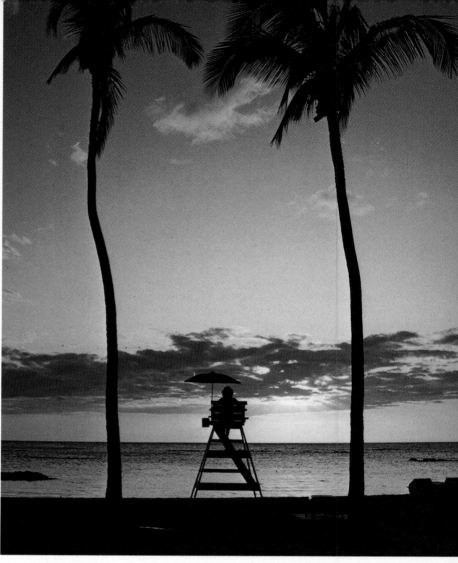

Manmade greens *and fairways combine with natural black lava obstacles to form Mauna Lani Hotel's oceanside course, one of the state's most beautiful and most challenging.*

THE KOHALAS & WAIMEA

In the Big Island's northwest corner, the two districts of North and South Kohala encompass a vast region of great contrasts. Ranches and truck farms spread over cool, windswept Waimea Plateau. North of the plateau the old Kohala Mountains rise up to 5,000 feet, flatten out into cropland, and then break apart into a series of awesome roadless canyons. South Kohala's sunny coast offers luxury resorts, popular beach parks, and remnants of old Hawaii.

You can make a loop trip along the west coast to the island's northern tip, down the center to Waimea, and return to Kona.

South Kohala

Continuing north from Kona along the Queen Kaahumanu Highway (19) through the South Kohala district, you may well wonder where all the people are. The road traverses miles of black lava fields, their monotony only occasionally broken by a clump of *kiawe* trees.

South Kohala's attractions lie off the main highway along the coast. Here, historic sites help bring Hawaii's past to life, and resorts foretell of this area's future.

Luxury resorts. In spite of the fact that this part of the Big Island contains some of the island's most beautiful beaches, it remained relatively undeveloped until recently. The first hotel to claim a spot along this sundrenched coast was Laurance Rockefeller's Mauna Kea, followed by Royal Waikoloan and Mauna Lani.

Today, Mauna Kea is Mauna Kea Beach Hotel, run by Prince Hotels, which has opened another hotel at Hapuna Beach. Royal Waikoloan Hotel is now part of Waikoloa Beach Resort, a planned development that includes Hilton Waikoloa Village and Kings' Shops arcade. (The inland portion of Waikoloa Village lies in the neighboring highlands.) Mauna Lani Bay Hotel and Bungalows is part of Mauna Lani Resort, which also includes Ritz-Carlton Mauna Lani.

These resorts boast some of the Big Island's finest dining rooms, a collection of luxurious condominiums, and an ever-growing number of championship golf courses (for details on golfing, see page 172).

Royal Waikoloan Hotel lies adjacent to Anaehoomalu Bay's palm-fringed, crescent-shaped beach. In addition to the usual amenities, the hotel has several historic attractions. The turquoise waters of old royal fish ponds lie between the hotel and the beach. Markers indicate the sites of preserved petroglyphs and burial caves on the Waikoloa Beach Golf Club courses.

Hilton Waikoloa Village incorporates 62 oceanfront acres and 1,244 rooms in three separate towers. This megaresort features a man-made, sand-edged lagoon filled with tropical fish, a dolphin pool, and a variety of swimming pools and restaurants. Canal boats and trams transport guests to their rooms.

Waikoloa Village's condominiums, stores, and golf course sprawl across lava fields 2,500 feet above the coast. At this elevation, the air is usually cool and refreshing.

Amenities include nearby riding stables. The turnoff from Highway 19 is a mile north of Royal Waikoloan.

Mauna Lani Bay Hotel and Bungalows sits on a lovely stretch of beach a few miles north of Waikoloa Beach Resort. The hotel features a dramatic five-story atrium and garden of flowering plants and cascading pools fit for Hawaiian royalty. Scattered around its spectacular grounds are petroglyphs, restored fish ponds, and an ancient coastal footpath.

Ritz-Carlton Mauna Lani's decor reflects that chain's flair for elegance. Queen Liliuokalani would have felt right at home amid the hotel's massive and intricately carved highboys and marble-topped tables, glittering chandeliers, and Oriental carpets.

Mauna Kea Beach Hotel, farther north, overlooks another beautiful crescent beach. Undergoing remodeling, the hotel is closed until 1996, but the golf courses are open. Its sister hotel, Hapuna Prince, rises above a nearby beach.

Puako. Just north of Mauna Lani Resort are the Puako petroglyph fields, an extensive collection of ancient rock art. A new ¾-mile trail and viewing area protect the art and provide visitor access. Take the paved side road to Puako. En route you pass modest vacation homes, the restored Holu Loa Church (completed in 1860), and a Catholic church in the round, with soaring roof and a fine use of lava. Near the end of the Puako road, a Hawaii Visitors Bureau warrior marker points out the trail.

Hapuna Beach State Park. This popular beach is less than a mile south of the entrance to Mauna Kea. Its 300-acre recreation area includes pavilions, picnic facilities, and a good sand beach. Tent camping is not permitted, but A-frame shelters are available (see page 171). Winter waves attract body surfers, but caution is advised if you swim here.

Pu'ukohola and Mailekini heiau. Just south of Kawaihae, on the road to Spencer Beach Park, you can visit two outstanding heiau that are the nucleus of a national historic site. Pu'ukohola Heiau guards the road like a giant fortress. It's even more impressive when you walk closer to its 224 by 100-foot platform composed of lava rocks and boulders carefully fitted together without mortar. Kamehameha built this last sacrificial temple in 1791 for his war god Kukailimoku because a prophet said Kamehameha would then be assured of becoming ruler of all the islands. Keoua Kuahuula, his last rival for control of the island of Hawaii, was slain when he arrived for the heiau's dedication. His body was offered as the principal sacrifice.

Mailekini Heiau, an older temple across the road from Pu'ukohola, was converted into a fort to protect the Kawaihae area during Kamehameha's time.

Spencer Beach Park. Located on Ohaiula Bay, Spencer is one of the island's most popular beach parks. It has a sandy beach, shallow waters for children, a *kiawe*-shaded lawn for picnics, good snorkeling areas, and showers.

Kawaihae. This tiny community is the site of an important harbor. In early days Kamehameha I sailed from this port to conquer the neighboring islands; in 1820 the first New England missionaries paused here. At one time, Parker Ranch cattle had to swim through the harbor and be hauled aboard steamers bound for Oahu. With the construction of an actual port, cattle can now be loaded directly on board barges. Today, Kawaihae is one of the island's major commercial ports.

North Kohala

Near Kawaihae, Highway 19 turns inland, heading across the island through cattle country and Waimea to Honokaa on the east coast. Highway 270, the road north from Kawaihae, spans a raw coast of black rock under a blanket of *kiawe*, passing a string of coves splendid for snorkeling. The parched country of the west turns green as you move into the normally rainy belt of North Kohala.

Here is the Hawaii of several decades ago, remarkably untouched, somnolent, but with a secure position in history as the birthplace and boyhood home of the first Kamehameha. When Kamehameha was growing up, taro covered the hills and valleys, and the region was the island's most populous. Taro and native villages gave way to sugar plantations, each with mill towns and gracious baronial estates, but now the last sugar mill has been phased out.

Lapakahi State Historical Park. Between Kawaihae and Mahukona stands the partially restored site of a 600-year-old seaside village. Strolling through this former home of Hawaii's working class, you'll see house plots, burial sites, family heiau, fishing shrines, and a garden of sugarcane, sweet potatoes, and gourds. The archeological dig connected with the discovery of Lapakahi has answered many questions as to how average Hawaiians lived down through the centuries. The park is open Monday through Saturday from 8 A.M. to 4 P.M.

At Mahukona, once Kohala's sugar-shipping port and now nearly abandoned, you can swim and fish from the old landing or at the beach park.

Kapaa Beach Park. You reach Kapaa Beach Park, north of Mahukona, on a mile-long paved road that winds downhill from Highway 270. Though there's no sand, snorkeling here is excellent—try the area around the park's old canoe landing. If you walk five minutes north and then around a fence, you'll find the ruins of another village occupied until 1915.

Mookini Heiau. The turnoff to Upolu Airfield takes you to Mookini Heiau, the state's first registered national historic landmark and one of two sacrificial temples of the highest rank built in A.D. 480. An Hawaii Visitors Bureau warrior marker points the way down a dirt road. Much remains of the 250 by 130-foot platform and surrounding walls. Kamehameha I was born just west of the heiau; his birthsite is marked with a plaque.

Hawi. This once-thriving plantation town, 7 miles/11 km from Mahukona, is the best known of a handful of settlements with colorful old houses, stores, churches, and temples along the northern coast. It's also the Big Island's northernmost town.

Kapaau. If you follow Highway 270 east from Hawi, you come upon a gilt-and-bronze figure of Kamehameha in front of the Kapaau Courthouse. Completed in 1880 by an American sculptor working in Italy, it was lost at sea, recovered, and placed here near Kamehameha's birthplace. A replica, the better-known of the two statues, stands across from the Iolani Palace in Honolulu.

Kapaau has a couple of quaint temples: diminutive St. Augustine's Episcopal Church, dedicated in 1884 by a largely British congregation, and the district's prize—Kalahikiola Church. Located ¼ mile up a side road marked by a warrior sign, Kalahikiola Church was designed by missionary Elias Bond, who also started Kohala's first sugar plantation to provide work for the Hawaiians. For six years, until 1855, parishioners hauled stones from ravines for the church's meeting house. To make mortar, they brought sand from the shore, coral from the sea, and wood (for burning the coral) from the mountains.

Beyond the grounds, set off by a stone arch, are the empty frame buildings of the old Kohala Girls' School that Bond started. The road to the church passes macadamia nut groves and the mission homestead—white buildings framing a generous lawn with fruit and shade trees.

About 2 miles/3 km east of the church turnoff, another warrior marker points to Kamehameha Rock, a huge boulder said to have been carried up from the sea to a nearby heiau by Kamehameha.

East to Niulii. In gulches between Kapaau and Niulii, villagers still grow wetland taro and sweet potatoes in the old Hawaiian way by diverting a stream through rock-terraced plots and letting the water dribble down from one to the next (look down Waikane Gulch as you pass to see how it's done).

In the late 1800s, Chinese laborers were hired to build a narrow-gauge railway for the sugar industry in this area. The railway, connecting Niulii and the port of Mahukona, was eventually abandoned and dismantled. The Chinese remained to work in the sugar mills. Among them were Hakka men who founded a Tong Wo Society in Halawa. The society's main building, once the scene of gambling and opium smoking, has been restored. Plaques engraved with proverbs edge the ornate building's doors and windows and scrollwork enhances the beams and posts.

Niulii is a scattering of houses in jungle. A thick pandanus forest now screens the quaint Japanese graveyard from the ocean it once overlooked. Take a side road down to the cove below the Keokea Beach Park, a grassy flat with an old heiau crowned by a jaunty lookout pergola. Another pavilion shelters picnickers from the region's heavy rains. Though the sea may be too wild for swimming, you'll find an inlet protected enough for boats and a stream bed to explore. An adjacent bluff is faced with caves; according to legend, one leads into the heiau that crowns the top.

Pololu Valley lookout. The road ends at a view point about 1½ miles/2½ km beyond Niulii. From here you can look over broad, green-carpeted Pololu Valley and down a coastline of spendid, uninhabited gorges. A trail leads from the parking lot and lookout to a black sand beach; figure about 1½ hours for the round trip.

Waimea—a Ranch Town

From Hawi, Highway 250 winds for 20 miles/32 km back to Waimea along the steep flanks of the Kohala Mountains. The hillsides are covered with sweet grasses, cactus, rocks, wild fennel, and morning glory. Windbreaks of Norfolk Island pines, eucalyptus, and ironwoods border high-country grazing pastures.

About midway, stop at Kahua Ranch picnic shelter for an expansive view of the Kawaihae coast. At 3,564 feet, the road crests above Waimea. Some say Kamehameha planned his island-conquering strategy here, using the plateau to represent the sea and all the visible peaks (the three big volcanoes, Puu Waawaa, and Maui's Haleakala) as the islands.

Parker Ranch. The major portions of this 250,000-acre ranch, one of the largest privately owned ranches in the United States, spread across the slopes of neighboring Mauna Kea and the Kohala Mountains.

In 1809 John Palmer Parker, a 19-year-old seaman, left his ship and went to work for Kamehameha I rounding up cattle that had strayed and gone wild. The cattle had originally been given to Kamehameha by the British Captain George Vancouver. Parker developed a domestic herd from the captured stock and established his ranch around 1815. He also married Kamehameha's granddaughter. Now the ranch has about 50,000 head of cattle. A few of the cowboys (*paniolos*) who work on the ranch today are descendants of the first ranch hands.

At the Parker Ranch Visitor Center and Museum, located in Waimea's Parker Ranch Shopping Center, artifacts, photographs and a 15-minute multimedia show tell the history of the ranch and the Parker family. In a smaller section of the museum, you'll see a collection of memorabilia relating to Duke Kahanamoku, the famous Hawaiian Olympic swimmer and surfing champion. The center is open Monday through Saturday from 9:30 A.M. to 3:30 P.M.; there is an admission fee.

Surrounded by gardens, Hale Kea ("White House" in Hawaiian) is a turn-of-the-century frame house on the west side of town. Built by a former Parker Ranch manager, the property has gone through several incarnations, including serving as an upcountry annex for the Mauna Kea Beach Hotel. Currently, the main house and outbuildings contain shops and Hartwell's restaurant.

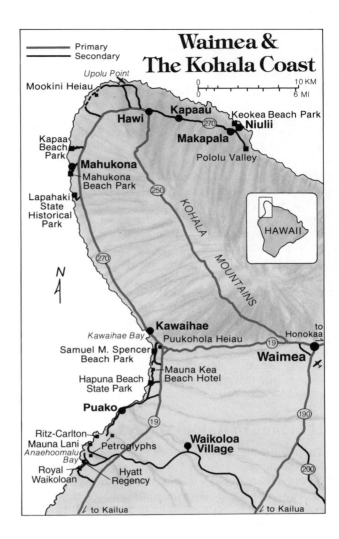

Waimea town. Cool and pastoral Waimea faces out over the tableland to Mauna Kea. The town's post office carries the name Kamuela, and the town itself is sometimes referred to by that name.

It's a village of gingerbread houses, flower gardens, picket fences, and carpenter's Gothic buildings. Notice the ornate bandstand, Lanakila Park pavilion, and Parker Ranch headquarters. Newer buildings contain shops, markets, a theater, and restaurants. This is one of the islands' best places for a steak dinner.

On the east side of town, several churches and temples surround an open green. Visit well-preserved Imiola Church, built in 1857 by Waimea's missionary, Lorenzo Lyons, who composed Hawaiian hymns that are still sung. Sporting a New England style spire, the church has interior walls paneled in koa and chandeliers that are koa bowls.

On the western edge of town at the junction of highways 250 and 19, private Kamuela Museum has a collection of artifacts dating back to days of the monarchy. The museum is usually open from 8 A.M. to 5 P.M.; you'll pay an admission fee.

A bird's-eye view of the Big Island's northeast coast reveals a gently rolling plateau carpeted with sugarcane and dotted with tiny towns. Subtropical canyons complete with waterfalls and lush vegetation veer inland from the rugged cliffs. Though you won't find resorts in this area, you can wander down side roads to jungled gorges, ponds, rocky points, and quiet villages on portions of the old highway now replaced by a straighter, wider Belt Road, Highway 19.

The drive from Waimea to Honokaa, largest town along the Hamakua Coast, and then down the coast to Hilo is a distance of about 55 miles/88 km. For the first 16 miles/26 km, from Waimea to Honokaa, you'll see truck farms, new subdivisions, pastures punctuated with eucalyptus, misty forest, and finally an expanse of bright green sugarcane.

At Waimea's outer edge, a gravel road (the middle part of which calls for 4-wheel drive) wanders off over the side of Mauna Kea for some 40 miles/64 km to Humuula in the Saddle (see page 170). About 8 miles/13 km up the road stands Mana, the Parker family's original home. A museum at one time, it is now closed to the public.

From Honokaa to Hilo, the wide, smooth highway follows the coast along Mauna Kea's long northeastern slope. Cane fields still carpet the slope all the way down to the cliffs that rise high above the sea.

Honokaa to Waipio Valley Lookout

Though the highway by-passes Honokaa, be sure to detour through this strongly Portuguese settlement perched on the hillside about a mile down a spur road from the highway. Fruit trees adorn the front and back yards of the pastel-colored buildings lining the main street. Note the many restored structures: the 1930s People's Theatre, the Honokaa Club (a popular restaurant with spartan hotel rooms above), and the United Methodist Church on the main street; another eye-pleasing frame church, Our Lady of Lourdes, is uphill on a side street.

Drive downhill to the classic sugar plantation camp at Haina, overlooking the Hamakua Sugar Company mill above the sea. Halfway down the hill is solid evidence—the Hawaiian Holiday Macadamia Nut Company—to support Honokaa's claim as macadamia nut capital of the world. The retail store (open daily from 9 A.M. to 6 P.M.) offers free samples. Self-guided tours of candy making and nut processing take place in the factory next door on weekdays from 9 A.M. to 3:30 P.M.

Honokaa and environs provide a few good places to shop for local crafts. Kamaaina Woods, just off Highway 19, offers a look at craftsmen producing bowls, dishes, and vases from koa, monkeypod, and other island woods. At Waipio Woodworks in Kukuihaele you can buy paintings, sculpture, pottery, and woodwork from local craftspeople. The general store in Kukuihaele also sells regional handicrafts.

Paved road (Highway 240) continues beyond Honokaa for 10 miles/16 km to the lookout park on Waipio Valley's east rim. From here, you gaze down on one of nature's masterpieces. A stream below lazes along the 6-mile/10-km-long valley, checkered with taro patches and bounded by 2,000-foot-high cliffs. Up the coast, a white ribbon of surf unwinds and disappears behind a bold headland. The old horse trail that zigzags up the opposite bluff crosses deeply furrowed tableland to the next big valley, Waimanu.

The lookout has rest rooms and drinking water. You can hike into the valley, but you'd be wise to make arrangements for a 4-wheel-drive or mule-cart tour (see page 168). A small hotel offers rustic accommodations.

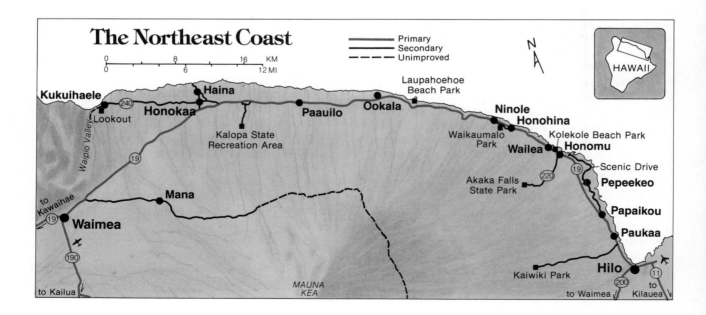

The Northeast Coast

Primary
Secondary
Unimproved

HAWAII

KM
0   8   16
0   6   12 MI

N

Kukuihaele   Haina
Honokaa   Laupahoehoe Beach Park
Lookout   Paauilo   Ookala
Waipio Valley   Kalopa State Recreation Area   Ninole
Honohina
Waikaumalo Park   Kolekole Beach Park
Wailea   Honomu
to Kawaihae   Mana   Akaka Falls State Park   Scenic Drive
Waimea   Pepeekeo
Papaikou
Paukaa
Kaiwiki Park   Hilo
to Kailua   MAUNA KEA   to Waimea   to Kilauea

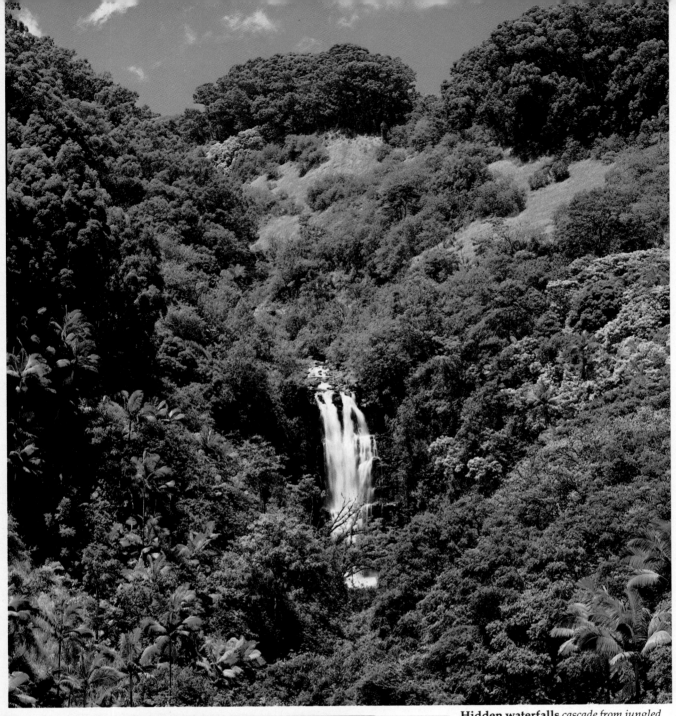

Hidden waterfalls *cascade from jungled slopes, tumble into deep gorges along the Hamakua Coast in northeastern Hawaii.*

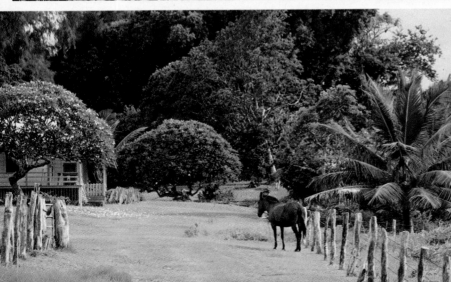

Once the birthplace of Kamehameha *and later a sugar-growing region, North Kohala retains a sense of history and a feeling of old Hawaii. Today, the countryside is a pastoral scene of small farms.*

...Along the Northeast Coast

The Hamakua Coast

If you stick to the main highway, you'll pass through mile after mile of cane fields, span jungle-clad gorges on the widened bridges of an old standard-gauge railway, and arrive in Hilo before you know it. Even if you're in a hurry, stop at one of the bridges to see the trestle underneath and the old road winding in and out of the canyon.

Kalopa State Recreation Area, between Honokaa and Paauilo, is reached by a side road that heads inland up the slopes of Mauna Kea. Over 600 acres of mountainside and narrow ravines comprise a native forest reserve of ohia lehua, koa, and other trees.

A detour into Paauilo, a classic plantation town, provides a glimpse of old Hawaii. Graceful gardens surround original old plantation houses. A large sugar mill stands at the end of the road.

A trio of coastal parks lie within 10 miles/16 km of each other: Laupahoehoe (monument lists people lost in a tidal wave), Waikaumalo (uphill along a stream), and Kolekole (under the highway bridge).

Akaka Falls State Park is reached by turning off the highway at tiny Honomu. The charming street displays a Catholic church, two temples, and the balustraded Honomu Plantation Store. Stop here for ice-cold sugarcane, fresh macadamia nuts, and photos showing the Hamakua Coast in the early 1900s.

The 4-mile/6-km road into the park goes through cane fields to this 66-acre arboretum of giant gingers, ferns, ti, azaleas, orchids, and bamboo. An easy trail loops through the lush, thickly canopied gorge past Akaka Falls, which drop 442 feet over a mossy precipice in Kolekole Stream, and Hapuna Falls, which drop from a height of 100 feet.

Hawaii Tropical Botanical Garden lies 7 miles/11 km north of Hilo overlooking Onomea Bay. Near Pepeekeo, a 4-mile scenic route leads to the coast. Van tours depart for the garden every 20 minutes from the visitor center near Old Yellow Church. The 45-acre nature preserve encompasses a tropical forest, flowering plants, waterfalls, streams, a lily-filled lake, and rugged coastline. Visitors can wander miles of trails. The park (tax-deductible admission) is open daily from 8:30 A.M. to 4:30 P.M.

INTO WAIPIO VALLEY—REALM OF ROYALTY

Honokaa is the gateway to Waipio Valley, the awesome gap that is the most accessible place along the *pali* coast of the Kohala Mountains. The only road leading in calls for a 4-wheel-drive vehicle, mule cart, or horse. Narrated tours of the valley are given by Waipio Valley Shuttle (775-7121) from Waipio Woodworks Art Gallery, Kukuihaele; Hawaii Resorts Transportation Company (885-7484) from Kohala resorts; and Waipio Valley Wagon Tours (775-9518) from Last Chance Store, Kukuihaele. Waipio Na'alapa Trail Rides (775-0419) arranges horses.

Down In the Valley

It's a steep mile down into the valley; the grade reaches 26 percent. Then you follow dirt roads and wheel tracks, splash through mud and across streams, and plow through thickets of ferns, ginger, guavas, and *noni* apples.

A fork to the beach lands you close to the mouth of the main stream, where you can dip (ocean swimming here is dangerous). Though the road inland turns into a network, you'll probably find your way to the delapidated buildings that were built as examples of native houses (a Borneo longhouse, Nepalese stone house, and Thai, Philippine, and Malaysian huts) when the Peace Corps operated a training camp here.

It's easy to spot the broad road near the camp that goes back into the valley to a pavilion of steel and bronze-colored glass up on the hillside. The building was designed to be a restaurant but never opened.

Hiilawe Falls, behind the pavilion, drops 1,000 feet from the top of a side canyon, but the stream that feeds it is used for irrigation, and the falls are not always running. You'll discover other waterfalls, large and small—some with swimming holes. Nanaue Falls, on the far side of the valley, drops into a series of pools; you can safely climb rocks to two of them.

The small, utilitarian Hotel Waipio (% Tom Araki, 25 Malana Place, Hilo, HI 96720) has a few rooms at rock-bottom rates. You must bring your own food and cook it in a community kitchen. Mosquitoes can be a problem.

A Short History

When white men first visited Waipio, in 1823, they found a continuous garden of taro, bananas, and sugarcane. There were fishponds, several *heiau*, and a place of refuge. The visitors learned from the nearly 1,500 inhabitants about sojourns of early kings, one of whom had sacrificed 80 people before the demands of his god were satiated. Here, in 1780, Kamehameha received his symbol of authority from reigning chiefs and was singled out as future ruler.

Chinese immigrants arrived in the late 1800s and grew rice until the 1930s. You'll meet taro growers (a few still live in the valley) and fishermen. Some people have weekend cabins in the valley. There is a poi factory, but most growers stuff their crops into gunny sacks and haul them out by jeep or truck for processing.

ANCIENT TEMPLES
LINK HAWAII'S PAST AND FUTURE

Traditional Hawaiian society was organized according to the *kapu* (taboo) system, strictly enforced codes dictating political, social, and religious activity. The *heiau*, or temples, played a major role in this system (see page 160). As the domain of *alii* (chiefs) and *kahuna* (priests), the link with gods and goddesses, and a sanctuary for refugees, these sites commanded great respect. A visit to a heiau helps visitors understand this important part of ancient Hawaiian life.

Ramparts of Lava Rock

Some heiau date back to A.D. 600; most were completely abandoned early in the 19th century when Kamehameha the Great died. As the kapu system was abandoned, the growing influence of American missionaries filled the void.

With their cluster of lashed wood and thatched grass huts, atop mortarless foundations of black volcanic rock, heiau resembled tiny settlements; the stone bases are usually all that remain today. Once, carved wooden figures and stone altars for offerings to the gods (occasionally human sacrifices) rested on the massive lava rock platforms. Structures on the upper level served as prayer houses and storage for ceremonial materials.

But even the heiau's stark platforms are impressive sights; larger temples measured about 125 by 250 feet within 13-foot walls that rose as high as 30 feet. Their usually desolate coastal locations lend an eerie sense of isolation and displacement. Often, the only nearby sign of human presence is a crushed rock and stone footpath leading to the temple.

A "Hawaiian Renaissance"

Interest in the archeological and social significance of heiau has grown since the 1960s; several heiau were restored and given national park or historic site status. Like Pacific versions of Independence Hall or Jamestown, the rescued heiau provide tangible evidence of Hawaii's history.

Used as settings for cultural awareness festivities, heiau are helping rekindle interest in the islands' heritage. Coupled with the preservation of the physical traces of Hawaii's culture is a growing awareness of the less-enduring legacies—language, arts, crafts, music, and sports.

Heiau To Visit

A brief summary of several of the major heiau follows. For further information, consult the Bishop Museum (see page 48), the University of Hawaii (see page 51) in Honolulu, or major bookstores.

Puuhonua O Honaunau National Historical Park (see page 160) south of Kailua, Hawaii, is one of the best examples of heiau preservation in the state. The *puuhonua* (place of refuge) gave sanctuary to war refugees, vanquished soldiers, children, women, and the elderly or diseased. Persons violating the kapu system could avoid a death sentence by reaching the heiau. Purification rites performed by a kahuna allowed a criminal to return to society in safety.

Sitting at the edge of Honaunau Bay, the site features a 1,000-foot-long wall and three heiau. Construction dates back to 1550.

Mookini Luakini Heiau at Hawaii's Upolu Point (the island's northernmost spot) is another major archeological site (see page 164). The heiau and an ancient fishing village a few miles away make up the Lapakahi Historical State Park. In addition to being one of the state's oldest known sites, this area is also the birthplace of Kamehameha.

Wahaula Heiau, one of the oldest and most picturesque in the islands, is also the hardest to visit at the moment. It is the sole survivor of a 1991 eruption by Kilauea volcano that destroyed much of the eastern edge of Hawaii Volcanoes National Park. Gone is the Wahaula Visitor Center (behind which the heiau spread). Today, the only access is via a rough trail off Chain of Craters Road (see page 153).

Kaneaki Heiau in Oahu's Makaha Valley traces its origins to the 17th century. Under the aegis of the Bishop Museum, Makaha Historical Society, and National Park Service, it is one of the islands' most thoroughly renovated temples.

Originally built for Lono, god of agriculture and fertility, the heiau was converted to a war temple by Kamehameha the Great in 1796. Supposedly, after an invasion fleet headed for Kauai was thwarted by fierce storms, the war god Kukailimoku was appeased by human sacrifices.

For information and directions to Puu O Mahuka above Waimea Bay on Oahu's North Shore, see page 59.

Other heiau can be found throughout the islands. The Southeast Molokai Archeological District contains a large concentration of temples. Iliiliopae, near Pukoo, is exceptionally well preserved (see page 127).

Mauna Kea rises high enough
above the Pacific to cast a shadow on the atmosphere at dawn and dusk.

The scenery is entirely different on this alternate route of about 55 miles/88 km between Waimea and Hilo. The Saddle Road (Highway 200) leaves Highway 190 just 4 miles/6 km south of Waimea and crosses the lonely pass between Mauna Loa and Mauna Kea. Though paved, it's rough, narrow, and off-limits to rental cars. It gives access to hunting grounds and to rugged roads that climb the state's two highest mountains. Big Islanders tell of mysterious happenings—such as rattling cars and eerie lights—that are said to occur in the windy, desolate Saddle before eruptions.

Lofty Mauna Kea, home to the Hawaiian goddess of ice, Poliahu, has become the most important astronomical site in the world. Nine observatories have sprouted on the austere summit of the inactive (although not extinct) volcano. Operated by the United States, the United Kingdom, France, Canada, and the Netherlands, they are used by astronomers from around the world who vie for time at the telescopes. Newest, largest, and most powerful of these is the W.M. Keck Telescope, built by the California Institute of Technology and the University of California.

For the first 15 miles/24 km, you climb 3,000 feet through fine pheasant country with views of the lava-scarred mountains. The Pohakuloa Area of Mauna Kea State Park is set in game bird grasslands at 6,500 feet, where the air is dry and crisp—and downright cold at night. Here you'll find picnic tables, rest rooms, drinking water, and cabins. You'll also see Hawaii's state bird, the *nene*, a native Hawaiian goose which had become almost extinct when a breeding project was started here some 30 years ago. Several hundred birds have been released into their preferred habitat: the arid land at 6,000 to 7,000 feet on Mauna Loa, Hualalai, and Haleakala. The nene is about 2½ feet high, gray and white, and has a black head and semiwebbed feet.

Mauna Kea Roads

If you have a 4-wheel-drive vehicle, you can drive to the 13,796-foot summit of Mauna Kea. Even in an ordinary passenger car (not subcompact), you can make it up to a viewpoint at the 9,400-foot level. On the way, look for pheasant and quail, grazing cattle, and wild game, particularly the big mountain sheep.

You can easily reach the Onizuka Center for International Astronomy at Hale Pohaku by car. Exhibits here explain work going in the laboratories atop Mauna Kea. Call the center (961-2180) for hours of operation.

Tours of Mauna Kea's summit depart from the University of Hawaii observatory Saturday and Sunday at 2:30 P.M.; you need 4-wheel drive to get there. No children under 16 are allowed. Weather is unpredictable at the summit, so take warm clothing. There are no facilities for gas, food, or lodging.

From Humuula Junction, a gravel road winds northeast along Mauna Kea's slope, through grazing lands interrupted by clumps of trees. At 7,000 feet you are above the Hamakua rain forest and often enveloped in clouds. The route becomes a 4-wheel-drive trail. It passes close to a monument in a grove of Douglas firs—a memorial to botanist-explorer David Douglas, who was found dead in a cattle trap at this spot in 1834 and for whom the Douglas fir tree was named. About 20 miles/32 km farther along, near Mana, the trail turns again into a graveled road and comes out on Highway 190 at the edge of Waimea.

Mauna Loa Road

The next side road off Highway 200 goes south up to Mauna Loa Observatory. This road is unique in two respects: it's the highest in the Pacific open to passenger car travel, and it climbs terrain said to resemble the surface of the moon more closely than any other place on earth. Choose a clear morning—after you've had your car tuned for high altitude.

On a 17-mile/27-km paved road, you wind from the Saddle up to an isolated scientific community at 11,150 feet, site of a geophysical observatory, solar research unit, and Department of Energy facility. Because many of the instruments are so sensitive that automobile pollution would invalidate the data, a locked chain is placed across the road about 9 miles/14 km below the observatory from 10 A.M. Monday until 5 P.M. Friday. It is lowered over the weekend. Hikers are welcome to use the road any time.

Roadside features are hardened lavas—jet black, silvery, brown, reddish—of shapes so fantastic as to stimu-

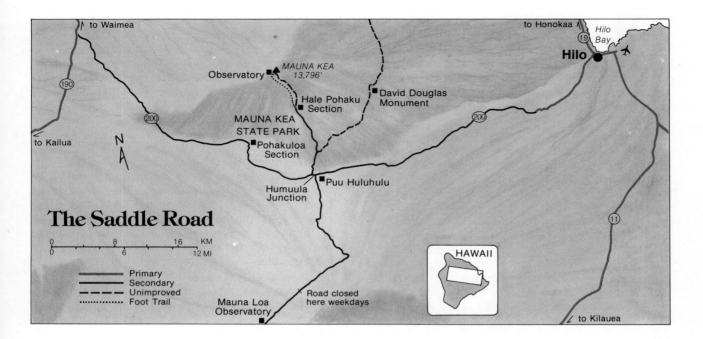

The Saddle Road

	KM
0 8 16	12 MI
0 6	

Primary
Secondary
Unimproved
Foot Trail

to Waimea · to Honokaa · Hilo Bay · Hilo · to Kailua · Observatory · MAUNA KEA 13,796' · Hale Pohaku Section · David Douglas Monument · MAUNA KEA STATE PARK · Pohakuloa Section · Puu Huluhulu · Humuula Junction · Mauna Loa Observatory · Road closed here weekdays · HAWAII · to Kilauea

late even the most sluggish imagination. About 3½ miles/ 6 km up, you cross a road that ends nowhere—a prisoner-built segment of an abandoned Hilo-Kona route. From 8,300 feet on, you follow Stainback Highway and take in sweeping views of the Saddle and Mauna Kea—unless clouds hang low. In winter, snow banks are not uncommon.

Highway 200 to Hilo

East of the side roads that climb the two mountains, Highway 200 continues toward Hilo across lava flows that have crisscrossed the Saddle over thousands of years.

On the south side of the road, just beyond the Mauna Loa road turnoff, swirly *pahoehoe* surrounds Puu Huluhulu, a Mauna Kea cinder cone that looks as if it had been set upon the Saddle floor. Sandalwood grows on its south side.

Farther on, you cross lava from a 1935 outburst that threatened Hilo's water supply until the course of the flow was changed by aerial bombing. You traverse 9 miles/ 14 km of an 1855 flow from a Mauna Loa eruption that lasted 13 months—longer than any other in recorded time. As you near Hilo, the landscape changes from barren plateau into *'ohi'a* and fern forests.

Why Drive the Saddle?

Though Highway 200 is the shortest route across the island, it's not the quickest, but it is used by hunters in search of sheep, goat, boar, and game birds in season; campers; hikers; and 4-wheel-drive enthusiasts. Ski buffs try runs over the fast, wind-packed corn snow that usually covers Mauna Kea's summit cones in winter. There are no ski lifts; a shuttle carries skiers back to the summit.

CABINS IN BIG ISLAND PARKS

Booking a cabin in one of Hawaii's parks gives you a choice of environment and climate. In both Hawaii Volcanoes National Park and Mauna Kea State Park, temperatures dip sharply at night, though beach areas usually remain quite warm. The parks listed below provide ir.formation on rates and reservations. Reserve well ahead; residents also enjoy cabin camping.

Hawaii Volcanoes National Park
Volcano House
P.O. Box 53
Hawaii Volcanoes National Park, HI 96718
(808) 967-7321
(10 cabins in the Namakani Paio Campground at 4,000 feet)

Mauna Kea State Park
Division of State Parks
P.O. Box 936
Hilo, HI 96721
(808) 933-4200
(15 log cabins, 5 with fireplaces, at 6,500 feet)

Hapuna Beach State Park
74-5543H Kaiwi Street
Kailua-Kona, HI 96740
(808) 882-1095
(6 A-frame cabins on the beach)

Hawaii, the state's youngest and most geologically diverse island, is a land of snow-capped volcanoes, black sand beaches, verdant grasslands, lava wastelands, dense rain forests, and vividly colored flowers. There is much to do and see—so much, in fact, that we've provided the following guide to help sort through all the activities found on the Big Island.

For further details on any activity listed below, consult your travel agent, hotel activities desk, or the Hawaii Visitors Bureau, Kona Plaza Shopping Arcade, 75-5719 W. Alii Drive, Kailua-Kona, HI 96740, 329-7787; or 250 Keawe Street, Hilo, HI 96720, 961-5797. The local area code is 808.

Boat cruises. What better way to become acquainted with Hawaii's waters than to skim across them in a sailboat, peer at the life below the surface from a glass-bottom boat, or descend deep into their depths in a submersible? Among your choices are Atlantis Submarines, 329-6626; Captain Beans' Cruises, 329-2955; Captain Zodiac, 329-3199; Fair Wind Sail & Dive, 322-2788; Hawaiian Cruises, 329-6411; Hawaii Sailing Academy, 329-9201; Kamanu Charters, 329-2021; Nautilus II, 329-7700; Red Sails Sports Waikoloa, 885-2876; and Sea Breeze Cruises, 326-7898.

Cycling. For a close-up, slow-paced view of Hawaii, get on a bicycle. If you didn't bring your own, you can rent one; check with your hotel activities desk, look in the Yellow Pages under "Bicycles," or stop by one of several rental locations in Kailua-Kona. Dave's Bike and Triathlon Shop in Kailua-Kona, 329-4522, rents mountain bikes and bike racks for rental cars so you can tour on your own.

One cross-country route heads north from Hilo along highways 19 and 220 to Akaka Falls; the round trip is 32 miles/51 km. The last 4 miles/6½ km are a steep climb; you'll find drinking water at the top.

Another route heads north from Hilo on Highway 19 for about 50 miles/80 km along the beautiful coast to Honokaa and Waipio Valley. Along the way are rest rooms and places to stop for water. For a traffic-free route with spectacular scenery, take sections of old, winding Mamalahoa Highway, which parallels the main highway for the first 30 miles/48 km out of Hilo.

On the west coast, a 6-mile/10-km ride south on Alii Drive along the Kona Coast leads to Keauhou Bay.

Backroads Bicycle Touring, (800) 245-3874, offers well-paced, escorted circle tours of Hawaii and other islands.

Deep-sea fishing. Hawaii is renowned for its spectacular sportfishing. The Kona Coast, in particular, has yielded world-record Pacific blue marlin, mahimahi, tuna, and wahoo only minutes from Kailua-Kona's waterfront. The Hawaiian International Billfish Tournament, an annual event held here around the beginning of August, attracts anglers from all over the globe. No seasonal restrictions or limits apply, and no licenses are required for ocean fishing. The free *Hawaii Fishing Guide,* available at stands around the island, provides detailed information.

Half, 1, and 2-day fishing charters can be arranged by Kona Coast Activities, 329-2971; Kona Charter Skippers Association, 329-3600; and Resort Activities Desk at Mauna Kea, (800) 228-3000. A number of independent charters on the west coast operate out of Kona, Honokohau Harbor (just north of Kailua-Kona), and Kawaihae Harbor in South Kohala.

Golf. The Big Island's famed golf courses look like green oases in their landscaped lava settings. Fees at public courses are low, but at most resort courses fees are substantial. More than a dozen additional courses will open during the next few years, including Kaumana Country Club, 5 miles above Hilo, and two Jack Nicklaus-designed courses at Kaupulehu, north of Kona's Keahole Airport. All the 18-hole courses listed below have restaurants and pro shops with cart and club rentals. Yardages are from the regular tees.

Public courses. Discovery Harbour Golf & Country Club, Naalehu, 929-7353, par 72, 6,410 yards; Hilo Municipal Golf Course, 959-9601, par 71, 6,006 yards; Volcano Golf & Country Club, Hawaii Volcanoes National Park, 967-7331, par 72, 5,800 yards.

Resort courses. Mauna Kea Beach Golf Club, Mauna Kea Resort, 882-7222, par 72, 6,737 yards; Hapuna Golf Course, Mauna Kea Resort, 882-7222, par 72, 7,114 yards; Francis H. I'i Brown Golf Courses, Mauna Lani Resort, 885-6655: North Course, par 72, 6,335 yards, South Course, par 72, 6,370 yards; Waikoloa Beach Golf Club, Waikoloa Beach Resort, 885-6060, par 70, 5,920 yards; Waikoloa Kings Course, Waikoloa Beach Resort, 885-4647, par 72, 6,010 yards; Waikoloa Village Golf Club, Waikoloa Beach Resort, 883-9621, par 72, 6,142 yards; Kona Country Club, 78-7000 Alii Drive, Kailua-Kona, 322-2595: Ocean Course, par 72, 6,165 yards, Mauka Course, par 72, 5,828 yards; Sea Mountain Golf Course, Pahala, 928-6222, par 72, 6,106 yards.

Hiking. If trekking in the great outdoors is your pleasure, the Big Island has plenty to keep you busy. High mountains, volcanoes, beaches, and rain forests provide endless exploration opportunities. You can hike without worry; there are no snakes or poison ivy.

The Alii Trail (an ancient route of Hawaiian royalty), hacked into the Kohala Coast's black lava, is still marked with white coral. In Waipio Valley on the island's north coast, you walk through lush wilderness (mosquitoes can be a problem).

Hiking trails abound in Hawaii Volcanoes National Park; the visitor center has information on easy hikes, such as Devastation Trail, as well as the more difficult foray up to Mauna Loa's summit. Overnight hikers must register with park headquarters and carry maps, water, and safety provisions.

A good guide for hikes all over the islands is *Hawaiian Hiking Trails* by Craig Chisholm; check local bookstores for a copy. For maps, guides, and other information, contact Hawaii Geographical Society, P.O. Box 1698, Honolulu, HI 96806; Hawaii Trail and Mountain Club, Box

2238, Honolulu, HI 96814; or Hawaii Sierra Club, Box 11070, Honolulu, HI 96828.

Conducted hikes are also offered by Big Island-based Hawaiian Walkways, 325-6677.

Horseback riding. Get out into the countryside and experience Big Island scenery from the back of a horse. Reservations are usually required for escorted trail rides.

Several of Hawaii's stables are located around Waimea: Hawaii Trail Rides Waimea, 685-6508; Ironwood Outfitters, 885-4941; and Waikoloa Countryside Stables, 883-9335. Horses can also be found at Mauna Kea Beach Hotel Stables, 882-7222, and at Kings' Trail Rides O'Kona at upland Kealakekua Ranch, 323-2388. Waipio Na'alapa Trail Rides, 775-0419, and Waipio on Horseback, 775-7291, take riders into isolated Waipio Valley.

Kayaking. The Hawaiian islands were first discovered by Polynesians piloting canoes. Perhaps that's why it seems so appropriate to see the Big Island from the vantage point of a small craft paddled over the waves. Outfitters lead guided kayaking tours ranging from half-day paddles to overnight trips.

Kona Kai-Yaks, Kailua-Kona, 326-2922, has 2-hour beginner's tours, customized half or full-day tours, and overnight adventures. Ocean Sports Waikoloa, Kohala Coast, 885-5555, offers a 3½-hour morning tour for novices that combines 2 to 3 miles of paddling along the flat, cove-dotted lava coast with snorkeling and lunch.

Skiing. It's hard to imagine skiing in the middle of the tropics, but you can schuss down Mauna Kea peak on beginner to expert runs that are nearly 1 mile/1½ km long. Just don't expect lifts, warming houses, restaurants, or accommodations. A 4-wheel-drive vehicle transports skiers to the top. For more information, contact Ski Guides Hawaii, 885-4188. The ski "season" is generally February and March, but snowfall is possible from late November to early June.

Snorkeling and scuba diving. The Big Island offers dramatic diving along its western coastline, which is strewn with lava flows, submerged caves, coral reefs, and more than 40 regularly used diving sites. Sheltered from the trade winds by Mauna Kea and Mauna Loa volcanoes, the coast is nearly all lava with little soil runoff to muddy the visibility, but this means few sandy beaches. Beach diving is best in the calm morning seas.

Most of the island's most popular snorkeling sites, including Kealakekua Underwater State Park, are accessible only by boat. Three types of boats are used: small, high-performance inflatables (called Zodiacs) that zip along the coast, detouring close to reefs; catamarans, which are twin-hulled sailboats; and larger tour boats favored by dedicated landlubbers.

Many trips depart from Kailua-Kona and Keauhou piers to Kealakekua and elsewhere in early morning; other boats operate daily from Kohala resorts. Check with your hotel activities desk. Outfitters include Captain Zo-

diac, 329-3199; Fair Wind Sail & Dive, 322-2788; Royal Hawaiian, 848-6360; and Kona Coast Divers, 329-8802.

For a list of dive stores and sites, get a copy of *Dive Hawaii* ($2), published by University of Hawaii Sea Grant Extension Service, 1000 Pope Road, MSB 205, Honolulu, HI 96822.

Stargazing. The air is so clear atop 13,796-foot Mauna Kea that several nations have built high-tech observatories there. Visitors are restricted at the summit (see page 170), but Onizuka Space Center at Kona's airport shows videos of space exploration at 7 P.M. Friday and Saturday.

Paradise Safaris, 322-2366, runs 7-hour guided tours from the visitor center to Mauna Kea for a look at the summit observatories at sunset and stargazing through a portable telescope. Waipio Valley Shuttle, 775-7121, also offers daytime weekday tours that include a look inside some of the science facilities and lunch.

Surfing. Surfing is not popular on this island because of the small waves and dangerous reefs. Around Hilo, surfers head for Honolii Beach Park. On the Kona side, try Kealakekua Bay off Napoopoo or Waiulua Bay north of Kailua.

Swimming. As the youngest of Hawaii's chain of islands, the Big Island has had the least amount of time to develop stretches of white sand. This is not to say that there aren't beaches on Hawaii; there are many—black, green, beige, white, and speckled. But beaches tend to come and go here. Harry K. Brown and Kaimu beaches were covered by Kilauea's recent eruptions, but a new black sand beach more than half a mile long was formed by the molten lava near Kamoamoa campground in Hawaii Volcanoes National Park.

The best beaches for children include Old Kona Airport and Napoopoo County Park in Kona, Spencer Beach Park in Kohala, and James Kealoha and Onekahakaha beach parks in Hilo.

Tennis. Courts, both public and private, are scattered around the Big Island. Major hotels and many condominium complexes provide tennis courts for their guests. Nonguests can play for a fee at Kona Hilton, Kona Surf, Ritz-Carlton Mauna Lani, Royal Waikoloan, Waikoloa Village, and Sea Mountain.

Hilo has a number of free courts, including those at University of Hawaii, 333 West Lanikaula Street, and at Lincoln Park, Kinoole and Ponahawai streets. Hilo Tennis Stadium, Piilani and Kalanikoa streets, has 8 courts (3 lighted) available for a small fee.

Windsurfing. A new sport on the Big Island, windsurfing is catching on, though the dangerous offshore reefs and tame surf will never make Hawaii a wave capital. Anaehoomalu Bay, behind Royal Waikoloan Hotel, is one of the best sites. Here, Captain Nemo's Ocean Sports can provide equipment and instruction.

INDEX

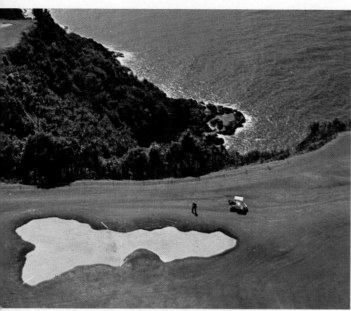

Challenging play and spectacular view at Princeville

Surfer at sunset

Photographers

Ken Bates: 14 all, 30, 103, 105 bottom. **Glenn Christiansen:** 10 left, 13 top right, 43 all, 79, 81. **Peter Christiansen:** 44. **David E. Clark:** 20. **Ed Cooper:** 36, 71, 154, 167 top. **Chris Fesler:** 8 left, 98 top. **David Franzen:** 10 top right, 12 center left and top right. **Mark Gibson:** 37, 50 left, 58 right, 151, 159 bottom. **Jeff Gnass:** 2, 38, 46 top, 95, 118, 123, 126 top, 159 top. **Hawaii Tourist News:** 27. **Vern Hawkins:** 89. **Cliff Hollenbeck:** 9 top right, 10 bottom right, 11, 15 top right, 19, 22, 28, 46 bottom, 55 bottom, 63 bottom, 87 bottom, 98 bottom, 162 top. **Saxon Holt:** 162 bottom. **Dave Houser:** 29, 134 bottom. **Hyatt Regency:** 15 bottom right. **Greg Kaufman:** 106. **Rene Klein:** 111 bottom. **Dorothy Krell:** 105 top, 126 bottom.

Greg Lawson: 1, 58 left, 96, 131. **Ells Marugg:** 12 bottom right. **David Muench:** 6 right, 146 bottom. **Suzanne Murphy:** 35 left, 104, 111 top. **Don Normark:** 16. **Norman Plate:** 6 left, 7 bottom right, 87 top. **Radlauer Productions, Inc.:** 115. **Richard Rowan:** 15 left, 35 right, 175 all. **William Rubenstein:** 97, 167 bottom. **Ron Sanford:** 8 right. **Marc Schechter/Photo Resource Hawaii:** 170. **Elliott Varner Smith:** 9 bottom right. **South Sea Helicopter:** 82. **Ted Streshinsky:** 13 top left and bottom, 45, 74, 88, 134 top. **Tim Thompson:** 21, 50 right. **Tom Tracy:** 12 top left, 63 top. **Larry Ulrich:** 90, 146 top. **Darrow Watt:** 12 bottom left. **R. Wenkam:** 3, 7 top right, 55 top, 112, 139, 142. **Walton Wimberly:** 66 all.